Shipwrecks and Rescues

Hulk of former U.S. Naval bark *Intrepid* wrecked
February 23, 1954 after slipping her tow line. Site just
north of Long Beach. When lost was used as a 1,110
ton commercial barge. Built in San Francisco between
1903-1907.   —Photographed by Don McArthur

Tuna seiner *Bettie M* was wrecked below Cape Disappointment lighthouse in 1976. The ship and cargo were a total loss.　　　　　　　—Photographs by Sam Foster

Shipwrecks

and Rescues

on the
Northwest Coast

World War-II Japanese Torpedoing of
Ships on the United States West Coast

—Documentary—

Bert and Margie Webber
Introduction by James A. Gibbs

WEBB RESEARCH GROUP PUBLISHERS

Published by
WEBB RESEARCH GROUP PUBLISHERS
Books About the Oregon Country
P. O. Box 314
Medford, OR 97501

The photographs are primarily from the authors' collections or were taken for this book by the authors. Other photographs are credited under each picture. We trust that no omissions of credit have occurred for if so, it was surely not intentional.

Cover pictures:

Front: *SS Larry Doheny* sinking after being attacked by Japanese Imperial submarine *I-25* off Oregon, October 1942.
Back: Coast Guard Life-Savers rescue some of crew from stranded cruiser *USS Milwaukee* near Eureka, California, January 1917

Library of Congress Cataloging in Publication Data

Webber, Bert
  Shipwrecks and rescues on the northwest coast : documentary : World War II Japanese torpedoing of ships on the United States West Coast / Bert and Margie Webber : introduction by James A. Gibbs.
     p.   cm.
  Includes bibliographical references and index.
  ISBN 0-936738-90-1 (pbk)
  1. Shipwrecks – Pacific Coast (U.S.) 2. United States. Coast Guard– Search and rescue operations. 3. United States. Life-Saving Service– Search and rescue operations. I. Webber, Margie. II. Title
  G525.W328   1996
  363.12'381'09116432–dc20   95-50880
                                                          CIP

Foreword and Acknowledgments

If one was to include stories of every ship that ever was wrecked along the Pacific Coast of the United States in one book, such a book would be so thick that the price of the tome would be so great that nobody could afford to buy a copy. The authors are aware of a over 2,000 shipwrecks on the Pacific Coast and for the most part, this number does not include fish boats and pleasure craft. Therefore, making the decision what to include and what to exclude can be a real dilemma. With this challenge in mind, the authors have made the effort to locate

1) Shipwrecks that other writers did not include
2) To revisit some popular shipwrecks for which new information is available
3) To offer some of the traditional shipwrecks that folks love to read about
4) To report on some contemporary shipwrecks that happened after earlier books appeared.
5) There has never been any series of concisely written and illustrated articles of all those ships along the west coast of the United States that were attacked by Japanese submarines during World War II. There are a bunch of them.

> The Japanese submarine attacks section will be illuminating to many readers who may find it hard to believe that folks could stand along the beach and watch American ships sink before their eyes.

As the Pacific War (as the Japanese called it) is now half-a-century in the past, and most of the principals have died, we have assembled everything that could be found about these affairs.

From a geographic standpoint, this volume has two sets of parameters. For the section relating to ship losses in the Pacific War, this book covers all the space within a broad arc from Hawaii to Anchorage then from Hawaii to the foot of Baja California. For the non-war section, this book's "Northwest Coast" runs from the Strait of Juan de Fuca to about Cape Mendocino.

One of the most intriguing of the war-time incidents is that of the mysterious "Q" ship that patrolled the coastal waters. Thanks

to Leonard W. May, Cheyenne, Wyoming, who was a sailor on board, we have the story and his pictures.

Our long-time friend Don D. McArthur, Aberdeen, Washington, has haunted the beaches around Grays Harbor since he was a teen-age kid with a "Harley." On his bike, he could out-run the Navy demolition teams when the teams exploded Japanese floating mines found on the beach and Don wanted some of the pieces for his collection. And, he unearthed, literally, an old newspaper clipping of the long lost *Nora Harkins* – she stranded in 1894 – as the hulk was exhumed from the sands of the beach by coastal erosion. And there he is in a snapshot sitting on it in 1948.

A fellow with whom the author was in conversation, said he was studying ship losses by submarine during the First World War and had been frustrated about the *USS Milwaukee.* He said he knew the Navy had a heavy cruiser by that name but he could not find it in any of the battle-actions. I told him it had been lost within a few days of the loss of a submarine that it had been sent after. This whetted his imagination and he demanded to know with rapid-fire speech when and where this "battle" had taken place, where had the submarine been sunk, how many men were lost and what was the damage to the cruiser? And he had a few more questions....

I related how the cruiser had been "mortally wounded" but as the ship lay damaged, the crew was able to get off, many of them only one-at-a-time in a breeches buoy. His face lit up. Where had all this happened? – He squirmed to learn!

By now he was vividly interested declaring this "stuff" I was relating must be fiction as he could never find any of this in his war-books. But he did know the *Milwaukee* had been stricken from the list of ships in 1917. Why? What was this submarine business? <u>What submarine?</u>

After some minutes of toying with this and not wanting him to have an acute anxiety attack right where we stood, I finally related how the U. S. sub *H-3* had stranded on a beach in Northern California and how the *USS Milwaukee* had been sent to pull it back into the water, when the cruiser, in a mishap, also became stranded and was declared to be a total loss. Indeed it was during the First World War but the incident was <u>before</u> the United States got into it. He looked shocked. The full story of the *H-3* and the *Milwaukee* is in this book.

And we have the story about the Pan American Clipper, a four-engine passenger flying boat whose pilot spotted a Japanese sub that had, a few days earlier, sunk an American freighter. PanAm's radioman reported it and ... – the story is in this book.

How the Coast Guard could lose three of its rescue boats and some of its crews while trying to save a fishing boat is an involved and serious incident to relate, and how the Coast Guard lost again, in a similar rescue *near the same place thirty years later* is not only amazing but true. These incidents are in this book.

Just writing a book of this type is an adventure in itself. We are certain readers will live right along with the actions, actually find themselves involved, just as we became involved while doing the research and then the writing. Enjoy!

It is important to acknowledge the kind assistance of many folks. We have already introduced Leonard May and Don Mc Arthur. There is Glenn Barkhurst who, during WW-II, was in Coast Guard Beach Patrols and shared his experiences and his private photographs with us. Professional photographer Sam Foster, Seaside, shot pictures for the *Oregonian* and for KGW-TV. Sam helps whenever he can. Jim Gibbs, author of shipwreck and lighthouse books allows us to pick his brain then he reviewed the manuscript. Our friends at the Curry County Historical Society, Gold Beach, and Westport – South Bay Historical Society, Westport, willingly provided assistance. The volunteers at the Humboldt Bay Maritime Museum in Eureka, California, were eager to assist. At the museums we were given access to their artifacts, files of shipwreck clippings and photographs, some of which are

Early-day U.S. Life-Saving Service crew has launched their boat and are pulling for a ship wrecked on Peacock Spit near mouth of Columbia River.

included here.

We wish to acknowledge the keen interest and technical assistance of eldest son Richard E. Webber, New Jersey. His globe-circling days at sea in the Coast Guard qualified him to edit the data on the *USS Milwaukee*. Coast Guard officials, particularly at Humboldt Bay Station, were also helpful. We thank them all.

The Reference Department of the Jackson County Library System, Medford, Oregon, provided numerous books through the inter-library loan system, and helped locate microfilm and other material. In many instances, the staff of librarians searched for various factors important to this work. And the Del Norte County Library, Crescent City, California forwarded data to us about the current saga of the plausibility of a treasure hunt on the hulk of the *Brother Jonathan* lost over a century ago. Bruce Berney, Director of the Astoria Public Library, located data for us on the 1961 and 1991 losses of Coast Guard vessels and the deaths of Coast Guardsmen and fishermen. We are indebted to all these professional librarians for their interest and for their help.

Many individuals, far too many to include here by name, answered questions and encouraged us in many different ways. We appreciate these fine folks and their willingness to be helpful.

The authors will accept letters of constructive criticism which may be sent to the publisher whose address is on page iv.

Bert and Margie Webber
Central Point, Oregon

Spectacular Coast Guard rescue effort saved the fishboat which was sinking at sea west of Tillamook Bay. Helicopter lowered several pumps which were put aboard the boat with Coast Guard boarding party while the 44-foot motor lifeboat steadied the fishboat with a closely tied line. A nearby commercial fish boat later towed the re-floated vessel back to port.
—Coast Guard photograph by Lt. Ralph Yetka, USCG

Contents

Vessels in Table of Contents are Listed Chronologically
For Alphabetical List, See Index on Page 257
There are More Vessels in the Index Than Appear in the Table of Contents

Washington Shipwrecks

Wreck of the *Elizabeth Olson* on north jetty Coquille River on November 30, 1960, Tug *Rebel* (Capt. Peterson) standing at left is in process of rescuing the 10-man crew. *Rebel* was wrecked in same location just four months later –March 27, 1961. Captain Peterson was drowned.

Introduction by
James A. "Jim" Gibbs*

At sea as on land, life is like a brief candle which flickers down from generation to generation only to flare again. Ironically, it is often the barriers, reefs, rocks and shoals that have torn ships to pieces more than the cantankerous open ocean with its pulsating, gale-driven billows. The death of a ship and those who people her decks is a sight once seen never forgotten. When a seafarer dies at sea and his final chronicle is read, it always casts a shadow over those who hear the traditional above the sough and whisper of the waves.

The cruise of another sailor is over, his battles are all fought, his victories won, and as in other days he lies down to rest awhile under the arching sky awaiting the bugler's call. Behold, the silver cord is loosed, the golden bowl is broken. We therefore, commend the soul of our brother departed unto Almighty God and we commit his body to the deep....

—*Book of Common Prayer* (Episcopal) 1839

What is there about the sea that so attracts people? Man has a kinship with the ocean for it is essential to life. Furthermore, each of us like the ocean, has salt in his veins and salt is a cleansing power.

The call of the sea is many faceted. From the mammoth commercial ships, tantamount to floating islands, on down to the modern day ski jet boats, craft come in all sizes and all descriptions and represent a variety of interests. As surface ships world-wide number in the thousands, there are also those undersea marauders

---

* Jim Gibbs attended the University of Washington then joined the U. S. Coast Guard during World War II. Among his assignments he was part of the wartime Beach Patrol, served aboard a cutter, and he did a stint on Tillamook Rock Lighthouse. After the war, as a journalist, he was the editor of the *Marine Digest*, a trade weekly paper in Seattle. Also in the post-war years, Jim wrote many books on lighthouses and shipwrecks. For Webb Research Group, Publishers, he did *Oregon's Seacoast Lighthouses* in 1992, and *Oregon's Salty Coast* in 1994. Jim built Cleft of the Rock Lighthouse on the north spur of Cape Perpetua near Yachats, Oregon in 1976. This private aid to navigation gained official Coast Guard approval in 1979. The light is at 44°15'5"N - 124°6'5"W. Its red and white beams flash through an acrylic bulls eye lens generating 80,000 candle power and can be seen 16 miles. Jim and his wife, Cherie, make their home at the lighthouse. The lighthouse has no access for visitors but full particulars about it are in *Oregon's Seacoast Lighthouses* which is included in the book list at the front of this book.

U.S. Lifesaving craft and crew attached to the Yaquina Bay Station undergoes drill in preparation for the real thing in the early part of the century.

Cleft-of-the-Rock Lighthouse Cape Perpetua, Oregon

armed with genocide weapons silently listening for a call to action which even their crews hope will never come.

The bleached ribs of many ships, whose names have been forgotten in the eons of time, lie buried amid the beach sands and shoals and occasionally surface after a storm or a tidal sweep. Other vessels lie buried deep in Davy Jones' locker victims of teredoes that honeycomb their wooden planks, while steel and iron hulls that have not completely rusted away offer sanctuary for a host of creatures that populate the undersea.

Occasionally divers find treasure of gold, silver, ancient anchors or cannon which alone mark the grave of some mystery ship. Some ships have vanished with all hands, their chronicles forgotten, those who manned their decks entombed within deteriorating walls – a marine crypt.

Semper Paratus is the motto of the United States Coast Guard. Translated, it means "always ready," and indeed that moniker is strictly applied. Forerunner of the Coast Guard, the U. S. Lifesaving Service, also had a motto, "You have to go out, but you don't have to come back."

There was no place for cowards in the old service, and the much more sophisticated modern counterpart demands a similar application. Its service personnel in their sleek motor lifeboats, cutters and helicopters, are far removed from the old salts who manned the oar-propelled surfboats of yesteryear.

At every station from Alaska to Maine the day begins with

"colors," a salute to the flag often followed by perhaps a drill with flags, a boat drill, or apparatus drill. Though there are times of inaction, personnel must be constantly ready to launch out in any type of weather. Aircraft are primed for immediate action in addition to routine flights along America's coastline.

In days of yore, a "capsize drill" was traditional with the old pulling boats. The modern rescue craft are self-righting but a nightmare experience for their crews when the craft takes a 360-degree roll in rough surf. In the beginning, the life-saving personnel had routine drills which required the men to purposely capsize their own boat. By planting their feet on the starboard gunwale, they would throw their weight till the craft was over-balanced; then as the boat rode bottom up, they would jump clear. Scrambling atop of it, they would then grab the life hoops on the far side, let themselves off again and slowly over-balance the weighty craft until it lifted out of the water and turned right side up. This accomplished, they would drop free in the water. With the boat rightside up, the men would have to climb back in to the confines of the watersoaked craft via the life hoops. It was a demanding and often chilling exercise but not nearly as demanding as when under adverse surf conditions on an actual rescue.

To be sure in old times those bold men of the sea often invited girl friends, family and citizens of their respected communities to watch the exercises. It was a thrilling sight to watch, but only a dress rehearsal for the real thing.

The feats of rescue of souls at sea by the United States Coast Guard and its forerunner are legion, but the modes of rescue have changed through the years. Before the advent of high technology, the general course for coastal vessels was close inshore where they could be guided by beacons in lighthouses and shore-based fog signals. These often had limitations in adverse weather conditions. Thus, shipwreck was a common occurrence and the shores of the Pacific Northwest adhere to this fact. Scores of wrecks occurred when a light was blotted out or a foghorn muzzled.

Today, equipment such as radiobeacons RADAR, SONAR, ECHO, LORAN, OMEGA and GPS (Global Positioning System) can see through the thickest weather. Ship-to-shore and ship-to-ship communications keep any seagoing ship in touch with powers that

(TOP) **Popular self-righting 36-foot motor lifeboat was mainstay of U. S. Coast Guard for several decades.** (LOWER) **modernized 44-foot boat.**
—Coast Guard

Coast Guard 44-boat off Umpqua River bar

stand ready to assist in an emergency because of modern innovations. Shipwreck *per se* have been greatly lessened as larger ships now operate well offshore. This results in the main rescue operations of the Coast Guard being involved with commercial fishing vessels and pleasure craft. When trouble with a large ocean going vessel occurs offshore, a search and rescue helicopter can be immediately dispatched.

At this writing, there appears no concern about a hostile nation engaging the United States in war at sea, but during World War II, there was not only great concern about enemy action, but several of the ships operating off the West Coast became victims of torpedoes and shelling. Though nothing like the Nazi submarine menace along the East Coast, ships did take their final plunge in Northwest waters and their remains lie silently in the depths. Nothing is as dramatic and at the same time troublesome as when one is a witness to the sinking of a large seagoing vessel, whether it be a cargo ship, a passenger liner or a warship.

Nothing that moves on this earth is larger than a great ship. This crowning achievement of man goes back to ancient times, and through maritime evolution has reached its apex with mammoth creations representing the ultimate in cargo transport and palatial cruise liners. Noah's Ark, the first vessel of colossal size, was about the dimensions of a World War II "Liberty Ship" but it

Following World War-II, helicopters of several designs have aided traditional surface search and rescue —Coast Guard

had no propulsion except by divine intervention.

The United States Coast Guard antedates our Navy. In 1790, the need for a Revenue Marine Service to assist in enforcing payment of customs and tonnage dues was recognized by an Act of Congress and for nearly a decade, that service was the only armed seagoing operation in the United States. From that humble beginning, down through the years, the service encompassed duties involving lifesaving, lighthouses and guardianship of all United States shoreline, culminating with the United States Coast Guard which has become a vital and necessary streamlined operations in our present day. In 1878, the Lifesaving Service became a bureau of the Treasury Department. The Coast Guard took over that branch in 1915, and the United States Lighthouse Service in 1939. (In time of war, the Coast Guard operates under the auspices of the U. S. Navy.) On our Northwest waters, the Coast Guard has proven itself time and again in search and rescue operations and seagoing law enforcement.

This book reveals some of the dramatic episodes involving maritime disaster in a vital corner of our great nation.

Despite the fact that men and ships perish, the candle burns ever brighter with each generation.

Jim Gibbs
Cleft of the Rock Lighthouse
Yachats, Oregon

World War-II Japanese-related Incidents on West Coast U.S.A.

> **NOTE**: Despite the writings of various authors, the United States Strategic Bombing Surveys (USSBS) and the Japanese Maritime War History Office, Tokyo, do not list sunken Japanese submarines anywhere along the west coast of USA from southeast Alaska to the tip of Baja California because there were no such losses. Losses of all Japanese submarines are found in Watts and Gordon (see bibliography). The loss of or damage to vessels in this list are directly related to wartime actions.

→Shown if known are tonnage, ship length, latitude/longitude, actions

- *SS **Cynthia Olson*** freighter. 2140T. De 7 1941 shelled & torp/sunk by *I-26* (29° N 140° W) between Hawaii and San Jose (Chapter 1)
- *SS **Montebello*** tanker. De 23 1941 nr Piedras Blancas torpedoed by *I-19* (Chapter 2)
- *SS **Samoa*** freighter. 2,000T. attacked De 18 1941 probably by *I-10* near San Diego (Chapter 3)
- *SS **Emidio*** tanker. 450ft. De 20 1941 torp/shelled by *I-17* near Cape Mendocino (Chapter 4)
- *MV **Tahoe*** garbage scow. De 27 1942 rammed and damaged *I-23* / damaged by *I-23* nr Farallon Isl (Chapter 5)
- *SS **Agwiworld*** tanker. 8242T. 440-ft running battle De 20, 1941 with *I-23* nr Santa Cruz (Chapter 6)
- *SS **Larry Doheny*** tanker. 7038T 450 ft. (twice) Oc 5 1942 torp by *I-25* off Cape Sebastian 5 mi s of Gold Beach (Chapter 7)
- *SS **Anacapa*** freighter. 7,420T 335 ft. TOP-SECRET U.S. NAVY "Q" SHIP rescued *Doheny* crew (Chapter 8)
- *SS **Absoroka*** freighter. (*I-19 or I-21*) De 24 1941 nr San Pedro (Chapter 9)
- *USAT **Gen. Gorgas*** transport. 4638T. 371ft. My 24 1942. (46° N 146° W) in Gulf of Alaska shelled, damaged by *I-9*
- *SS **Coast Trader*** freighter. Je 7 1942 torp sunk by *I-26* (48° 15′ - 125°45′W) off entrance to Str. of Juan De Fuca (Chapter 10)
- *SS **Fort Camosun*** freighter. Je 20 1942 torp/shelled by *I-25* (47° 05′ W - 125° N) 70 mi sw of Cape Flattery (Chapter 11)
- *SS **Camden*** tanker. 6600T. Je 23 1942 attacked 50 mi w of Coos Bay - escaped. Oc 4 1942 torp by *I-25* then sank under tow off Grays Harbor (Chapter 12)
- *L-16* Soviet submarine. Oc 11 1942 torp/sunk by *I-25* 800 mi w of Washington coast (Chapter 13)
- *I-180* Jpnse submarine. 2000T. 333½ft. Ap 26 1944 sunk by *USS Gilmore* at (55° 10′ N - 155° 40′ W) 120 mi sw of Kodiak (Chapter 14)
- *SS **John H. Johnson*** freighter. Oc 29 1944 torp/sunk by *I-12*. (29° 36′ 30″ N - 141° 43′ W) midway between San Francisco and Hawaii (Chapter 15)
- *I-12* Jpnse submarine. 2390T. 355¾ft. Nv 13 1944 sunk by *USS Rockford* (31° 55′ N 139° 45′ W) in Pacific Ocean (Chapter 15)

Aircraft-carrying _I-15_-class Type B-1 Imperial Japanese Navy submarine.

—1—
The Mystery of the *Cynthia Olson*
Position at sea on December 7, 1941 when sunk by Japanese submarine
I-26: approximately 33°N - 145°W

About the time that bombs started dropping on Pearl Harbor on December 7, 1941, Japanese Imperial submarine *I-26*, Commander Minoru Yakota, was patrolling 1,000 miles northeast of Diamond Head. This is about 1,200 miles west of Cape Flattery, Washington. His lookout spotted the *SS Cynthia Olson* (Captain Berthel Carlsen). She was a freighter of 2,140 tons displacement with $75,000 in lumber on board under charter to the U. S. Army. She had sailed from Tacoma, Washington.

Arguments still pop up over which came first: The attack on Pearl Harbor or the sinking of the *Cynthia Olson*? Commander Yokota, who changed his name by marriage to Hasegawa after the war, explained what happened by letter in 1973 then reinforced his recollection when we talked about it in Tokyo in 1975.

The claim that I wish to make clear is that my attack on *Cynthia Olson* was <u>after</u> Pearl Harbor. I had a strict order from Japanese Navy Superior <u>not to do anything</u> before 3:30 a.m. December 8, 1941 (Tokyo time), the planned time to attack Pearl Harbor, so that Pearl Harbor might be the real sudden attack against U. S. forces.

The most important element in the entire debate as to the event seems to be that throughout the world, the Japanese Navy was using <u>Tokyo time</u>. Thus, the day of Pearl Harbor was to us the 8th of December, while it was the 7th [in North America].

I did not come up to the sea-surface until 3:30 a.m. Japan Tokyo time to attack *Cynthia Olson*. I did not use any torpedo against the *Cynthia Olson* [on first attack] but gun shells as the attack was from the surface.

21

Hayashi-san's photograph of the sinking of the *Cynthia Olson*, the testimony of the submarine commander as well as that of Hayashi, established what happened to the ship. The Japanese language data, written by Hayashi, identifies the incident.

Takaji Komaba
Torpedoman

昭和16年12月8日
0410頃 撮影

14糎砲の命中弾を受け火災を起し、漂流する
シンヒアオルソン号 エ喬ココトに星候調揚s

    I shot the shell so that it would not hit the ship directly but go over it as the warning to stop, and give them some chance to escape from the ship.

    Men left the ship in small boats. Our radio man caught the SOS from *Cynthia Olson* which S.S. *Lurline* was said to have heard. And we noticed a mistake in their message, that they were saying of being attacked by "torpedoes" when actually they were gun-shells.

    We shelled the ship effectively, but at that time we could not sink it. In order to avoid the counterattack [we expected] from the air force in reply to the radio [SOS] our *I-26* went into the water without seeing the last moment of the ship. After awhile I came on the surface again and saw the ship now on fire but not yet sunk. I shelled some again and went into the water again to avoid the possible counterattack. For the third when time I came up to the surface, I could see it almost sunk. I could not see in person the very moment when the ship sank into the water. Then *I-26* went on southward on the surface of the sea.

    Chief Gunner Saburo Hayashi told me in 1975 why the attack on the *Cynthia Olson* took a long time.

The ship would not sink. More than 20 [of our] 14-cm [5.5-inch] shells were consumed with about 10 hits. The first firing was from 3,000 meters. Immediately after the first shot, Mr. Osawa, our radioman, reported that the ship was sending SOS. Then we saw the American flag being raised. Two boats were put into the sea and I believe all of the crew got off the ship. After firing and fearing an air attack in answer to the SOS, *I-26* crash-dived. When no enemy appeared, the submarine resurfaced and found the ship still floating but on fire.

We switched to torpedo attack, but because the submarine was drifting too close to the flaming ship, we had to back off before we could fire. One torpedo was fired by Chief Torpedoman Takaji Komaba from about 400 meters. This was our first torpedo attack of the Pacific War. We were dismayed because the [10-year] old torpedo went wild, turned in mid-course, missed the target by a hair's breadth, then went dead in the water.

Still fearing an air attack, we dived again. When we resurfaced, the ship was in heavy list. The gunners went back to the deck gun for more shooting. Although I was Chief Gunner, my duty during the attack was in the control center. While the sub-gunners were shooting, I received permission from First Officer Saito to go on the bridge to take a picture with my Zeiss 6 x 9 cm camera.

Mr. Hayashi said that Imperial authorities never quizzed him about the sinking and apparently did not know he had taken pictures. He was pleased with my interest* and he presented his pictures to me. Hayashi-san's fine picture of the last moments of the *Cynthia Olson* is in this book.

Although the crew of 33 plus 2 Army soldier passengers from *Cynthia Olson* left their ship in lifeboats, they were never rescued from the sea.* Mr. Hasagawa wrote to me in September 1983 that before the lifeboats with survivors disappeared, submarine *I-19* saw them drifting helplesssly and pulled alongside. *I-19's* medical officer observed the sailors closely, then directed the submarine's skipper to make food available to the men in the boats. This done, *I-19* departed for a patrol position off Los Angeles, California. The *I-26's* next duty was to take a patrol position off the entrance to the Straits of Juan de Fuca. □

---

* Bert and Margie Webber were the Guests of Honor at the reunion of officers and men from submarines *I-25* and *I-26* in Tokyo's Navy Shrine in July 1975. It was then that former skipper Hasagawa and former gunner Hayashi (and others) answered additional questions that had not been covered in letters. Officials of the U. S. Naval History Division, Washington, D.C. wrote to Webber after they saw the photograph of the sinking by the I-26 in his book saying that they could then (1975) close the file on what really happened to the *Cynthia Olson.* For additional details and pictures, refer to *Siege Siege-III.* (see biblio.)

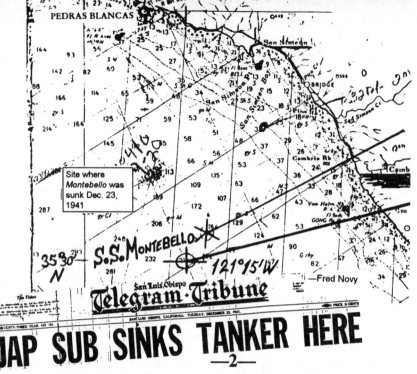

JAP SUB SINKS TANKER HERE

—2—

Townsfolk Watch Torpedoed *Montebello* Sink

Position on December 23, 1941 when sunk by Japanese submarine
I-21: 35°30'N - 121°15'W

> SAN FRANCISCO, Dec. 23 (UP) –A Japanese
> submarine sank the Union Oil tanker *Montebello* ... in new
> attacks on U. S. shipping off the California coast during
> the night, 12th Naval District Hq. announced today.

— so started a newspaper account of a stirring night's activity. The paper's writer included that the tanker *Larry Doheny* had been also attacked but had escaped by running in to Estero Bay.

The *Montebello* (Captain Olaf Eckstrom), with a full load of crude oil, was bound for Vancouver, B.C. This was a big vessel of 8,272-tons, and 440-feet long. This early in the war it did not have deck guns and was traveling alone. It had loaded at Avila but did not get very far.

An eye-witness on shore, M. F. Waltz, editor of the newspaper in nearby Cambria, reported:

> We counted 14 flashes of gunfire and we could see the dim outline of the tanker. The firing continued for about 20 minutes. The *Montebello* seemed to

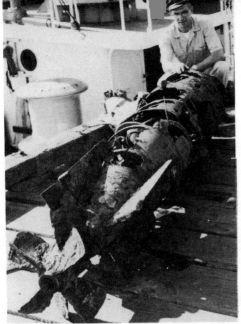

Japanese World War-II torpedo netted by Morro Bay fisherman about 1960. It was probably fired at tanker *Montebello* by Japanese sub *I-21* which sank the ship on December 23, 1941 near Cambria.
—Fred Novy collection

be listing when the firing commenced then when it finally sank, there was no fire or explosion about the ship that we could see. When it sank it upended like a giant telephone pole and slowly settled into the sea.

The Navy said the water at the sinking site was about 230 feet deep.

Later, lifeboats were seen making for the shore. One boat contained the *Montebello's* skipper, Captain Eckstrom, First Mate Kenneth McClean, Second Mate John Young, Fireman Edgar F Smith and two seamen, Bill Frez and John Smith.

Waltz stated that as the boat with the captain and other officers came in:

...it was caught in a heavy surf and was smashed against rocks causing all the men to be dumped into the sea. They were all rescued by the heroic efforts of the townspeople who had lined the shore.

After being escorted to a private home near the beach, the survivors "had something warm to drink," the skipper said. He was interviewed by a reporter from the United Press and related:

...one torpedo from the Japanese submarine struck the *Montebello* directly under the bridge and that was plenty. We had been proceeding along the coast when the torpedo struck. After the torpedo, there were eight or nine shells fired apparently from the submarine's deck gun with one of the shells hitting the fore part of the ship.

While the sub was firing at us, over a period of half an hour, we

25

Montebello on the bottom off coast at Cambria as viewed by SONAR.
—Fred Novy

zigzagged the *Montebello* in an attempt to make as small a target as we could, but we soon saw that the boat was sinking and we took to the lifeboats.

When the torpedo exploded, the sound was so loud it broke windows in some beach-front homes.

There were 38 members of the crew. The submarine continued to fire as the boats were lowered and fired at two of the boats with a small (25mm) machine gun after the boats were in the water. The captain said as far as he knew none of his men were hit or otherwise hurt seriously in the violence.

The Standard Oil Company's tugboat *Alma* (Captain Merle Molinari) served as a rescue ship for survivors taking aboard the men from two lifeboats.

The *Montebello*'s captain stated that the submarine ran quite close in to his ship and "we could see the outline of the superstructure in the water." He said the sub first appeared on his stern.

The crew members on the *Montebello* were mad and yelled curses at the Japanese. They declared that they could have hit the submarine if the tanker had been armed with naval deck gun.

The attack happened off shore from Cambria, six miles south of Point Piedras Blancas. □

—3—

SS *Samoa* Escapes 'Davy Jones' Locker

Position on December 18, 1941 when attacked by unidentified
Japanese submarine not determined

Captain Nels A Sinnes, skipper of the lumber steamer *Samoa,* reported to Navy officials at San Diego that a "giant submarine" fired five shells at the 2,000 ton vessel just before dawn on December 18th as the ship plodded along at 7 knots north of San Diego. His precise position was never revealed. The submarine was not identified but the *I-10* was known to be patrolling in that vicinity at the time.

One shell, apparently aimed at our radio antenna, burst in the air above our stern then rained fragments all over the deck. We saw the telltale wake of a torpedo coming directly amidships. It was too late for us to do anything but just wait for our destiny. None of the shells actually hit us.

He said "the miracle happened" when the torpedo didn't hit the ship but passed directly under the *Samoa's* hull then continued some distance beyond when it exploded sending a geyser of water into the air.

The sub was within hailing distance of us. It was so big that First Mate John Lehtonen, who awakened me at first sighting, and I could clearly make out its black-painted hull in the pre-dawn haze. We saw several men on its deck. One cupped his hands with a shout of 'Hi.' I replied with a megaphone, 'What do you want of us'? The several men on the deck of the submarine did not answer but immediately we heard the telegraphs ring then the roar of the vessel's engines filled the air as the submarine disappeared into the night.

At this point the *Samoa's* engine room was quickly summoned to make "full speed." All of the crew was now fully awake and many had come to the deck. The vessel responded with a lurch and raced for San Diego as the cook handed out mugs of steaming coffee to the excited crew.

In port, a Navy inspection team combed the vessel's decks picking up over a bucket full of shell fragments. The pieces were of various shapes from fingernail size to several jagged pieces up to about 6-inches long. One piece was described as "flat on one side, about 2-inches thick and about the diameter of a pancake." This example was later determined to be the "base" of a shell and measured close to 5½ inches – a 14 cm shell had been fired.

27

The ship's log has this entry by Captain Sinnes:

The sub disappeared evidentaly thinking that we were sinking on account of our heavy port list.

The *Samoa's* "list" was due, the skipper said, to the manner in which the fuel oil tanks happened to be trimmed at the time and "represented no danger to the ship but the Japs were fooled."

Post-war records reveal the attacker might have been the *I-7*, the *I-10* or the *I-19* as all had patrol stations stretching from San Pedro to Guadalupe Island (29°N - 118°45'W) Mexico. □

---4---

A Ship That Would Not Sink – *Emidio*
The latitude and longitude where torpedoed on December 20, 1941 was not recorded

The first submarine attack on a commercial ship close to the Northwest coast occurred, according to the *Emidio's* skipper, because the U. S. Navy goofed.

Captain Clark A. Farrow, of the ship, a General Petroleum tanker, was on a course set by the Navy. The Navy had told him there were no Japanese submarines in the vicinity. But as we know now, the Japanese High Command had *nine* (9) long-range aircraft-carrier (Type B-1) submarines positioned along the west coast of the United States at that time. These arrived immediately after the attack at Pearl Harbor. They were stretched from the Strait of Juan de Fuca to below the Mexican border.*

The *Emidio* was a 75,000 barrel capacity tanker but was running empty, southbound, from Seattle to San Pedro.

Captain Farrow was about 18 miles west of Blunts Reef Lightship when the lookout spotted a submarine traveling in the same direction about 10 miles landward of the 450-foot long tanker. Both vessels were going about the same speed. As *Emidio's* men could not identify the submarine as "ours of theirs – it was just BIG," Captain Farrow turned his ship toward Eureka, about 25 miles to the north, signaled his engine room to move at full speed and raced for that port. He didn't make it.

---

* For map and further explanation, see *Silent Siege-III* in bibliography.

SS *Emidio* resting at Steamboat Rock, Crescent City.

The Captain recalled:

As the tanker came about so did the sub. Although [we] were at top speed, the submarine was much faster and soon closed the distance. When a quarter-mile off, the submarine's first shot went though one of our cargo tanks amidships.

The *Emidio's* radioman sent a MAY DAY call within seconds of the hit which was answered by a passing Navy bomber on a flight between San Francisco and Seattle. The airplane dropped two bombs, one at a time, narrowly missing the submarine with the first but the second bomb failed to explode.

The attack was by Commander Kuzo Nishino in Imperial aircraft-carrying submarine *I-17*. His deck crew had raced to the 5.5-inch gun on Nishino's command and with careful aim through the optical sight, made everyone of the six shots effective. Three men on the tanker were killed as they attempted to lower a lifeboat. The same shot also toppled the ship's radio antenna. A little later, the *Emidio* took a torpedo.

There were five deaths. The three at the lifeboat station plus two in the engine room. The remaining 43 men, including the skipper, took to four lifeboats as the Japanese gun crew continued to shoot over their heads into the now abandoned hull.

When Commander Nishino observed the crew abandoning the ship, he also noted that the tanker was settling rapidly by the stern. He broke off his action, submerged, then disappeared from the scene. Nishino radioed Tokyo that he had "sunk" the ship. But we shall see.

Captain and Mrs. Clarke Farrow visit *Emidio* monument at Crescent City. Life ring and porthole frame exhibited at Battery Point Lighthouse Museum. Steamboat Rock, viewed through porthole was where hulk of *Emidio* rested for many years.

Life-ring from *Emidio* exhibited at Battery Point Lighthouse

The survivors kept their lifeboats together and rowed to the lightship where they were taken aboard about 11 p.m. The next day, the Coast Guard cutter *Shawnee*, from Eureka, picked them up and landed them at Crescent City.

The *Emidio* never did sink.

The ship drifted on the Davidson Current until it ran up on Steamboat Rock. This is adjacent to Battery Point Lighthouse, at Crescent City's front door. The battered hulk remained on public display there for the next 18 years. Finally, declared a menace to shipping by the Coast Guard, as well as an eye-sore by the local people, bids were let for its salvage. The hull was patched, refloated, then it was towed to Long Beach where it was cut up for scrap.

But there is a piece of the *Emidio*'s hull and an anchor windless in a permanent exhibit at Beachfront Park in Crescent City. Artifacts are also exhibited in the museum in the Battery Point Lighthouse nearby. □

—5—
The Strange Affairs of the *Tahoe* and the *I-23*
The *Tahoe* and the *I-23* position on December 20, 1941 was approximately 37°42'N - 123°W

Captain William Vartnow, of the obsolete steam schooner now serving the City of Oakland, California as a garbage scow, was declared to have "lived up to the highest traditions of the sea." This quotation appeared in a short news story appearing in the San Francisco *Chronicle* in January of 1942.

Some weeks earlier, on December 20th, 1941, the *Tahoe* was on a routine garbage dumping run and went to the Farallon Islands to relieve itself of its load. These several rocky islets extend northwesterly for 7 miles and are located 23 miles west of the Golden Gate. The largest of the group consists of two islands, the highest rising to about 350 feet. These rocks are a federal bird sanctuary and there is a Coast Guard lighthouse tower. Noonday Rock, covered by the sea, is a danger marked with a lighted whistling buoy. The clipper ship *Noonday* hit the uncharted rock

Garbage scow *Tahoe* at Mare Island Navy Yard about to go into dry-dock to inspect her bottom where an 80-foot long gash 1-foot wide was discovered. The skipper said he rammed a Japanese submarine. The sub's commander, Shibata, did not survive his next mission to tell about it.

on January 1, 1863. It sank within an hour thus the rock's name.

Skipper Vartnow returned from his garbage chore and put directly into Mare Island Navy Yard at Vallejo. He said that he had sighted a Japanese submarine near the islands and he had rammed it and he claimed he probably sank it with his wood-hulled *Tahoe* in broad daylight – a fanciful story on which a novel and a made-for-TV movie could be based. But Captain Vartnow was deadly serious as he talked with the Navy so officials decided to put his scow into the dry-dock and look for evidence.

In the dry-dock, marine inspectors announced that the 37-year old vessel had indeed "struck a steel object" that left an 80-foot long gash, one foot wide, in the hull. It was observed that if the damage had been caused with a ramming against a submarine, it was a wonder the hull of the wooden ship had not been punctured and the *Tahoe* sunk on the spot.

The Navy disavowed any knowledge as to what could have caused this damage but the Navy acknowledged it surely didn't happen by striking any rock. Nevertheless, the Navy had a tradition of not talking about strange things especially if its own information was limited or even, worse, if it was true there was a

Japanese submarine in its front yard and the U. S. Navy was not about to publically admit it.

What had the *Tahoe* struck? The Navy claimed there was no Japanese submarine there. But, using the advantage of 20-20-hindsight from a post-war standpoint, we know that right after the attack on Pearl Harbor, the Japanese Imperial Navy dispatched 9 of its best submarines to the U. S. west coast plus one more (*I-7*) to patrol off the northwest coast of Mexico near Guadeloupe Island. Was there a sub near the Farallon Islands? The Japanese chart reveals that *I-23* was assigned to patrol in the vicinity of Monterey Bay. That's pretty close to the Farallones. But *I-23* was not sunk that day.

Commander Genichi Shibata of the *I-23,* attacked the tanker *Agwiworld* nearby and chased the vessel into the harbor at Santa Cruz. This was the same day as the *Tahoe* incident. In the post-war conferences where the two sides sat down to discuss all ship losses, the U. S. Navy appears to have mentioned the *Tahoe* matter, but the Japanese disclaimed any knowledge about it. This may have been because the *I-23's* skipper didn't have a chance to report it if indeed it had happened as the *I-23* was later lost at sea.

When the flotilla of submarines was recalled from the U. S. west coast just before Christmas, they were ordered to Kwajalein Atoll for refueling, general resupply and rest and recreation for the nearly 1,000 crewmen who had been confined in their steel fishes for over a month. While they were enjoying themselves, and also preparing for the second air raid on Pearl Harbor, the American Navy staged an air raid at Kwaj that caught the Japanese totally by surprise. In the confusion in the lagoon, as the 46 U. S. dive and torpedo bombers rattled the palm trees and some anchored ships were sunk with bombs, the several submarines were ordered to crash dive to save themselves. During this raid, *I-23* sustained some undisclosed damage that was locally fixed, that was shrugged off.

Very shortly thereafter, the *I-23* cast off to participate in "Operation K" the second Pearl Harbor attack. The submarine made its daily noon position reports to Tokyo, but it was never heard from after February 14th, 1942. The post-war analysis by the Japanese declared it was lost due to some kind of a "marine disaster." Was the sinking of the *I-23* caused by some strain and ultimate damage done by the *Tahoe*, the after-effects of the Kwajalein air raid, or was the submarine lost due to the compound damages from both incidents or even some factor unknown? It makes a better story to say, "the *Tahoe* did it"! ☐

—6—
Agwiworld Fights Back
Position at sea when attacked on December 20, 1941 by *I-23* 37° - 122°W.

Richfield tanker *Agwiworld* loaded with oil (Capt F. B. Goncalves), was running off Cypress Point on December 20, 1941 on the north side of Carmel Bay (City of Carmel, California), when Japanese submarine *I-23* (Cmdr Genichi Shibata) suddenly surfaced and with the 14cm (5½-inch) deck gun started to shoot at the tanker. The tanker's skipper was not going to have any part of that so commanded his engine room to go to FULL SPEED and prepared to ram the submarine. The startled submarine commander seeing the threat to his health, headed out to sea followed by the churning tanker. The submarine continued to shoot but never did hit the vessel probably due to the smoke screen being made by the *Agwiworld*. The tanker then sought refuge in the harbor at Santa Cruz.

—7—

Not a Good Day for the *Larry Doheny*

Position on December 23, 1941 when first attacked by *I-25*
was not determined.
Position on October 5, 1942 when sunk by Japanese submarine
I-25: 42°20'N- 125°02'W

The day after the *I-25's* encounter with the *Camden*, Commander Meiji Tagami again sounded battle stations. In the late evening of October 5, he sighted another tanker off Cape Sebastian, five miles north of Gold Beach, Oregon. This was the Richfield Oil Company's *Larry Doheny* (Captain Olaf Brelland), 7,038-tons and 450 feet long. The vessel was on a northerly course at 10 knots. His load was 66,000 barrels of oil.*

---

* The *Doheny* had been attacked on December 23, 1941, during the wild submarine hysteria but had escaped by running into Estero Bay, California. An unidentified submarine, plausibly *I-21*, launched two torpedoes that missed the ship. One exploded near the port side of the ship and blew off the chart room door. The other exploded in the breakers. This was immediately after the attack on Pearl Harbor, when the Imperial Navy sent nine *I*-class submarines, most of them with aircraft on board, to the U.S. west coast to harass shipping. The full details of this matter is found in *Silent Siege-III*. Refer to bibliography.

Let Your Answer to Bombs be — BONDS!

Use The
MAIL TRIBUNE
Want Ad Way
Quick Results
at Small Cost

NO. 175

MEDFORD MAIL TRIBUNE

PULITZER AWARD 1934

United Press—Full Leased Wire

Thirty seventh Year.   MEDFORD, OREGON, TUESDAY, OCTOBER 13, 1942.

TANKER TORPEDOED OFF MARSHFIELD

Bill to...

SECOND ATTACK WITHIN 4 DAYS TAKES ONE LIFE

Damaged Craft Sinks While Being Towed to Port — First Torpedo Misses.

Let Your Answer to Bombs be — BONDS!

Use The
MAIL TRIBUNE
Want Ad Way
Quick Results
at Small Cost

NO. 173

MEDFORD MAIL TRIBUNE

PULITZER AWARD 1934

United Press—Full Leased Wire

Thirty seventh Year.   MEDFORD, OREGON, SUNDAY, OCTOBER 11, 1942.

JAP SUB TORPEDOES SHIP OFF COAST

SHIP SET AFIRE, 4 DIE, 38 SAVED NAVY ANNOUNCES

Attack on Recent Foggy Night, Location Untold— Schooner Makes Rescue at Dawn.

Kelly's Comment

From Washington, D. C.

Ickes Orders New Cut in Petroleum

Copper Mining Revives in Baker

Capital Housing Grows Scarcer

By John W. Kelly

Comment

It was common for the Office of War Information (OWI) to release stories to newspapers about off-shore attacks by enemy submarines on the Atlantic coast but so few were the attacks, by comparison, on the Pacific coast that when they happened, the stories got big headlines. (TOP) The paper in Medford, Oregon's front page story was about the attack on the Camden – "Second Attack Within 4 Days Takes One Life," with sub-headline "Damaged Craft Sinks While Being Towed to Port –First Torpedo Misses." Marshfield is the old name for Coos Bay. (LOWER) Headline two days earlier, reports sinking of Larry Doheny but of course the ships' name and place was not mentioned. The sub-head reading "Schooner Makes Rescue at Dawn" referred to the "Q" ship USS Anacapa.

HENDERSON MAPS PLAN TO PROVIDE ESSENTIAL TIRES

Five Point Program Told— Violators To Be Denied Rubber, Gas.

Aft gun on fantail, either a 4-inch .50 or 3-inch .38 on the *Doheny*. **Gunners saw nothing to shoot at but stayed at the gun until ordered to abandon the sinking ship.** —Frank Geelan collection

It was a very dark night with very poor visibility. Sonar operator Kou Maki had detected the *Doheny* but Tagami put off an attack because the target was too far away and dinner was ready. He considered that the risk of being spotted in the dark was minimal so be pursued the ship on the surface until in better range. Finally, when Torpedoman Kenji Takezawa was ordered to fire the first torpedo, he mashed the button. The 21-inch torpedo squirted from its tube and raced toward the target. No hit. Still too far – continue pursuit. About one hour later, Takezawa fired a second torpedo. Shoji Aizawa, who was nearby, recorded in his diary:

Success – heard tremendous sound. It hit just under the bridge and caused a huge fire.

Sadao Iijima wrote to me:

[There was] the huge fire-explosion on the ship."

Kou Maki recalled that *I-25* was low in the water at a distance and obviously not visible to men on the now sinking *Larry Doheny*. Because of the success of the attack, Captain Tagami allowed all of the approximately 100 crew men to come on deck two at a time for a brief view of the scene. The Japanese submarine had validated its existence by sinking a ship, the victim now being viewed by all members of the crew.

On the tanker, crew members remember hearing a strange sound about 8 p.m. This was probably the sound of the first torpedo hitting the hull but failing to explode.

At 9:20 p.m., the lookout on the flying bridge yelled out his sighting of what he thought was a torpedo wake. The forward lookout confirmed this but the Third Mate believed these sightings were merely porpoises so he took no action. Maybe they were. The diaries of the former Japanese sailors only tell of two shots.

When Takezawa's second torpedo slammed into the port side of the *Doheny* with a dull thud followed by a loud snapping crack at 2207 Pacific War Time, the blast caused No. 2 and 3 tanks to explode and burst into flames. The torpedo hit six feet below the water line and the starboard side buckled. The torpedo caused a 14-foot-long rip and opened the hull to the sea. It was all over for the *Larry Doheny*.

With the blast, all steering gear failed, the engines stopped, and the ship drifted, dead in the water within two minutes of the attack. Because of flames and fumes, the radioman was unable to send a distress message. A man of the Naval Armed Guard stayed at the after gun until ordered into a lifeboat. He had nothing to shoot at. The *I-25* was never seen.

Within minutes, the crew lowered lifeboats Nos. 3 and 4 and got into them. They quickly rowed away to escape the burning ship. Confidential code books went down with the ship.

A vessel, about 12 miles away, the USS *Anacapa*, a secret U.S. Navy decoy – a "Q" ship – was probably never observed by the *I-25*. It appeared on the scene early the next morning. At 0545 the "Q" took the men aboard from one lifeboat, then found the other lifeboat at 0745 and rescued those men. She searched for survivors and dropped depth charges as the *Larry Doheny* sank.

The lifeboats contained 34 of the 36 crewmen and 6 of the 10-man Navy gun crew. Of the 6 not found, 3 were known dead and 3 Navy men were listed as missing. The survivors were put ashore at Port Orford the next evening while the *I*-25 hid from Navy search ships by sitting, undetected, on the bottom of Port Orford's harbor. It was October 6, 1942. □

> The sinking of the *Larry Doheny* was the final loss, the final attack, and the final visit to American shores of Japanese submarines, during the Pacific War.

—8—
USS Anacapa – The Mystery "Q" Ship
Although not attacked during World War II, the *Anacapa*, under name
George Olson was wrecked on January 30, 1964

For about 18 months, the *Anacapa* was, to all who saw her, just an old 1919 lumber carrier. She could hold a steady 8 knots. Her role was to poke along by herself at sea as a "sitting duck" for Japanese submarines that might be looking for an easy target. This was a pretty husky "duck" for the *Anacapa* was of 7,420-tons, 335 feet long and 49 feet beam. (This was the same displacement as the U. S. Navy "Omaha" class cruisers, but the cruisers were longer and wider.)

Hidden on her decks were powerful guns. Two 3-inch guns were below bow plates and two 5-inch 50's amidships and on the fantail, were hidden in false deck houses. When the ship was in port, she was the *Coos Bay* and her crew wore civilian clothing. But at sea, she was the *USS Anacapa* (AG-49). She carried double papers. Her specially trained crew looked like merchant seamen but all were pure Navy. The *Anacapa's* skipper was Cmdr. Albert M. Wright, USN, San Diego.

From the deck of this cloak-and-dagger ship, electrician Leonard W. May, Cheyenne, Wyoming, shot the picture, with his Argus C-3 35mm camera, of the smoking *Doheny* as the doomed ship slipped beneath the waves,

USS Anacapa / Coos Bay
—Leonard W. May col.

The U.S. Navy had four "Q" ships. Three operated in the Atlantic as bait for German subs and the *USS Anacapa* was in the Pacific. But the Americans were not alone with "Q" ships. The Germans also had them.

According to records, the *Anacapa* started out when launched at Wilmington, Delaware by Pusey and Jones Corp. in 1919, as the *Castle Town*. When she was sold her name became *Lumberman*, then the *Coos Bay*. When purchased by the Navy on June 20, 1942, the ship became *USS Anacapa*. After the war and decommissioning by the Navy, the vessel, again in the lumber business, was the *George Olson*. Then the ship was dismantled to its deck and became a 3,321-ton Columbia River lumber barge still carrying the same name.

On January 30, 1964, the tug *Mikimiki* lost its tow line to the barge while crossing the Columbia River Bar at 1:20 in the morning. The Coast Guard responded to the calls for assistance with its 52-foot *Triumph*, a 40-foot and a 36-foot boat from Cape Disappointment Station. With lines attached, the rescuers started back over the bar toward Astoria but the barge started to sink. To try to save the vessel and is load, as well as to keep the channel clear of a wreck, the Coast Guard grounded the barge along side Jetty A about 1,300 feet from the Cape Disappointment lighthouse. When the cutter *Yacona* surveyed the scene, it discovered the barge had broken and the stern third of it had disappeared along with much of its lumber. The *George Olson*, x-*Anacapa*, was declared a total loss.

Notes from Leonard W. May, Cheyenne, Wyoming who served on the *Anacapa*, indicate that 1 million cu.ft. of lumber was stored in the hold to make it as unsinkable as possible. When

Larry Doheny's last moments before sinking into the Pacific Ocean off the Oregon Coast as viewed from the *Anacapa*. —Leonard W. May

the *Anacapa* was northbound along the coast, its dummy cargo was empty oil drums as deck load. On southward voyages, it had a deck load of lumber. The crew was 30. If the ship was stopped by an enemy submarine, the idea was that the Japanese wouldn't waste a torpedo on such a target, but would shell it. If challenged, about half of the ship's crew would make a pre-rehearsed scramble with abandoning the ship by lowering a lifeboat while the remainder stood at the "ready" to drop the falseworks and hopefully shoot the submarine out of the water.

Should the *Anacapa* be required to rescue a large number of survivors – it picked up 40 from the *Larry* Doheny – these could be accommodated for a few days depending on how far it was to a suitable port. (It could handle up to about 100.)

An all-steel room was constructed in the bottom of No. 1 hold which held under-water detection gear. The transmission and detector head protruded from the ship's bottom. In the radio room, standard Merchant Marine equipment was retained but special Navy radio equipment was installed. There were Y-guns on the aft well deck for dropping depth charges. To make the ship look "current," there were fake wooden 2-inch guns on the stern. The crew was all volunteers from the regular Navy, picked from submariners, in addition to war-time reservists who had special skills such as SONAR and RADAR. □

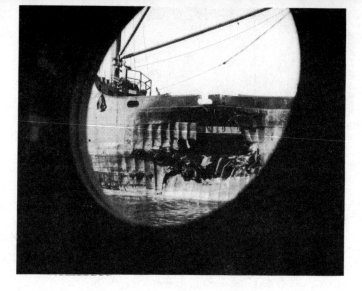

This picture of the torpedo damage to the *Absoroka* was made through a porthole from a nearby ship by a sailor, Nathan R. Deaver.

—9—
The *Absoroka*

The position on December 24, 1941 when attacked by
Japanese submarine was not recorded

The steamship *Absoroka*, a freighter, inbound to San Pedro, was shelled by a Japanese submarine almost at the harbor's door on December 24, 1941. But it would not sink as the holds were loaded with lumber. The attacking submarine, off Whites Point, plausibly the *I-19*, fired a torpedo at the ship hitting the hull on the starboard side. Folks on shore watched the adventure in wonderment that a Japanese submarine could be shooting at American ships that far from Japan.

Fortunately, no one on the crippled ship was hurt. The *Absoroka* was able to get to port under her own power then it was towed to Bethlehem Shipyard at Terminal Island to be fixed.

Before being repaired and returned to sea, Jane Russell, a voluptuous actress, was pictured standing in the hole while holding a huge sign close to the famous boson reading:

A slip of the lip will sink a ship!

☐

10

The Sinking of the *Coast Trader*

Position at sea when sunk on June 7, 1942 by Japanese submarine
I-26: 48°15'N - 125°45'W

The Imperial Japanese Navy ordered two submarines, the *I-25* (Tagami) and *I-26* (Yokota) to take up patrol positions across shipping lanes between the Pacific Northwest and the Aleutian Islands in the spring of 1942. The subs were to be on the lookout for U.S. Navy war ships that might interfere with the Japanese attacks in the Aleutians.

Commander Tagami was ordered to take his *I-25* to watch the mouth of the Columbia River.

The *I-26's* patrol offshore of Vancouver Island and prowling around outside the Straits of Juan de Fuca was a long one. He arrived on station May 30th and hung around until July 22 (U.S. dates).

On Sunday afternoon, June 7th, while cruising at periscope depth, he sighted a steamer just off the mouth of the strait. This proved to be S.S. *Coast Trader* (Capt. Lyle G. Havens). She was owned by Coastwise Steamship Company and was under charter to the U.S. Army. The ship had just put to sea from nearby Port Angeles. The skipper had set a course of 180° true at 10 knots but was not zig-zagging. He maintained radio silence. There were four lookouts: one forward, one aft, one on the bridge and one on top of the bridge. The freighter was bound for San Francisco with 1,250-tons of freshly made newsprint. The weather was ideal with a smooth sea and light variable winds. To all outward appearances, it seemed to be a nice bright, spring day for sailing in a ship at sea.

It was 1:55 p.m. and just as the cooks were about the take a break having finished the lunch chores, without warning, there was a terrific explosion that rocked the ship. In a split second the peace and tranquillity of a moment ago turned to chaos.

The shock came from slightly to starboard of the amidships section under No. 4 hatch toward the stern. As the engines quit, the hold filled with steam. The refrigerator was demolished which triggered the ammonia gas alarms. The hatch cover was blown about 40 feet into the air and with it loads of confetti – paper from the 2,000-pound rolls of news print – rained down on the decks. The mast that held the radio's transmitting antenna toppled to the deck. The starboard deck buckled upward with jagged holes and bulwarks were flattened to the side of the hull.

Looking over the rail, Captain Havens was amazed to see a huge, gaping, jagged round hole with the edges pointing inward and extending both about three feet below and above his water line. Although the Army gun crew was scanning the ocean, there was not a single thing in sight. The lookouts had not seen any submarine and there had been no visible torpedo wake. All 38 of the crew as well as the 9-man gun detail, got away safely in two life rafts and one lifeboat.

The *Coast Trader* went down in only 40 minutes.

After spending an uneventful night in the ocean, a fishing boat, the *Virginia I*, sighted the lifeboat the following afternoon and towed it into Neah Bay.

There had been no radio SOS so there had been no response from either the Navy or the Coast Guard. The next day, a Canadian corvette from Victoria, B.C., which was guided by a U. S. Coast Guard airplane, located the rafts. The corvette rescued the men then drove for the Port Angeles Navy Section Base. There had been some injuries. One man, a cook, died in the boat apparently from exposure. Those hurt were admitted to a hospital in Port Angeles. Mr. Hasagawa wrote to be about his meeting with the *Coast Trader*:

It was our *I-26* that torpedoed [the *Coast Trader*] near the Strait of Juan de Fuca. I did not go into the strait [as] it seemed too dangerous for us to enter [so] we attacked *Coast Trader* as she came out from the strait [into the ocean]. Takaji Komaba was the torpedoman at my side in the conning tower at the time of the attack. In firing the torpedo he was assisted by Yukio Oka. We could not see the last moment of her [but we saw] many things [flotsam] from the boat floating on the surface. I did not meet any U.S. forces in the area except one patrol frigate-type boat [the Canadian corvette *Edmonston*] cruising eastward. But we could not ascertain its nationality whether American, Canadian or other. However, we were much aware of the aircraft frequently flying over us.

The U. S. Navy's patrol craft the *YP89*, a Coast Guard motor surf boat (probably a 36-foot self-righting life boat). and several airplanes were sent to look for the submarine. The corvette, HMCS *Edmunston* and the American armed yacht *Sans Peur* searched the waters to the north of the strait. The American destroyer *Fox* put to sea from Port Angeles with such haste it left a liberty party ashore. Regularly patrolling PBY Catalinas were messaged to be especially alert in the search area. On June 9th, the air search group reported sighting a submarine 420 miles northwest of Tatoosh Island. This was *I-25* then enroute to its station off the Columbia River.

The Navy appoints a Board of Inquiry for every ship sunk, damaged or as some say, "if anyone stubs his toe." The Board considered the testimony of the *Coast Trader's* officers and crew then, inspite of what it had heard wrote:

> The ship was sunk by an internal explosion and not by a torpedo or mine.

Not a single member of the crew agreed with the findings.

The Navy particularly did not want any bad press by acknowledging there were enemy submarines lurking in or near the straits, so directed the late Nard Jones of the *Seattle Post Intelligencer*, then writing for the Navy as a Lieutenant, to "give the matter negative publicity" – silence! □

Corvette *Edmundston* alongside *Fort Camosun* low in water after taking Japanese torpedo from *I-25*. (lower) Crew drifts away in life boats.

11

The Attack on the *Fort Camosun*

Position at sea on June 20, 1942 when torpedoed by Japanese submarine
I-25: 47°05'N - 125°W

Commander Meiji Tagami (*I-25*) and Minoru Yokota (*I-26*) had been classmates at the Imperial Naval Academy at Etajima. They were friends. When they were assigned to the Aleutian Patrol then ordered to the west coast of North America in hostile waters, there was a feeling of comradeship knowing they were not really alone although 6,000 miles from home.

The *I-25* had been sighted by American patrol bombers in the Gulf of Alaska some 400 miles northwest of Cape Flattery. But Tagami went deep and changed course to avoid contact. He was successful. By June 1st, the *I-25* was near the north end of his patrol assignment (approximately west of Seattle) – Straits of Juan de Fuca to the Columbia River.

The daily ship-board routine could become very boring. Tagami's ward room maintained a continuing card game as did some of the 100 man crew in their cramped quarters.

On board the SS *Fort* Camosun (Capt. T. S. Eggleston) a brand new coal-burner built at Victoria, B.C., ship-board life had not yet assumed a routine as the vessel had just left port. The general cargo ship was under charter to the British Ministry of War and was on her maiden voyage. The destination was England by way of the Panama Canal. She never made it.

Just after midnight on June 20th – 12:06 a.m. to be exact – Tagami's torpedoman placed a torpedo into the port side of the ship just under the bridge. Number 2 and 3 holds were opened by the explosion. The freighter started to settle, evenly. It was a dark night. The lookouts saw nothing.

At about 1:15 a.m., *I-25* surfaced and the gun crew, led by Sadao Iijima, raced for the gun on the aft deck, uncovered it and prepared to fire. Five minutes later, the first 5.5-inch shell was fired across the vessel's bow.

The deck guns on Japanese I-class submarines were generally the same models used on the destroyers. They were long barreled and had optical sights. They were big for submarines. (Many

American submarines had 3-inch guns).

Iijima was a "regular" Navy man and had not really joined the force in peacetime with any idea of going to war and hurting anybody. *

Iijima's second round struck the starboard side amidships. A newspaper in Vancouver, B.C., the *Sun,* described the attack as "determined."

The radioman on the *Fort Camosun* got of a quick message asking for immediate help. Within six hours, the Canadian corvette *Quesnel,* which was returning to British Columbia from convoy duty along with its sister the *Edmonston* (*K-106*) which had been on anti-submarine patrol off Vancouver Island, sighted the damaged *Fort Camosun.* During this period, Tagami watched his prey through the periscope. He told me that his was a very "cautious" peaking at the scene as up scope, take a quick look, down scope, then repeat the activity at odd intervals.

The *Quesnel* dropped a pattern of depth charges around the damaged freighter but as this activity as well as the sudden arrival of other traffic was getting too much for Commander Tagami, he headed south toward the Columbia River. He entered into his log that he had "sunk a tanker."** But we know the ship was not sunk and it was not a tanker.

The freighter's crew took to two lifeboats then rowed them to a safe distance from the wrecked ship. With the *Edmunston* as lookout, the *Quesnel* picked up the 31 men from the boats.

The *Fort Camosun* was totally dead and wallowing in the water as if waiting to sink. It was slowly settling on an even keel but its prognosis for staying afloat was in jeopardy. But the ship would not sink. It was full of plywood!

Twenty-fours after the torpedoing and shelling, the *Edmonston* was able to put a tow line on the freighter then headed for

---

* Sadao Iijima told the author in Japan in 1975: "Through my optical sight I could see the crew running on deck at the front of the ship so I aimed the gun carefully to avoid the men." The philosophy of war had not struck him and being a kindly type, it plausibly didn't throughout the war: The object of war is to kill as many of the enemy as possible and to break as much of his stuff as possible.

** When I asked the Tokyo War History Institute in June 1972 about this incident, the correspondent confirmed Tagami's claim and then identified the victim as "...tanker *Fort Camosun.*"

port. The stricken ship, like most modern vessels, had "power steering" – motors to move the rudder. But with the ship dead in the water, and without any manually-operated steering apparatus, the vessel would not turn.

About 2:30 a.m., on June 22, two tugs arrived. These were the *Henry Foss*, a large commercial sea-going tugboat from Tacoma, and the USS *Tatnuck ATO-27*, a 149-foot fleet tug of 1919 vintage that mounted a 3-inch gun. By dawn, the tugs took the *Fort Camosun* in tow. At 3 p.m., another tug, the *Salvage Queen*, joined the outing. Although the torpedoed ship was by now even deeper in the water and yawed wildly, the task of getting her out of the ocean and into the strait though formidable, was accomplished. Her condition was growing more critical by the minute. As an emergency measure, all the tugboats lashed themselves to the crippled ship in an effort to hold her on course and to provide a little extra buoyancy.

Captain Leighton Evans, Royal Canadian Navy Reserve, commanding the *Quesnel*, boarded the tow and directed the movement steering for the closest port, Neah Bay, Washington. As the flotilla proceeded at a snail's pace, the foredeck of the freighter was awash but her cargo of plywood was keeping her afloat. When 8 p.m. rolled around on the 23rd, the vessel was anchored with her bottom resting in the mud of Neah bay.

The *Quesnel* crossed the strait to Esquimalt near Victoria and landed the rescued crew. Word that they were coming had leaked, so those reporters with a nose for news moved into the scene. Pathe's noted newsreel cinematographer Will E. Hudson, based in Seattle, had his (100-foot long film capacity) Bell & Howell "Eyemo" 35mm camera whirring as the survivors straggled across the gangplank.

The U. S. Navy's divers examined the hull of the *Fort Camosun* while the vessel was resting on the bottom of Neah Bay. Assured that the freighter had sufficient integrity to make it to home port, the tugs pulled her our into the strait and at only 4 knots, pulled the ship across to Esquimalt harbor arriving at 4:15 a.m. on June 25th. Repairs in Victoria and then in the dry-dock in Seattle made her seaworthy again. But that's is not the end of the story.

In the fall of 1943, the *Fort Camosun* was attacked by *I-27* in the Gulf of Aden. This time she limped into port under her own power. The freighter was still working as late as 1959 when it was acquired by the U.S. Dept. of Commerce. It was later sold for scrap. Commander Meiji Tagami's claim that he had sunk her back in 1942 was more hopeful than accurate. □

—12—
The Death of the *Camden*

The position at sea on June 23, 1942 when reported attacked by Japanese
submarine *I*-25 was 43°38'N - 124°48'W
The position at sea on October 4, 1942 when torpodoed
by *I-25* was 43°43'N - 124°54'W
The position at sea on October 10, 1942 where the ship sank was
46°46'38N - 124°31'15"W.*

The Operations Report entry for June 23, 1942, in the *War Diary, Northwest Sea Frontier* reads that at 4:40 a.m., information was received that the *SS Camden* (Captain N. A. Davidson) had been torpedoed by a submarine less than 50 miles west of Coos Bay, Oregon. Other reports of the *Camden* being struck were received and United Press began calling about tips it was getting. Planes sent to investigate reported seeing the tanker heading north apparently undamaged. A crew member of the tanker with whom I visited does not remember any such attack in June.

SS CAMDEN

* Various sources differ with the positions. Those shown are copied from the *Memorandum for File*. Re: *SS Camden* Navy Dept. Oct. 23, 1942 CONFIDENTIAL Op-16-B-5.

Lyczewski

Signalman Arnold Lyczewski a member of the Navy Armed Guard detail on the ship, vividly recalls the real attack on October 4, 1942. This 6,600-ton tanker, owned by the Charles Kurz Company out of Philadelphia, then under lease to Shell Oil Company, had left San Pedro and was enroute to Puget Sound. The ship carried 76,000 barrels of gasoline in tanks 1,2,3,4,5,6,7 and oil in tank 8. The ship stopped for engine repairs at 43°43'N - 124°51'W close to the spot where the phantom attack had been reported just four months earlier.

Imperial submarine *I-25*, nearing the end of its third and final cruise into American waters, was always on the watch for a nice, juicy, "target of opportunity."

At about 7 a.m., the sub's lookout reported a large ship dead in the water. No lights were showing but the sun was just coming up. The sea was choppy and there was a light northwesterly wind. It was almost ideal weather and the *Camden* was an ideal target. Commander Tagami called his crew to "stations" then zeroed in on what he thought was a freighter.

On board the *Camden*, the skipper and the mate were on the bridge. Signalman Lyczewski was on watch at the stern near the the 4-inch gun. He saw one torpedo miss the ship then realizing there would probably be another quickly, he wrapped himself around a steel ladder and hung on.

He wrote to me many years later:

> The second torpedo hit the starboard side and the blast was terrible. Fire and smoke and black oil flew higher than our masts. I lost my grip on the ladder and was knocked flat on the deck. I immediately got up and turned on the General Alarm. The ship's steward, Ray Jones, of Laguna Beach, California, was out on the deck with me when all this started. Right after the blast, he jumped overboard and started swimming. I threw him a cork life ring but he kept right on swimming. We never saw him again.

When the torpedo hit the starboard bow 10 feet from the stem, smoke and flames immediately appeared from the tank containing fuel oil. After the hit, the tanker immediately settled by the head. Decks were awash from the bow to the bridge with her propeller out of the water. A radioman sent a distress message on

The two-fingered "V" for victory salute is given by crew members who survived the torpedoing of the *Camden* then were rescued by the Swedish ship *Kookaburra*. The men disembarked at Seattle. —Picture from microfilm of Seattle *Post Intelligencer*.

Tugboat *Kemal* has cut the tow line as *Camden* starts her death-plunge

500 kc. At 7:05 Captain Davidson ordered "Abandon Ship." The Navy guard manned the gun until the last minute but did not fire because no target appeared. By 7:20, 47 crew members including the Armed Guard detail, were off the ship in three lifeboats and one life raft.

The Swedish motorship *Kookaburra* picked them up about 11 o'clock. The men were off-loaded at Port Angeles the following afternoon. Although another ship, the *Victor R. Kelly* had been sighted from the *Camden's* bridge at an estimated 7 miles to the north, the ship did not assist with the rescue. Apparently *I-25's* lookouts didn't see the *Kelly* either or Commander Tagami would surely have attacked it.

Commander Tagami's claim of the sinking of the *Camden* was only slightly premature.

A Navy boarding party recovered the Confidential documents and codes that had been left on the bridge then succeeded in controlling the fire. The tug *Kemal* took the damaged ship in tow then headed for the Columbia River as the initial plan was to repair the ship at Astoria. On arrival at Cape Disappointment, it was determined that the *Camden* was too deep in the water to cross the always treacherous Columbia River bar so the orders were changed to take the wreck to Seattle.

At 6:30 p.m. on October 10, the *Camden* suddenly burst into flames. In just 15 minutes the ship sank in 52 fathoms. Her position was just west of Gray's Harbor, Washington at 46°0' 46"N - 124°31'15"W. □

—13—
The Soviets Lose Their *L-16*
The position at sea on October 11, 1942 was not reported —sank

Kou Maki, the submarine *I-25's* SONAR operator, reported to Captain Meiji Tagami that he had determined there were two submarines on the surface about 800 yards apart moving southward. Presuming them to be American, the skipper ordered his crew to battle stations and prepared to launch his last torpedo.

The *I-25* had been cruising on the surface about 800 miles west of the Washington coast on the great circle route to Japan. Tagami went to periscope depth as quickly and quietly as possible then closed the distance to about 500 yards. As this was his last fish, he wanted a sure hit.

Morikazu Kikuchi was a diesel machinist. He recalls that the SONAR report indicated that the enemy submarine's main engine was turning at 150 rpm. At Commander Tagami's request, Kikuchi figured the target was moving between 11 and 12 knots. This would be a cruising speed as if the subs were headed somewhere and not necessarily just out on a patrol. And two of them close together?

Tagami, basing his firing data on this speed, scored a direct hit. Shoji Aizawa, who was keeping a diary wrote:

> The torpedo was fired by Kenji Takezawa at 4.07 a.m. [Tokyo time]. The explosion followed in about 20 seconds with shock and damage to *I-25* because of closeness.

The torpedo obviously hit a vital spot for witnesses on the *I-25* and on the second submarine that was following close by, describe the resulting explosion as "devastating." Nobuo Fujita, pilot of the GLEN aircraft housed on the *I-25*, who was often detailed to control room duty, told me that it was a...

> ...terrific explosion. The shock was very severe [on *I-25*] like a near-miss bomb or depth charge."

Aizawa, a torpedoman, wrote to me relating that:

> ...the shock broke glass covers on instruments, put out some of the lights and *broke the porcelain toilets* in the submarine.

An officer who was in the submarine that was following reported that a sailor on watch said he ...

> ...heard a violent explosion [and] saw a column of water approximately 100 feet high [and] pieces of what appeared to be plating and black smoke rise from the sea.

He also reported seeing periscopes of a submarine about 1,500 yards to port. The remaining sub, the *L-15*, fired five rounds from her deck gun at them but without apparent results.

The stricken submarine sank in about *20 seconds*. It took with it all hands on board. Right after the explosion, the *L-15*

Sergi A. V. Milhailoff, USNR
1890 - 1942

Chief Mihailoff, a naturalized American, was lost with the 50-member crew of *L-16*. He was detailed to serve as translator and liaison officer and had boarded at Dutch Harbor. Here was an American citizen in the U. S. Navy, on a Soviet warship, torpedoed by the Japanese, when the Soviet and Japanese were not at war with each other. Mihailoff, an American hero of the Pacific War, died without notice until the matter was brought up in the author's books. Refer to *Silent Siege-III* for additional details. See bibliography.

started a zig-zag anti-submarine course.

Sadao Iijima remembers his feelings at the time and told me:

For a moment I shudder thinking of the lives lost of the enemy crew and their poor families. I realized that this very destruction could have been us but we were at war, a sad situation. I still pray for the souls of the dead and for the happiness of their families.

Commander Tagami reported to Tokyo that he had sunk an American submarine on October 11, 1942 (Tokyo time). It was also listed in the War History Institute as an American submarine. When Mr. Fujita wrote about this in a Japanese magazine in the 1950's, he also still assumed it was an American submarine.

But the U. S. Navy has always claimed there were no American submarines operating in the area at that time.

Two Soviet subs were. These were the *L-15* and the *L-16*. They were out of Vladivostok enroute to the U.S.S.R. with stops at Dutch Harbor, San Francisco and the Panama Canal. U.S. officials had offered partial air coverage from Alaska to California but the Soviet commander refused, preferring not to follow a definite course.

The loss of the Soviet submarine presented a potentially embarrassing international situation. The U.S.S.R. and Japan were not at war. Although American naval officers suspected at the time that the Soviet sub had been sunk by the same Japanese submarine that had attacked the *Camden* and the *Larry Doheny* within the week, no such announcement was made.

When the matter was presented to Messers. Fujita and Tagami in 1973 by the author, Fujita replied:

I believe that none of our crew knew that the submarine was Russian. Both Commander Tagami and I, discussing the matter in 1973, feel very lucky that this affair did not bring serious diplomatic problems between Japan and the U.S.S.R. at the time. □

I-180 Japanese Submarine Located —sunk

Position at sea on April 26, 1944 when sunk: 55°10'N - 155°40'W

No Japanese submarines had come prowling into the waters off Alaska since the troubles in the Aleutians in 1942-43. It was now the spring of 1944. And there she was, the Imperial government's 333½ feet long *I-180*.

The *I-180* was a new submarine having been launched at Yokosuka Navy Yard in 1942 and ready for sea just 15 months later. She was out to intercept targets of opportunity and was parked on the great-circle course. *I-180* was watching for allied ships that regularly ran between Seattle and the Aleutian Islands. If lucky, a freighter out of Seattle with Lend-Lease material for the Soviet Union with destination Vladivostok might happen by. The sub, whose displacement was somewhere between 1,833 and 2,602 tons, had six 21-inch torpedo tubes and carried 12 torpedoes. On deck was a 4.7-inch long-barreled cannon.

On April 26th, a pair of freighers, guarded by two destroyer escorts, entered the effective range of the *I-180*. The freighters were the *Frank G. Drum* and the *Greenup*. Their escorts were the *Gilmore* and the *Edward C. Daly*.

At 2230, the destroyer-escort *Gilmore's* night-duty crew in the RADAR room came alive when they saw a blip that indicated a surface contact just 4 miles away. The escort received radio permission to leave the convoy so turned in the blip's direction. Just 5 minutes later, now only 2 miles off, the *Gilmore* challenged with blinker. Instead of replying by blinker, the contact quickly disappeared. *Gilmore's* crew was summoned to general quarters therefore starting the deadly game of cat-and-mouse. The game lasted only 2 hours and 37 minutes.

The target turned out to be *I-180*. This KD-7 class submarine had been caught on the surface recharging its batteries.

Gilmore attacked several times with patterns of Mark-10 then Mark-6 projectiles while *Daly* sent a coded message to Alaska Sea Frontier Command that a contact had been made.

At Kodiak Naval Air Station, four OS2U-3 KINGFISHER observer planes with wheels, instead of the usual pontoons, were quickly fitted with 350 pound depth charges and readied for a search and destroy mission. It would be about a 2-hour flight to the interception site. The weather was the usual putrid. The four pilots were Lt.Cdr Robert E. Ellis, leader; Lt. Ray Compton; Lt. jg. Peter Klein; Ensign James W. Spencer, USNR.

Meanwhile, back in the ocean, the *Gilmore's* patterns had brought forth a tremendous underwater explosion from about 280-feet under the sea. A little later, an oil slick appeared but in reality, it was not reported by the naval vessel as the oil was nearly impossible to see in the inky night.

The KINGFISHERS arrived at dawn. Although there was no sign of the *Gilmore*, which was now under a fog patch, the pilots saw and reported the oil slick. It was about one mile square and so thick that it prevented white-caps from breaking in the 35-knot wind.

The location was plotted to be 55° 10' N and about 50 miles from tiny Chirikof Island. As there was no need to waste expensive ordnance, the airplanes returned to Kodiak.

The Action Report rated the incident as "probable kill" on April 26, 1944. But no positive conformation would be available until after the war when the Japanese admitted it was their *I-180* that had been lost with all hands to the *Gilmore* that night. □

—15—
Sunk:
John A. Johnson and *I-12* Japanese submarine

John A. Johnson. Position at sea on October 29, 1944 when sunk by
Japanese submarine *I-12*: 29°36'30"N - 141°43'W
Submarine *I-12*. Position at sea on November 12, 1944 when sunk by
USS Rockford: 31°55'N - 139°45'W

By autumn of 1944, all was quiet along the west coast of the United States there having been no submarines sighted and no ships damaged or sunk for two full years. Admiral Shigeyoshi Miwa, Commander of the Japanese Sixth Fleet, felt he would like to disrupt American shipping along the coasts of Washington, Oregon and California. In this way, he reasoned, ships loaded

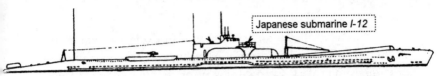
Japanese submarine *I-12*

with war materials bound for the South Pacific battle areas could be interrupted. In searching for a suitable method to conduct hit-and-run raids, he learned that the new "A-2" class submarine, the *I-12*, had just been completed.

The *I-12* was the only submarine in its class. It was intended as a long-range escort command ship. It was fitted with both electric and diesel power plants that were considerably less powerful (by over half) compared with other submarines of the same size and crew complement. But there was a compensating factor for the slower power plants. It was that the *I-12* had a range of 22,000 miles. This was 6,000 miles greater range than her counterparts that had been spread along the American west coast immediately after Pearl Harbor.

This submarine sailed from Japan early in October taking an evasive course to avoid the packs of American submarines that were now a threat to everything Japanese that floated. She left Kure Naval Base on the 4th by way of the narrow Tsugar-u Strait to the North Pacific Ocean. This is between Honshu and Hokkaido.

One of the ways Americans were plotting Japanese ship movements, was in being certain to plot the locations of all noon-time radio reports of positions. This daily reporting was standard practice in the Japanese Navy. But the *I-12*, and its home-base commanders, had agreed that the sub would not send position reports therefore the Americans would not know the *I-12* existed.

The waters between Hawaii and the U. S. mainland were considered to be an "American lake." This was because of no enemy troubles for months but on October 29th, this "quiet" was jolted awake. The freighter *John A. Johnson* was plowing through a placid sea at 8.9 knots on a course 239° true out from San Francisco. The freighter was not zig-zagging. It was totally blacked out and its radio was off. The ship carried a large detachment of Armed Guard personnel. On duty were four in gun tubs on the bridge and one, aft. Visibility was good with only a few clouds on an otherwise clear night. There were no other ships within view.

The freighter had a load of 140 tons of explosives and nearly 7,000 tons of canned foodstuffs. The ship was crammed full with this freight. On deck were dozens of crated and uncrated trucks lashed to closely there was little space to walk. There was an overly large population aboard made up of 41 in the merchant crew, 28 in the Armed Guard detachment plus 1 U. S. Army Security Officer – 70 in all. In the captain's cabin was a locked pouch of Registered Mail. From an attack standpoint, the scene was nearly textbook ideal.

The *I-12* was 372¾ feet long, displaced 2,390 tons and was a large, steady platform from which to operate. At 9:05 p.m., as the freighter was taking a roll to port, a torpedo struck the starboard side forward of the bridge below No. 3 hold. A few minutes later, the track of a second torpedo was sighted but it passed about 50 yards astern then exploded about 2 miles aft on the port side.

The explosion of the first torpedo was below the water line – the ship was drawing 27 feet due to its load – but the blast was muffled by the tightly packed canned goods so there was no upward damage to the deck other than the trucks were torn loose.

One starboard lifeboat was wrecked. Unbelievably, there was no damage to the engine room and the crew there shut down everything within about 3 minutes. Only No. 3 hold was flooded. The shock had damaged the main transmitting antenna so a quick change was made to an alternate transmitter. Although a distress signal was immediately sent, there was no reply. All this was happening very quickly.

Within about three minutes, the ship began to break into two sections forward of the bridge. It took only about 10 minutes for the ship to break completely in two. As no attacking submarine was seen, there was nothing for the Armed Guard to shoot at. The ship's captain sounded the Abandon Ship alarm on the freighter's whistle just 20 minutes after the attack started.

The large contingent of men took to the boats with some doubling for as we saw, one of the boats had been wrecked by the blast. Then another foundered when it hit the water. The location was recorded as 31°55'N - 139°45'W.

As the flotilla of life boats distanced itself from the wreckage, about 30 minutes later the submarine surfaced in the middle of the boats. In the confusion, four of the merchant crew and five of the guards as well as the Security Officer were determined to be missing and presumed dead.

The *I-12*'s gun crew rushed to the deck, pointed its 5.5-inch cannon first at one section then at the other section of the ship setting each half on fire. The sub stayed in the area for about three hours plausibly waiting to attack any rescue ships that showed up. Suddenly, the sub's diesels roared into action and the vessel left at high speed in an unknown direction. The men in the boats spent an anxious night.

About 10 the next morning, the Pan American Clipper, which flew scheduled flights between San Francisco and Honolulu, appeared overhead. Then it circled low to observe the scene. (During the investigation that followed, the airplane's pilot said he and the passengers had seen the submarine earlier that morning.) The radioman signaled Pearl Harbor reporting seeing only the stern of a ship on fire as well as seeing the men in lifeboats. About 5 that afternoon, a plane swooped over the site then dropped a "Gibson Girl" emergency radio by parachute. This was picked out of the sea, set up and immediately operated.

> The "Gibson-girl" radio transmitter was intended for use by pilots who had ditched in the sea. To operate it, one merely turned a crank which sent a signal that could be located by direction finders. It got its name because the radio had an "hour-glass" shape.

At about 9:30 that night, just 24 hours after the *I-12*'s attack, the Navy's *Argus*, (PY-14) picked up the survivors and sailed directly for San Francisco where it docked on November 3rd.

Two weeks after the sinking of the *John A. Johnson* the *Rockford*, (FP-48) a new 1,430-ton frigate over 300 feet long, with an all-Coast Guard crew, along with the new mine-sweeper *Ardent*, (AM-340) were participating in a routine 6-ship convoy between Pearl Harbor and San Francisco. This convoy was following the same "track" as had been the *John A. Johnson* in the "American lake." But the convoy was steaming in the opposite direction and was zig-zagging on a course of 58° true at about 11 knots. *Rockford* was on the starboard and *Ardent* on the port side . At 12:42 *Ardent* advised *Rockford* by code that *Ardent* had made sound contact and was investigating. All ships in the flotilla were ordered to make a simultaneous emergency turn to starboard.

Ardent's Mark 10 projectile attack had no results so the *Rockford* requested permission of the convoy commander, who was aboard the *Grant*, to leave its guard position to assist in attacking whatever had attracted *Ardent's* attention. Permission was granted and the frigate left the convoy. Ten minutes later, *Rockford* fired a full pattern of depth charges. There were no misfires.

The *Rockford's* deck log reveals that a

...terrific underwater explosion was heard; debris and oil came to surface [then] submarine was seen just beneath the surface on her side [then] bow broke the water pointed up at angle, remained motionless for about one minute, more hissing of escaping air then submarine disappeared.

Later, a whale boat was put over the side of the frigate with a salvage crew aboard. These sailors brought back

...many pieces of teak deck plants, pieces of cork insulation, wooden slat from a vegetable crate inscribed with Japanese writing listing name and address of produce dealer. Piece of varnished wood from an instrument case with loose fitting screws around the edges as if blown off remainder of box inscribed with Japanese writing; one piece of teak deck planking inscribed in Japanese with the builder's specifications. These trophies were all covered with diesel oil.

From the first report of the submarine's presence, until the destruction of *I-12* was only 79 minutes.* □

---

* Additional particulars about this action are in *Silent Siege-III*. See bibliography.

—16—
Northerner Lost Her Footing in a Slippery Sea
Lost January 5, 1860

When a ship in the 1860's hit uncharted rocks, there was little a skipper could do. There was no radio. He would fly his flag upside down hoping another vessel would see it. If the situation permitted, he might put lifeboats over the side with his crew and passengers in it. Sometimes a barrel of oil might be burned on deck to glow in the night.

The sidewheel steamer *Northerner* (Capt. W. L. Dall), left Francisco at 4:30 on the morning of January 4, 1860. Dall passed through the Golden Gate and turned to the north heading for Puget Sound with a planned stop on the Columbia River.

The ship steamed quietly on its course at 12 knots but the sea was running heavy. One hundred-eight people filled the crew and passenger lists. The ship was west of Cape Mendocino, off Blunts Reef, when the *Northerner* lost its footing in the slippery sea and had its bottom gouged on an uncharted rock. When a large swell lifted the ship off the rock, the vessel started taking water. The pumps were started and the lower reaches of the vessel were inspected for damage. It was pretty bad. Water was gaining against the pumps with risk that the boiler fires could be put out by the rising sea water in the ship.

Where was this?

One report said the stranding was on a rock 3½ miles north of Cape Fortunas – a cape of that name not on today's maps. It changed names several times over the years but finely, the name <u>Punta Gorda</u> was settled on by the Geographic Names Board. This is south of Cape Mendocino. The area is noted for fog. In 1911 a lighthouse was established 1 mile se from the point (40°15'N - 124°21'W) **with a fog siren but this was discontinued sometime after 1934. The description of the off-shore rocks is in *Pacific Coast Pilot No. 7*:**

The outlying rocks are not more than .7 miles offshore until about 2.5 miles s of Cape Mendocino where they extend offshore to Blunts Reef, 2.5 miles w of the cape.

The captain believed the only chance to save his passengers and his ship was to make a run for the beach. He made it almost all the way when the engines stopped. One of the lifeboats was lowered full of women and children under the charge of an officer. The boat remained upright on its wild ride shoreward and was soon dashed upon the beach by a thunderous breaker. A second boat was not so lucky for it turned over with all except two of the occupants drowned. When the third boat was launched, it lost most of its passengers when a big wave swamped it.

Finally, the Chief Engineer, Thomas O'Neil, tied a line to the ship and the other end around his body and jumped into the heaving sea. He gained the shore to establish a life line but as the night was very dark, those on the ship would not leave it.

A seaman, who knew there was a horse on board, set about to free the animal and bring it to the deck. Once topside, the desperate sailor forced the horse off the ship with him clutching to its tail. The horse headed for the beach with the soaked crewman desperately hanging on. Although badly shaken, both made it.

The people and the vessel were severely jostled by the storm which, along with the hole in its hull, caused the vessel to break. A large section of the deck, with many clinging to it, drifted toward shore. Finally, with breakers crashing over it, the piece of wreckage and its frightened passengers who happened to be on it only by chance, were flung onto the beach. The remainder of the ship, with many people still aboard, sank.

When dawn came and a head count could be taken, it was discovered that 70 had been spared a watery death. Thirty-eight were missing and presumed to have drowned.

Inspectors believed the cause of this catastrophe was inadequate navigation charts and the plausibility that the *Northerner* had not been properly inspected. □

—17—
Catastrophic Loss of *Brother Jonathan*
Position when stranded July 30, 1865 was approximately 41°50'N - 124°22'W

The wreck of the side-wheeled steamer *Brother Jonathan* (Capt. Samuel DeWolf), 1,359-tons, 220-feet long, which occurred on St. George Reef, a few miles from Crescent City, California, was a catastrophe beyond the imagination for the period. Some remnants of the ship are in the museum at Battery Point Lighthouse at Crescent City.

—0—

A severe storm was blowing and the headwinds the ship was trying to bite into were insurmountable. The ship, out of San Francisco and bound for Victoria, British Columbia, was making no headway. Finally, Captain DeWolf decided to reverse his

Brother Jonathan —Del Norte County Public Library

course and go back to Crescent City, from where he had just left after putting some cargo ashore, to wait out the storm. In spite of the stiff winds, the *Brother Jonathan* was successfully turned and was headed in the direction of the safety of the harbor just 6 miles away. The ship, and 166 of its 185 people on board, never made it. Only 19 survived. It was July 30, 1865.

> **Depending on the writer, some claim the vessel had no planned stops between San Francisco and its destination, Victoria, B.C. Others say there was a stop at Crescent City to off-load freight. Some conjecture that Captain DeWolf made an unscheduled stop to get rid of some of the overload due to the rough sea.**

Some claim the vessel was never intended for use in the open ocean. It had been built in 1850-51 to chug through the relatively clam waters of Long Island Sound. But the ship was just out of the yard when it was sold and undertook the long trip around South America for service on the Pacific Coast. At San Francisco, the ship underwent two changes. It got new owners and a new name: *Commodore*.

As the *Commodore*, the paddle-wheeler carried passengers and general cargo along the northwest coast. On a voyage in 1858, her joints were severely strained when she nearly foundered in a typically rough northwest storm with 350 passengers on board off the coast of Washington.

The owners decided their money-making venture with the

little ship was too risky so they sold the now creaking vessel to the California Steam Navigation Company. The first order of business was a complete rebuild which included another name change. She would henceforth be the *Brother Jonathan*.

In the early 1860's, the shipping business out of San Francisco was very good. It was so good that the line's ships were going to sea badly overloaded. When the *Brother Jonathan* was being readied for a trip to Victoria, the skipper vainly tried to stop the overloading be was observing. He asserted to the ship's agent that a voyage in the open sea with the overload would be unsafe. But money won over safety. He was sternly directed to get aboard and sail his ship or he would be fired.

The *Brother Jonathan* left its dock at noon on July 28th and drove through the Golden Gate into the North Pacific Ocean. On gaining the open water, the ship was immediately buffeted by a heavy sea churned by a steady northerly wind. The overloaded vessel did her best but under the conditions, the pitching deck sent most of the passengers to their beds. There is nothing so miserable than being seasick and there was no letup.

After losing headway due to the storm, a little north of Crescent City, Captain DeWolf decided to seek refuge so put about for that port.

The circumstances of the ships of the California Steam Navigation Company being overloaded may be laid to the speculations that the Confederate raider *Shenandoah* was thought to be in nearby waters. Was the plan to overload the vessels to compensate for fewer sailings thereby limiting exposing the ships to the Confederate Navy? Or was the overloading greed?

Captain DeWolf plausibly breathed a sigh of relief after successfully herding his top-heavy and ungainly ship through the 180-degree turn. Now to make the harbor's safety. In his way was St. George Reef. It has never been settled as to why the ship was lost other than the fact that it hit a rock. The reef is made of rocks and covered ledges extending 6½ miles northwest of west from Point St. George. There are nine of these rocks visible. The *Brother Jonathan* lurched to a stop when it hit one that apparently was covered by the raging swells and was not seen. Now, in memoriam, it is named Jonathan Rock. That rock breaks into the

Brother Jonathan sank after hitting a rock.
—Del Norte County Library

open only in a heavy swell but not continuously even then. Deep water surrounds it. In less than one hour, the ship slipped off the ledge into this deep water. Jonathan Rock lies 3.2 miles southeast of Northwest Seal Rock upon which the government opened the St. George Reef Lighthouse in 1891.*

The crash ripped open the bottom of the vessel and immediately there was great panic among the passengers and crew as people rushed for lifeboats. One boat was lowered but it was so overloaded that it turned over drowning all who had been in it.

James Patterson, the Third Mate, placed five women and three children in a boat and while his back was turned, ten of the crew piled in. Patterson, gained the stern of the boat which was lowered away. Whether it was his skill or Lady Luck, this lifeboat with 19 survivors, was picked up by the steamer *Del Norte* (Capt. Henry Johnson) which had been dispatched from Crescent City on a rescue mission. These 19 went down in history as the only survivors of the 185 who had left San Francisco.

Jacob Yates, a quartermaster, was at the ship's wheel when

* The lighthouse (41°50'N - 124°22'W) was discontinued May 13, 1975 in favor of an automatic floating buoy deployed 1 mile west of the lighthouse.

the *Brother Jonathan* struck the rock. At the hearing that followed, he reported:

I took the wheel at 12 o'clock. A northwest gale was blowing and we were four miles above Point St. George. The sea was running mountain high and the ship was not making any headway. The captain thought it best to turn back to Crescent City and wait until the storm ceased. He ordered the helm hard aport. I obeyed, and it steadied her. I kept due east. This was about 12:45. When we made Seal Rock the captain said, "Southeast by south" It was clear where we were, but foggy and smoky inshore. We ran until 1:50 when she struck with great force, knocking the passengers down and starting the deck planks. The captain stopped and backed her, but could not move the vessel one inch. She rolled about five minutes, then gave a tremendous thump and part of the keel came up alongside. By that time the wind and sea had slewed her around until her head came to the sea, and she worked off a little. Then the foremast went through the bottom until the yard rested on the deck. Captain DeWolf ordered everyone to look to his own safety, and said that he would do the best he could for all.

But the captain's hands were tied. His last words were reported to have been:

Tell them that if they had not overloaded us we would have got through all right and this never would have happened.

The 3rd Mate, James Patterson, one of those who gained the lifeboat and lived to tell about it sent a telegram to the owners, the California Steam Navigation Company. It was published in the newspaper in Jacksonville:

The steamer *Brother Jonathan* struck a sunken rock off of George's Point, eight or so miles northwest from Crescent City at 1½ o'clock today and went down in 45 minutes. All on board are supposed to be lost, except seventeen persons and three children, who came ashore with me in a lifeboat, about 5 o'clock p.m. All the small boats in this place have gone out to the rescue– no hope of saving anyone. Two boats swamped alongside of the ship; three boats are left on the steamer. The following is a list of the saved in my boat: Jas. Patterson, 3rd officer; David Fannell, steerage steward; Henry Miller, baker; Patrick Linn, fireman; W. Lowery, fireman; Edward Echields, water; Stephen Moran, waiter; Mrs. M. A. Medale, Mrs. H. Bernhard and child, Mrs. M. E. Walder, Mrs. M. Stott and child, and four colored seamen. At 8 o'clock p.m., boats all returned and reported nothing seen of the wreck. We have given up all hopes. The last that was seen of General Wright, he was standing on board holding a life preserver in his hand. There were two boats swamped before one that the fourteen and the woman and child made their escape in. Capt. Buckley had men out patrolling the beach all night and the next day, so as to pick up any bodies that might drift ashore, but there was no drift of the ship, nor did any wash on shore up to 2 o'clock on the 31st ult. The boat fired two guns, but it was thought that it was only a signal of some boat on her way up. There was nothing known of it until it was revealed by those who made their escape in the small boat.

Jas. Nesbit, editor of the Bulletin, was among the passengers. Major Eddy, Paymaster United States Army, had $200,000 Government funds, which were to be used in paying off troops. The Major, before sailing, balanced his Government accounts, settled his private affairs, and made his will, telling one of his friends that he felt a presentiment that he should never return.

—The *Oregon Reporter* Jacksonville Oreg. Aug. 5, 1865

Other wealth aboard included $80,000 of the ship's money and personal funds of passengers entrusted to the purser, John S. Benton. The Wells Fargo Agent, Mr. Joseph Lord, had $250,000. There was a cache of pure gold bars.

One of the more prominent passengers was General George Wright of the United States Army. His wife elected to stay with her doomed husband although she had been offered a place in a lifeboat. They went down into the sea together.* Other notables on board were Anson Henry who had been appointed Governor of Washington Territory and James Nesbitt, editor of the San Francisco *Bulletin*. Nesbitt's body was recovered seven miles at sea.

In the weeks that followed, the sea coughed up 75 bodies but the others were never recovered.

Many are the stories about the wealth that was alleged to be on the ship some thinking it was higher than a million dollars. Known values were the Army pay, Wells Fargo money and gold.

Adventurous amateur and some professional divers have sought to find the ship and from time to time there are reports of its discovery. The wreckage was finally discovered in the summer of 1994. In August of 1995, the State of California's State Historic Commission nominated the ship for listing on the *National Register of Historic Places*. A firm, Deep Sea Research, Inc., wants to dive on the ship to recover the "treasure" and filed a brief in federal district court to establish its right to do just that. While the company owns the salvage rights, a story in the Crescent City newspaper (The *Triplicate*) asserts:

---

* When a Colonel, Wright had led a punitive expedition against the Indians in the Battle of Four Lakes and Spokane Plains near Spokane. Many Indians died along with their ponies. Some critics of the colonel declared his death on the *Brother Jonathan* was his "just rewards."

Deep-sea divers ready
to descend, in 1915,
on suspected location
where *Brother
Jonathan*'s remains
are hidden. Almost
uncountable numbers
of searches have been
conducted but have
apparently been
fruitless until 1994.
Now, with the location
known, it will be up to
the courts to decide
what to do about it.
—Curry County Hist. Soc.

The judge ruled it [salvage] must be done under the auspices of a qualified archaeologist and that all artifacts found would be under the jurisdiction of the court.

Donald Knight, an archeologist and deep-water explorer had a video of the hulk. He said the ship seems to be sitting upright on the ocean floor, in one piece

...and it's most deninitely the *Brother Jonathan*. It is the culmination of a 19-year search. We have found a maritime graveyard, the last resting place of 221 lives.

Dwight Gregory, news director for KPOD radio, Crescent City, who viewed the 19-minute video, said:

You can see the hub of the paddle wheel on the port side, part of the steam boiler, part of the engine. It says 'Morgan Iron Works New York'

Knight declined to identify where the ship rests.

It may probably be some time before a decision is made to accept the application that the wreck be accepted for the *National Register* and quite some time before anything is done about diving on the remains of the *Brother Jonathan* to determine what is really there. Time will tell. ☐

HINDSIGHT: The impact of the *Brother Jonathan* tragedy moved legislators to pass a law requiring that all cargo ships be marked with waterlines to avoid catastrophies resulting from overloads.

—18—
Humboldt Bar Claims *Mendocino*
Stranded December 2, 1888 —abandoned

The Humboldt bar claimed another victim but it took from December 2, 1888 until March of 1889 for Davy Jones to secure the *Mendocino* in his locker.

This steam schooner met her end before she had any real experience in the water. Only months old, the vessel left San Francisco Bay and headed for Eureka. Her cargo was lumber.

The Chief Engineer, Frank Bragg, gave a heart-rending account to newspapermen. He said that the bar looked pretty rough so it would be preceeded in the crossing by the steamer *Tillamook*. But when the *Tillamook* neared the bar, her skipper decided against making any crossing and turned around.

Apparently the skipper made a signal to the *Mendocino* to also turn back for the open sea but the *Mendocino*, presumably not seeing the signal, headed in. In no time at all, the ship grounded on the south spit about half-a-mile from the bay and about 75 yards off center and south of the channel. When the ship struck, it was brutally turned around taking so much water the engine room became flooded.

Although a boat was lowered in which Bragg and his wife with their child took seats, along with three others, it was swamped by an incoming breaker. All wore the standard cork life preservers. They floundered for about half-an-hour when the rescuers from the Humboldt Bay Life Saving station arrived in their boat. But the child had drowned. Efforts to revive the youngster by the lifesavers, were unsuccessful.

News of the wreck had reached the Life Saving Station in a round-about manner. The stranded ship was first observed from the farm of Captain H. H. Buhne from which there was a clear view of the bay and bar. Buhne's farm had one of the new and very few telephones. With a twist of the crank, a call was made to Buhne's store in Eureka which notified the crew in the Humboldt Bay Life Saving Station. While this was happening, Captain Buhne sent his bar tug to the scene.

As the tug considered what, if anything, it might do with the stranded vessel, the lifesavers again rowed their boat to the scene to stand by if needed. Those still on the *Mendocino* included the skipper, the mate and six of the crew. Although, by signals, it was agreed they would leave the ship, nothing could be done until high tide. While the rescuers waited out the clock, the Lyle gun, for shooting a weighted line to a stranded ship, and other materials were transferred from the lifesaver's boat to the steam tug. On the third attempt, the line was landed and made fast on the vessel. All this time a storm was raging with huge breakers crashing in the middle of the operations.

One at a time, heavier lines were passed from the tug to the *Mendocino* as efforts proceeded to try to pull the vessel back into deeper water. While many tow lines have worked well over the years, just as many break thereby thwarting the salvage effort.

And so it was on this day when the line snapped.

The Life Saving Station men worked their boat up to the ship and under less than favorable conditions, succeeded in rescuing everyone but the captain. He was temporarily entangled in the maze of lines on the deck. But the captain was rescued on the next tide when the boat made another trip.

Time and tides await no man. By now, Christmas Eve, the weather had moderated somewhat so the lifesavers made another run to the ship. This trip was to recover the ship's instruments and what personal property as might be located.

The next night, King Neptune decided to move the ship without the help of the salvage tug. The *Mendocino* drifted off its sandy perch into the channel then quickly grounded on the north spit where the vessel promptly settled in the sand. Efforts were made to unload the lumber were started on the ship's owners' order. To do this, a tramway was installed on the spit to convey the lumber to the bay. With the ship lightened, some though was given to moving it over the spit then launching her in Humboldt Bay. It had been done before. Although work in this direction started, the soft beach sand made progress so difficult that after a mere start, the operation was discontinued.

The owners placed the vessel on auction "as is where is." There was a successful bidder at $2,107.50 but it seems unlikely that he profited and it was doubtful that he broke even. □

—19—
Tricolor – Lost in the Fog
Stranded July 26, 1905 —abandoned

> **The Way to Ruin A Perfectly Nice Day is to Wreck Your Ship**
> —Sign on skipper's desk, *USCG Tupelo* - 1973

The Wilhelmsen Steamship Company of Hunsbery, Norway received a cablegram from the *Tricolor's* Captain Wold, that he was forced to abandon their ship and it had been lost on the rocks of Blunts Reef off Cape Mendocino, California.

This freighter of 6,950-tons, was just eleven months old. It was carrying a cargo of coal with its most recent port-of-call being Ladysmith, British Columbia.

It had been a very black and very foggy night. The situation on deck was desperate for although Captain Wold thought he knew where he was, no fog signals and no lighthouse beams were heard or seen. However, when the ship hung up on a rock, the skipper ordered that his ship's whistle make repeated blasts. And the desperate blasting of the whistle was heard!

On Cape Mendocino, not all that far away, the whistle was heard by people at Ocean House. Someone there telephoned the U. S. Life Saving Service at Eureka notifying of what was being heard. It would be best, officials decided, to send a rescue boat to "check it out" rather than not respond and be sorry. Accordingly, the tugboat *Ranger* with the government lifesaving boat on a tow rope, left the shelter of Humboldt Bay, passed over the bar and turned south.

The *Ranger* headed for the *Blunts Reef Lightship* which could be used as a check-point. On arrival, the *Ranger's* crew was amazed to see men from the stricken ship already on board.

It was obvious that Captain Wold was in personal distress having just lost his ship. When a shout of "breakers ahead" was heard from a lookout, then the vessel hit the rocks, there was no doubt that the *Tricolor* was off course. He said he was sure the vessel had already passed Cape Mendocino in the heavy fog however, the Captain had taken the *Tricolor* between the beach and the offshore reef.

The ship reacted to the swells of the sea rising and falling and every time it came back down, it scraped rocks. Although every effort was made with the engines trying to run "ahead" then run in "reverse," trying to have the propeller grip the water and move the vessel, the effort proved fruitless as the rocks tore into the ship's bottom. It was only time before the water rose in the engine room to snuff the boiler fires.

At 7 o'clock the next morning, the skipper ordered his men to take to the boats. One lifeboat, lowered on the seaward side, swamped. The other three boats, put into the sea on the lee, made a successful getaway. Now there was a choice:

1) As the beach was just the equivalent of a few city blocks away, the loaded lifeboats could head for shore trying their luck in the breakers. It was assured that everyone would at least get wet and the probability existed that one or all of the boats would be upended spilling everyone into the sea with the risk of drowning. If they all made it to shore safely, they would have to fend for themselves until the few people in the area could be aroused to help.

2) The men in the lifeboats could take turns at the oars and pull for the lightship (40°26'N - 124°30'W) which was about five miles away. The sea, away from the shore, was calming and the fog was lifting. On board the lightship, there was at the least hot coffee and something to eat. The men decided the best chance of survival would be to row to the lightship.

A day later, the *Ranger* got within about a mile or so of the wreck but to avoid risk, would venture no closer. The determination was made that the ship and its cargo should be classed as a total loss due to inaccessibility and the high danger that the freighter would break up injuring anyone on it or close to it. Nevertheless, a few of the ship's crew went aboard from a small boat off the *Ranger* to salvage the navigation instruments and pick up personal belongings.

It was not long afterward that the ship, pinned to a pinnacle, twisted then broke spewing its cargo of coal into the ocean. □

From what ship did this propeller come? Why is it here at Battle Rock Park in Port Orford, Oregon?

—20—
Rocks Claim *Queen Christiana*
Stranded October 21, 1907 —abandoned

This 360-foot long Norwegian ship was running in ballast on October 21, 1907 when, in the fog, she piled up on the rocks off Point St. George. The *Queen Christina* (Captain Harris), a modern steel vessel, was only six years old. All the crew survived. Quite a bit of her above-decks instruments and fittings were salvaged before the vessel was abandoned. The ship eventually broke up and sank. □

—21—
Passengers Rescued from *Corona*
Stranded at 40°65'5"N - 125°14'9"W March 1, 1907 –sank

The passenger steamer *Corona* (Captain Boyd) 1,492-tons, was lost while trying to cross the Humboldt bar, inbound, on March 1, 1907. When the ship stranded at the north jetty, some passengers, anxious to leave the ship, launched a lifeboat only to see it capsize and drown one person. They climbed back to the *Corona's* deck to wait for the U. S. Lifesaving Service that was soon at the vessel's side.

Steamship *Corona* (TOP) **stranded at the north jetty on Humboldt Bay with U.S. Life-savers on the beach getting ready to take off passengers. (LOWER)** *Corona*, **down at the bow, is settling in the sand; will become a total loss.** —Humboldt Bay Maritime Mus.

Some claim as many as 5,000 people turned out to the Samoa beach to see the ship wobbling in the surf and to watch seemingly miraculous deeds by the lifesavers rescuing passengers.

The ship was quickly down by the bow and listing to port with 154 passengers lining the stern deck awaiting rescue. The storm was rough but the lifesavers knew their duty and they did it. The only life lost was the fellow who fell out of the lifeboat at the onset.

By 2:30 on the afternoon of March 2nd, according to the *Daily Humboldt Standard*:

Saloon Deck Is Now Awash

The vessel does not seem to have moved or changed her position a particle but some people believe that she is settling in the sand. As yet it has been impossible to ascertain with any degree of certainly the extent of the damage to her bottom. If this is confined to the forward hold there is the possibility of floating and saving the vessel by bulkheading her abaft the hole and then pumping out the rest of the hold.

Later — People returning from the wreck at 3:30 p.m. say that the vessel has sunk in the sand until the saloon deck is awash at high tide. This indicates little chance of saving the freight in the hold. Nearly all the baggage from the deck staterooms has been sent ashore and was being identified and claimed by the owners.

DAILY *Humboldt* STANDARD

FIGHTING TO SAVE
CORONA'S LOAD OF FREIGHT

Only One Life Was Sacrificed

Almost Miraculous Escape From Death Of a Large Passenger List—Life Savers Made a Royal Battle

If Weather Continues Favorable It Is Hoped To Secure a Large Part of the Cargo—Passengers All Safe and Well—Conflicting Stories As To How the Accident Occurred

Stories As To Cause Of Wreck

That Vessel's Master Blundered In Giving Orders Is Advanced as Reason For Disaster—What Pas-

—Humboldt Bay Maritime Mus.

76

The brass engine room gong from *Corona*, was later used on stern-wheeler *Antelope*. This bell is presently exhibited at Humboldt Bay Maritime Museum, Eureka. Visitors can ring the bell by pulling wire on right.

The *Corona* was indeed eating its way deeper into the sand and as the newspaper reported, there was "little chance of saving the freight" and none was recovered.

What caused the wreck?

Apparently Captain Boyd's order to the man at the wheel was misunderstood resulting in the helmsman turning the ship in the wrong direction. □

—22—

The Mysterious Japanese Junk at Samoa
Stranded August 1, 1913

The strange occurrence about a stranded Japanese junk on the Humboldt Beach near the mouth of the Mad River on August 1, 1913, brought federal and local investigators to the scene in a hurry. The junk was discovered grounded about four miles north

Japanese junk found stranded and abandoned on Samoa Beach.

Nine Japanese nationals rounded up in Humboldt County, shown with Immigration Officer, are believed to have been smuggled into the U.S. The western style clothing was provided by the Salvation Army.

JAPANESE DECLARES HE DRIFTED ACROSS OCEAN TO HUMBOLDT

SMUGGLERS ARE SUSPECTED

Immigration Inspector Arrests Mikado's Subject Who Tells Queer Story

ALIFORNIA, SUNDAY, AUGUST 3, 1913

NUMI

NINE JAPANESE ARE CAPTURED

UESDAY, AUGUST 5, 1913

JAPANESE IS IN A CRITICAL CONDITION NOW

AUTHORITY RECEIVED FROM OFFICIALS TO REMOVE JUNK TO BAY

ONE PRISONER IS IN HOSPITAL

Inspector Nicholls Arrests Full Complement of Craft From Japan

INSPECTOR WILL LEAVE FOR METROPOLIS FRIDAY AFTERNOON

It is probable that when Deputy Immigration Inspector W. J. Nicholls departs Friday afternoon for San Francisco with the smuggled Japanese whom he captured last week, he will be forced to leave one of the nine in Eureka owing to his serious condition. Yesterday the patient was in a critical condition, suffering with peritonitis.

It is thought he ate too many green apples after fasting for two or three

79

of Samoa by a local man, Walter H. Pratt. There was no sign of life on or about the vessel.

Apparently the craft came in on the tide then the junk was left high on the beach when the tide changed.

Had it drifted all the way from the Japanese home islands?

Where was its crew?

As the details slowly unfolded, it appears this was a plot to avoid U. S. Immigration officers by smuggling Japanese nationals into the U. S. A., according to Deputy Immigration Inspector W. J. Nicholls.

One Japanese, S. Inowua, who was caught, told in broken English that he and the others had crossed the Pacific Ocean in the grounded junk. They had used only the wind in the small sails for power.

The *Humboldt Times* reported:

Until the boat was found, the story seemed incredible until one glance at the clumsily constructed craft and its contents is sufficient to convince anyone that the Japs were not deserters from some tramp steamer carrying a Japanese crew. Articles found aboard the junk are typical of Japan while the hardwoods were never obtained on this coast.

Inowua and seven others were being held in cells in the city prison. One more man was in the hospital. Inowua said that he and eight others had crossed the ocean in the junk. After stern interrogation with an interpreter, it was announced that the "little brown men" were not a fishing party but had intentionally sailed from Iyo, Japan for the United States with Captain Osaki, who agreed to land the men in the United States for ¥70 – about $55 each. Observers declared the smuggling attempt was "crude."□

—23—
Stranded *Bear* Grabs Big Headlines
Stranded June 16, 1916 —abandoned

To state it bluntly, the ship's captain, in a miserable fog, mistook Sugarloaf Rock (40º26'20"N - 124º24'45"W) – just 250 yards west – for Cape Mendocino and the ship was wrecked.

The six year old 4,057-ton passenger liner with a manifest showing 100 passengers and a full crew of 82, experienced an incident none of the survivors would forget for the rest of their lives. Over the next several days, the boats that responded to radio messages for help included the steamer *Grace Dollar*, the tug *Relief*, the Coast Guard lifeboat *Liberator*, the salvage ships *Iaqua* and *Salvor*, and the great battleship the *USS Oregon* (Commander George Williams, captain).* The *Blunts Reef Lightship*, anchored on its station at 40º26'4"N - 124º 30'3"W, took on board so many survivors that activity on the ship ceased for lack of room to even move about.

---

* This war ship nearly single-handedly won the naval portion of the Spanish-American War, went to sea again in both the First World War and in World War II. See bibliography for *Battleship Oregon; Bulldog of the Navy*.

—Humboldt Bay Maritime Mus

The Humboldt Times.

Th 365 Day Morning Paper THE HUMBOLDT TIMES, EUREKA, CALIFORNIA SUNDAY, JUNE 18, 1916

Seaman On Steamer Bear Arrested For Theft Of Passengers' Valuable Personal Effects; Arrested By The Sheriff

Photo by Mrs. Mildred Mills, Ferndale

WRECK OF STEAMER BEAR ON BLUNT'S REEF OFF CAPE MENDOCINO

INSPECTORS WILL   LARIBEE CREEK   VESSEL IS LOOTED BY LABOR MEDIATOR   WRIT OF REVIEW

Captain Louis Nopander was on a routine passenger and cargo run from Portland to San Francisco when his ship, the *Bear*, ran onto sharp rocks about 300 feet off the beach. Before the wreck, he realized he had ventured into dangerous water but it was too late. How did he get there? Seafarer-author James A. Gibbs wrote:

The *Bear* could not have been brought into its position with the best of navigation, for to get through such a network of rocks as infested the Cape Mendocino area was a masterful machination, described as an 'act of God.'*

* *Shipwrecks on the Pacific Coast* page 209. See bibliography.

82

With the advantage of "20-20-hindsight," *United States Coast Pilot* now declares:

> The area as far W as Blunts Reef Lighted Horn [that replaced *Blunts Reef Lightship*] and for about 4 miles N and S of Cape Mendocino includes dangerous rocks and covered ledges. Vessels should not attempt the passage between Blunts Reef Lighted Buoy and the cape under any circumstances.

There was no serious lurch when the *Bear* slid up on a rock about 11:30 the night of June 14, 1916. The owners of The San Francisco and Portland Steamship Company considered Captain Nopander to be both wise in the ways to handle a ship and a competent navigator for their $1-million vessel. He had been on this coastwise run for them on this vessel for several years. The vessel had been running in the fog at a slow speed. There was no panic when the accident happened, but to be on the safe side, the skipper had his crew summon all the passengers and had them enter the lifeboats.

Early in this deadly adventure, two of the first boats into the sea were upset and the occupants were thrown into the surf that was breaking near the ship. From one boat, five drowned. From the other, 29 landed on the beach in various conditions, all were soaked to the skin, 10 with some injuries, 2 were critical. The old Country Hotel, close by, set aside a room for a hospital. The *Humboldt Standard* declared on June 16th that 205 were saved.

The oarsmen in the other lifeboats were directed to avoid the dangerous surf and to row for the *Blunts Reef Lightship*. The lightship's crew didn't know what to do with so many people as were suddenly clamoring over its rail, eventually 155 survivors, that a radio message was tapped out to the nearby *Grace Dollar* to do its duty and please come alongside – now – and assist with all these refugees. Once anchored about a quarter-mile off, small boats ran a shuttle service taking survivors of the *Bear* to the bigger vessel.

The last officers off the *Bear* were a quartermaster, a boatswain, a winch operator then the captain. They made it directly to the beach on a raft.

> If any disaster was at hand, the press was sure to turn up. But the "press" of 1916 consisted of just two "media." These were the "genuine" media – newspaper reporters and the accompanying photographers with tripod and cumbersome equipment – and men from the new fad, maybe newsreel cameramen. Here also was a large tripod on which was mounted a big hand-cranked box of a movie camera.

The "press" met the skipper as he alighted from the raft.

He addressed the reporters, who had come from Eureka and from San Francisco:

Name plate from the steamship _Bear_ is exhibited at Humboldt Bay Maritime Museum.

I realize that this is the worst thing that can happen to me. I feel it would be an injustice to myself or employers to make an extended statement. The proper time will come when I appear before the federal inspectors.

The disappointed members of the 4th Estate had no choice but to turn again to making notes and pictures of the beach scene and views of the stranded ship in the distance.

In the hold of the steamer was a valuable horse that was owned by the president of the steamship line. There were no horse-minded men in the crew so their handling put the animal at risk – at such a risk that the horse drowned.

The manifest described the vessel's cargo, in addition to the horse, as 1,000 cases of condensed milk at 24 cans per case. There were many dozens of 100-pound sacks of flour and newsprint worth $50,000 alone. In order to lighten the ship for possible salvage, all this was thrown overboard. But to no avail.

The salvage experts and their vessels, first the _Iaqua_ and then the Canadian _Salvor_ each exerted their best power. The _Bear_ was stuck fast. In the weeks that followed, the tides built up a lot of sand around the ship. Eventually in November, a company bid on the salvage rights with a plan to refloat the ship by digging a canal in the built-up sand. But as soon as the trench was dug and seawater admitted, the bow and the stern cleared leaving the hull on a perch. The inevitable happened on a high tide – the _Bear_ broke in half and that was the beginning of the end. The winter storms did the rest. □

—24—

H-3 and the Futility of the *USS Milwaukee*

H-3 Stranded December 16, 1916 – salvaged
Milwaukee Stranded January 17, 1917 – abandoned

The American submarine *H-3*, (Lt. Harry R. Bogusch, Commanding) also known as the *Garfish*, was on the way to Eureka out of Coos Bay when, during a heavy fog, she stranded on Samoa Beach just north of the entrance to Humboldt Bay. It was a little after breakfast on December 14, 1916. Even with radio communications, it took only about 30 minutes before sketchy information got to the U. S. Life Saving Service stationed at the mouth of the bay.

The *H-3* (SS-30), was one of only three vessels of its class. She was 358-tons surface displacement and 433-tons submerged. This sub was 150-feet 3½-inches long with a beam of 15-feet 9½-inches and draft of 12-feet 5-inches. She could do 14 knots on the surface and 10.5 knots under water. She had a diving depth of 200-feet and was commissioned on January 16, 1914. It had been built by The Moran Company in Seattle in 1911. When *H-3* hit the Samoa Beach she was less than two years old.

The lifesavers hitched their two-horse team to a cart to pull the various paraphernalia to the site but, because the horses and load bogged in the soft sand, the men put their rescue boat into the surf and rowed the rest of the four miles to the vessel.

The "little diver," or "submarine torpedo boat," as these submersibles were called, had no guns – just torpedoes. The *H-3* was being rolled from side-to-side as breakers crashed against it. The boat rolled one way then, when the water receded, the submarine rolled the other way. An observer noted that the only thing that stopped the submarine from being rolled completely over in the

Stranding of a submarine on Samoa Spit near Eureka, California was so unique that thousands of people crowded the beach to take a look.

breakers was the conning tower.

This scene was in the surf only about 200 yards off the beach. The officers and crew, 27 men, some of them injured, were being rattled around inside with every crashing wave. While maintaining the integrity of their vessel by keeping the hatches shut, there was trouble inside.

NEWS FLASH

Twenty-seven lives were imperiled and the United States submarine H-3 is being battered by the heavy surf on the ocean beach back of Samoa as a result of the craft driving ashore at 9 o'clock yesterday morning during a dense fog. The entire crew was rescued late yesterday afternoon from the perilous position in the gas-filled submarine which momentarily was in danger of destruction.

The H-3 [*Garfish* SS-30] accompanied by the H-1 [*Seawolf* SS-28] and H-2 [*Nautilus* SS-29] and convoyed by the mother ship *Cheyenne*, was enroute south from northern ports when the accident occurred. None of the officers of the H-3 or the *Cheyenne* would make a statement last night as to the responsibility for the wreck.

—*Humboldt Times. Dec. 15, 1916. Page 1.*

As the tide was on the way to flood stage, the pounding breakers kept moving the stricken vessel closer inshore.

U.S. SUBMARINE GOES ASHORE IN FOG AT EUREKA

Submarine H-3, En Route From Eremerton to San Diego, Strikes Shoal Off Samoa—Waves Pounding Tiny Vessel—Only Conning Tower Prevents Ship Turning Over.

EUREKA, Cal., Dec. 14.—The United States submarine H-3 commanded by Lieutenant Commander H. R. Bogusch, went ashore in a fog early today on a shoal off Samoa two miles north of the bar on Humboldt Bay. The diver was rolling heavily this morning to an angle of forty five degrees, but watchers ashore, a distance of 200 feet, heard the diver whistle "All safe" three blasts.

Life Savers at Hand

The U. S. S. Cheyenne, mother ship of the submarines H-1, -2 and -3, which were on their way to Mare Island navy yard from Bremerton, Wn. was standing by a mile northwest. The tug Relief was a quarter mile off to the east and a life saving crew from Humboldt bar was nearing the distressed diver to shoot a line aboard. It was feared the H-3 would be a total loss.

The water is too shallow for any adequate relief vessel to approach.

An attempt will be made later, it was said, to take the crew off in a breeches buoy as the diver is unable to free itself. Another alternative was to drive the H-3 farther ashore into the sand.

TRYING TO PULL SUBMARINE OFF EUREKA BEACH

EUREKA, Cal., Dec. 16.—It was possible to wade within twenty feet of the United States submarine H-3, still rolling today in the breakers two miles north of here, where she struck Tuesday morning. Salvagers under command of Lieutenant W. B. Howe succeeded in making fast a ten-inch hawser last night and it was hoped to get some of the rescued crew aboard the H-3 by noon to open hatches for the escape of chlorine gas and to empty the diver's tanks.

Lieutenant Howe, commanding the monitor Cheyenne, mother ship of the H-boats, said he expected to take a pull on the H-3 from off shore at high tide tonight. A coast guard crew will attempt to carry a line inshore from the U. S. S. McCulloch.

During the night the H-3 swung around bow to shore at right angles.

Boatswain's Mate Davidson of the monitor Cheyenne, boarded the wrecked submarine H-3 this morning and returned reporting conditions good under dock. Although he did not enter the craft, he said that it is possible to do so. There was nine feet of water under the stern of the submarine, he said. This afternoon, with conditions favorable, the coast guard cutter McCulloch will make the first effort to pull the submarine off the sand.

Newsboys sold thousands of papers to spectators at the beach. In 1916 there was no radio news.

88

Heavy hawser (ARROW) **to pull** *H-3* **off beach failed as sub was severely stuck in the sand.**

When the sub stranded, the radioman could not get off an SOS because the electrical system went out. (If there was a battery back-up system, no mention of it has been found.) Accordingly, no distress message was ever heard on the *Cheyenne* just a few miles away.

Word of the wreck appears to have been announced after some boys, wandering on the beach on their way to school, saw what they first thought was a stranded whale. They told their teacher. The teacher sent them back for a closer look and now the boys, with great excitement, announced their discovery of a submarine. The teacher sent them over to the Hammond Lumber Company's office, nearby, where there was a telephone. The clerk listened, then telephoned the Table Bluff Wireless Station where the word of the wreck was relayed to the Coast Guard.

By now most of the residents of the nearby lumber town of Samoa were on the beach watching the saga, bringing thermos bottles of coffee (and "spirits") for the men. The school teacher decided this was exciting history being made therefor classes were dismissed for the day and all the kids hurried to the beach to watch.

The lifesavers, directed by Captain Lawrence Ellison, shot a line to the sub but there was no one visible to pick it up.

Inside the boat it was dark. The badly mauled crewmen were having great difficulty doing anything as the craft rolled sickeningly in the breakers. Two crewmen had battery acid burns and others were suffering from chlorine gas that developed when leaking battery acid came into contact with sea water that apparently was shipped in through the main hatch when the sub was first grounded with men on deck. Two men got their fingers smashed in the rush of trying to close the hatch. To protect themselves from being gassed to death by the chlorine, the water-tight doors were closed and all the men jammed themselves into the main compartment.

Hours went by. The tide changed and was now on the ebb. In mid-afternoon, another line was shot to the vessel and again, no response from the submarine.

With the surfboat, the lifesavers went out to the sub and put one man on the boat and this time was met by a crew-member, Jack Agraz, a Chief Gunner's mate. The line was made fast, and along it was passed a heavier line for a breeches buoy.

Remembering there was no radio and no ship-to-shore communication, something had to be done to let rescuers on shore know of the severe injuries on the ship. It is unclear who started the signaling with wig-wag (semaphore) flags. But a sailor appeared on deck with flags and on shore were Harry Moreland and Kenneth Farley, Boy Scouts, with flags. With the wig-wags, the distress of the crew was told.

In the meantime, alerted by Table Bluff Wireless Station, the *Cheyenne*, the tender for the flotilla of "divers," apparently crossed Humboldt Bay and tied up at a lumber company dock at Samoa. With several officers in charge, members of its crew were detailed to assist as needed on the beach and to hike over there promptly. It was getting dark.

With the detail from the *Cheyenne* as well as volunteer civilians (some of whom got in the way, causing delays*), the 27 men

---

* In one instance, a civilian, meaning to be of assistance, tied a line from the submarine to a stump but the vessel rolled and the rope broke. The surfman from the lifesavers, had to struggle back to the submarine to attach another line. The surfman was Werner Sweins. The civilian volunteer was unidentified.

MONITOR CHEYENNE WILL PULL H-3 OFF BEACH AT HIGH TIDE

EUREKA, Cal., Dec. 18.— The United States Monitor Cheyenne had a line aboard the submarine H-3 today and was ready to put a strain on the diver which went aground in the breakers two miles north of Eureka last Thursday morning. Surfmen boarded the H-3 today from the beach without wetting their feet.

There was a smooth sea and no fog. The Cheyenne was waiting for a full tide.

The *Cheyenne's* skipper wanted to succeed with getting the "little diver" *H-3* off the beach. But the plan didn't work. The newspaper did not reveal how long the wait would be for high tide as the paper obviously did not own a *Tide Table*. Ship captains do.

on the diver were brought ashore. It took over fourteen hours from the initial grounding to get the rescue set up. Once running, the breeches buoy made short work of the task, finishing its business in a little more than one hour.

Following the tradition of the sea, the sub's commander, Lieutenant Bogusch, was the last man off the vessel.

What was to be done with the nearly new stranded submarine was left for higher authorities to be concerned.

Once on the beach, the crew were wrapped in what few blankets had been volunteered. The men were picked up by locals who took them home to be washed, fed, and bedded. In one instance, Duane Stewart a Navy Electrician said years later that the men were "naked, salty, gassed, [and some had been] covered with acid." He was taken home by Walter Pratt of the Hammond Lumber Company. There, Pratt and his wife gave him and a companion, a bath and supper.

Why the *H-3* Landed in the Surf

The *Garfish*, Navy Number *H-3*, along with *H-1* and *H-2* and the tender *Cheyenne*, were headed for Humboldt Bay when the mishap occurred. The *H-3* had a history of trouble with its diesel engines. One engine quit as the vessel neared the Humboldt bar. With but a single engine operating, the vessel drifted off course too far to the north. In the fog that was closing rapidly, the skipper lost eye-contact with the tender *Cheyenne*. But when there was a very brief cleft in the fog, he saw what he later described as smoke as if it was from the *Cheyenne*. The fog closed again. He set his bearing not on the *Cheyenne*, but on a smoke stack at the Hammond Lumber Company on the other side of the spit. In almost no time at all, the *H-3* landed on the beach.

Within the next few days, several efforts were made to get the submersible back into her element. The Coast Guard brought in its cutter *McCulloch* while the Navy ordered the sub's tender, the *USS Cheyenne*, to stay at Humboldt Bay to do what it could. Then came the *USS Arapahoe*, a sea-going Navy tug to try her luck. All got into position and all pulled. But all failed to salvage the submarine. The weight of the *H-3* and the wave action were too much, as they firmly held the diver in the sand.

It was believed that the various ships trying to pull the stricken vessel out of the sand were not of sufficient weight and power to do the job, so locating a really big ship to do the job was considered.

All there seemed to be to the matter was the mathematics of heavy weight and heavy power against light weight and no power plus "x," the unknown but significant drag caused by the sand. The Navy theoreticians would have the submarine back in the water within minutes of attaching a tow lime, or so they believed.

In the meantime, a local contractor, Mercer-Fraser Company, submitted the low bid of $18,000 to refloat the submarine. Other bids were between $72,000 and $83,000. The Navy considered the local bid way too low so it was rejected outright.

The Navy, with pride unabated, ordered the 9,700-ton armored cruiser, the *USS Milwaukee* to do the work. This fighting ship was very powerful. The *H-3*, should be hauled off the beach with ease, the investigating officers conjectured. For an assist to move the submarine in the water, until it might be under way with its own power, or if need be to tow it into a port, the Navy would send its venerable ocean tug the 1,000 horsepower *USS Iroquois*.

Lieutenant W. F. Newton, USN, was commanding the *USS Milwaukee* during the absence of Captain Charles F. Preston who had been detached while the vessel was being refitted in dry-dock. Lt. Newton was alerted to the situation when the cruiser was ordered in as the valiant rescuer. He, and another officer on the cruiser Lt. W. B. Howe, developed what became known as the *Newton-Howe Plan* for the recovery of the *H-3*. The Plan envisioned the *Milwaukee* as the major pulling force. This was a very big ship at 9,700-tons and 426-feet long. She had just been released from the Mare Island Navy Yard after a refit. As the flagship of the Torpedo Flotilla – Pacific Fleet, the *Milwaukee* would supervise the tender *Cheyenne* and the *H-1*, *H-2* and *H-3*. The cruiser would also do some shepherding on her own as well as be the major stores vessel for this flotilla. With a full sea-going machine shop, she was expected to handle at-sea repairs. With this powerful battle-ready vessel to work with – she could develop 22,454 horsepower – the *Newton-Howe Plan* was placed before Rear Admiral William B. Caperton, the Commander-in-Chief of the Pacific Fleet, for evaluation.

Lt. Newton was in a powerful position for a young Naval officer whose only previous command had been a submarine. Another member of the brain-storming team was (Lt.?) Harvey Haislip, who would be the executive of the operation. Mr. Haislip had never been in command of a ship and he did not have previous salvage experience. Lt. Newton had been aboard the *H-3* on an earlier grounding of that submarine, and undoubtedly had a false impression of what it would take in the present instance to move the submarine from the deep sand of Samoa Spit.

If Lt. Newton had but one single thing going for him, it was that he moved ahead positively.

He discussed his plan with Admiral Caperton and presented sketches of what he proposed to do. The Admiral approved the plan therefore the *USS Milwaukee* left Vallejo's Mare Island Navy Yard for Samoa on Humboldt County's coast.

On station, the Lieutenant backed the cruiser toward the submarine with a tow hawser over his stern to be attached to the bow of the *H-3*. The tugboat *Iroquois* would be at the end of another hawser that was tied to the cruiser's starboard bow to counteract the effects of currents. The *Cheyenne* would be on the end of another hawser from the peak of the cruiser's bow standing out about 45-degrees to starboard. In addition, two large anchors were placed ahead of the cruiser. One was dead ahead, the second was at about 50-degrees to starboard. The two small vessels and the two anchors were to stabilize the cruiser against the current as it pulled the sub off the beach.

Finally, two marker buoys were set 300-feet seaward of the breaker line on each side and outboard of the submarine. Everything needed to be in place by high tide at 3:00 a.m. January 13, 1917. Getting the final line from the cruiser to the submarine was the first inkling of the disaster to come. After much difficulty with the line, a surf boat started with it toward the beach. When under way, a great swell raised both the *Cheyenne* and the cruiser quite high. This comber enveloped the surf boat and threw everyone into the sea. One man, H. F. Parker, a seaman drowned. Others might have been drowned were it not for the quick work of husky spectators who were lumbermen and fishermen. The volunteers jumped into the rush of cold, white water and saved not only the men, but salvaged the end of the line from the cruiser. The injured were taken to the lumber company's infirmary in Samoa.

As there was only 3,600-feet of the special hawser, the cruiser had to be moved closer inshore than was anticipated – much closer to the first breaker line than Naval officers deemed wise from an escape standpoint. Accordingly, a commission of officers from the submarine and from the Coast Guard assembled with Lt. Newton to share their grave concerns. A part of this was the question: Was salvaging that little diver worth all the risk and expense? Lt. Newton was determined to proceed and as the on-site commander, his word was final.

Harvey Haislip, using the advantage of "20-20-hindsight" many years later wrote:

The *H-3* with all her equipment stripped out would be worth no more than a tin can. Yet here was $7,000,000 worth of ship and equipment with that tin-can tied to her tail.

The hawsers eventually attached between the *H-3* and the *Milwaukee* were twisted steel wire rope of 3⁷/₈-inches. Hooking this line to the cruiser was a challenge as the cruiser was never intended as a towing vessel and did not have any such facilities. The cruiser-end of the hawser was lashed around the armor of an 8-inch gun. One detriment was the lack of suitable size pelican hooks to fit the cable's size. Hooks were used as quick-release devices if anything went wrong. A substitute measure was agreed where the ship's machinists would be nearby with an acetylene cutting torch and could spring into action if ordered.

When the high tide approached, steam was up and engines ready. The *Iroquois* was standing out toward the sea with a line running from it to the *Milwaukee*. This kept the line between the cruiser and the sub taut and helped to prevent the cruiser from drifting into dangerous shallow water facing the beach. When all seemed ready, radioed signals sent from the cruiser alerted this "fleet" to start the pulling.

Even though it was in the middle of the night, the beach was lined with spectators. In their midst were the Coast Guard's "Always Ready" Life Saving men.

As if to say, "No, not tonight," the fog came in shrouding the entire venture with a cloak of ill-omen.

Objects planned to be seen during operations, became obscured or disappeared from view all together. Just what the conditions were aboard the *Cheyenne* were unknown when its cable to the cruiser was accidentally cut when run over by the ship's propeller. Even with this set-back, Lt. Newton was determined to get the *H-3* into the water during the high tide.

As the ship's radio cracked with the signal to "Heave away!" the lines tightened. Churning away in the dark and in the fog, with attentions directed at the sometimes visible beach the dragging anchors weren't noticed as the bow of the *Milwaukee* gradually but imperceptibly began to swing to port. At 3:42 a.m., the ship had swung so far around into the surf that the rudder dragged the sandy bottom sending a shiver throughout the ship. Reports came from various parts of the cruiser, some saying a shock had been felt. It apparently wasn't strong enough to transmit itself to the bridge because no such sensation was felt by Lt. Newton. Perhaps

Cruiser *USS Milwaukee* stranded in surf on Samoa Spit was great embarrassment to the Navy. Although massive salvage effort brought much of the warship's equipment ashore, hull was total loss.

it was disguised by the vibration of the ship straining on the tow lines attached to the still immovable *H-3*. Even so, the engines were returned to ALL STOP and all the officers on the bridge ran aft to investigate, leaving only the helmsman on the bridge. The hawsers were ordered cut, and Lt. Newton ordered the radioman to send a FULL SPEED AHEAD order to the *Iroquois* to keep the cruiser from drifting any further into the breakers and up onto the beach. Not realizing the *Milwaukee* was now nearly parallel to the beach and in only 4½ fathoms of water, he telegraphed to his engine room to go FULL SPEED AHEAD - PORT and 1/3 SPEED ASTERN - STARBOARD to attempt to pivot the mighty ship's bow back out to sea.

It took only a few minutes for Lt. Newton to appreciate the seriousness of the situation and, with the bow *still* swinging toward the beach, finally ordered FULL SPEED ASTERN - BOTH SHAFTS to try to back away from his position, now barely outside

VOLUME LXV — Humboldt's 365 Day Morning Paper — THE HUMBOLDT TIMES, EUREKA, CALIFORNIA, SUNDAY, JANUARY 14, 1917 — NUMBER 14

CRUISER MILWAUKEE IS BELIEVED TOTAL LOSS

Crew of 450 Officers and Men Saved By Heroic Work

TEUTONS ADVANCE ON RIVER DANUBE

AVIATORS ARE BEING SOUGHT BY 2 NATIONS

Two Army Officers Who Started From San Diego For Little James With Air Car Are Still Missing

WILSON IS HOPING FOR PEACE TERM STATEMENT

Wants Germany and Her Allies To Make Full Statement Similar In Tone To Entente Powers

President Has Made Clear That He Is Indifferent To Means Employed For Desires Early Peace

Cheers Given Brave Officer of Milwaukee

MILWAUKEE IS BEACHED IN PULLING AT DIVER H-3

Line From the Cheyenne Let Go Early In Evening and Later Line From Iroquois Also Slipped

When Officers of Milwaukee Saw Danger, Men Were Set To Cutting Huge Steel Cable To Stranded Diver

SAMOA BEACH IS SCENE OF WRECK

Flagship of Pacific Torpedo and Submarine Flotilla Swept Ashore By Treacherous Tidal Current While Pulling On Line Attached To Stranded Submarine H-3 Which Drove To Grief Month Ago Today

SAILORS LINE RAIL FOR TEN HOURS AND LONGER WAITING TO BE RESCUED

Valuation of $7,000,000 Placed On Second Naval Craft To Pile Up Opposite Eureka Within Thirty Days — Thrilling Rescues Held Great Crowd Breathless During Battle Against Heavy Odds

—Humboldt Bay Maritime Mus.

the breakers. Within only moments, the end of the venture was clear as the leviathan was finally sucked into the surf and slammed repeatedly on the bottom. By 4:10 a.m., it was all over. With the surf now on the *starboard* side the *USS Milwaukee* was sitting on the sand, almost next to the "tin can," with a matching 20-degree list.

Lieutenant Newton ordered a radio message sent to the other ships (Table Bluff Radio was monitoring) to stand clear of the cruiser, that the ship was lost. Table Bluff relayed to Life Saving Station, but those men were already on the beach assertively exercising their collective "wait-and-see" anxiety.

MILWAUKEE IS BEACHED IN PULLING AT DIVER H-3

Line From the Cheyenne Let Go Early In Evening and Later Line From Iroquois Also Slipped

When Officers of Milwaukee Saw Danger, Men Were Set To Cutting Huge Steel Cable To Stranded Diver

BULLETIN
(Associated Press)
SAN DIEGO, Jan. 18—The cru...
...San Diego, flagship of the Pacific...
...left with Admiral W. B. Caperton on...
...board left at nine o'clock tonight for...
...the scene of the stranding of the...

BULLETIN

SAN DIEGO, Jan. 18—The cruiser *San Diego,* flagship of the Pacific Fleet, with Admiral W. B. Caperton on board left at nine o'clock tonight for the scene of the stranding of the cruiser *Milwaukee* near Eureka. The *San Diego* is expected to reach its destination Tuesday morning.

The story of the stranding of the *Milwaukee* was gleaned piecemeal yesterday....

When the Admiral arrived, he was not pleased with what his eyes beheld.

97

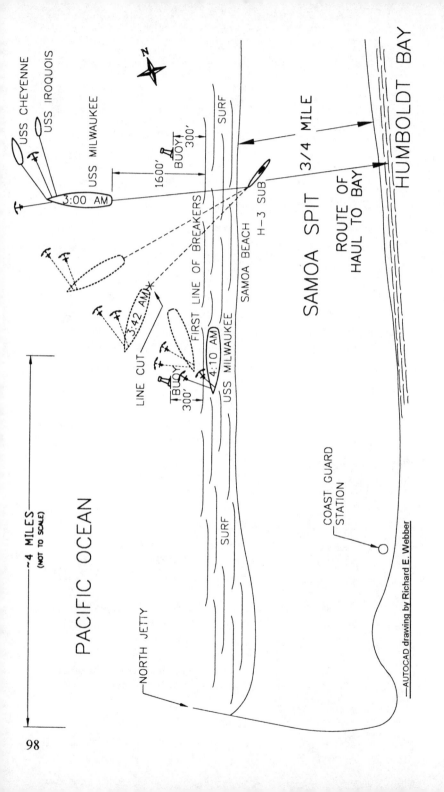

PACIFIC OCEAN

~4 MILES
(NOT TO SCALE)

NORTH JETTY

SURF

COAST GUARD STATION

USS CHEYENNE
USS IROQUOIS
USS MILWAUKEE

3:00 AM

1600'

BUOY 300'

SURF

FIRST LINE OF BREAKERS

LINE CUT

3:42 AM

4:10 AM

USS MILWAUKEE

BUOY 300'

SAMOA BEACH

H-3 SUB

SAMOA SPIT   3/4 MILE

ROUTE OF HAUL TO BAY

HUMBOLDT BAY

—AUTOCAD drawing by Richard E. Webber

98

The U.S. Life Saving Service brought most of the crew to shore by boat although many were landed by breeches buoy.

The great *USS Milwaukee* was stranded on the beach almost within shouting distance of the submarine. What had been conceived to be a mere take-a-big-ship-and-pull-the-little-ship-off-the sand, turned into a major disaster for the United States Navy.

The lifesavers swung into action, as if their part in the adventure had been a part of the script. They shot a line to the cruiser. Next they rigged their breeches buoy and started hauling off the 438 men of the crew, one man at a time. About 150 men were landed on the beach this way. In the meantime, the Coast Guard brought in lifeboats to take off the majority. The men who took the breeches buoy to safety left their ship only with the clothes on their backs. The miracle of the event was that not a single life was lost.

On the beach, the hundreds of civilian gawkers had gone into action and started bon fires for all to get some warmth. From nowhere coffee and spirits appeared.

The last man off the wrecked cruiser was her commander, Lieutenant Newton. He went ashore in a Coast Guard surf boat rowed by the lifesavers. He was accompanied by the executive officer, the chief engineer and the paymaster. But the paymaster left $90,000 in his safe. That amount of money made a very large bundle and to have it on the beach seemed unwise. (The next day the paymaster returned to the ship, picked up the treasure and took it to the Bank of Eureka.)

Of immediate concern was how to handle a large population of men now on the Samoa beach – the crew. Arrangements were quickly made with the lumber company to march the men about 1/2-a-mile to the cookhouse-dining room* where everybody was fed. Then the men were assigned beds in Hammond Lumber Company's bunk house with overflow into a pavilion in the park. The officers were, of course, put up at the Sequoia Yacht Club.

Some of the crew went back to Mare Island on board the *City of Topeka*, a steamship. It took three more days for arrangements to be made to have a special train come north to Samoa to pick up the remainder. This was on the Northwestern Pacific Railroad which took the men to the end of the line on San Francisco Bay at Sausilito. From there, a chartered ferry boat took them to Vallejo. They were marched from the ferry slip to Mare Island Navy Yard.

---

* The Samoa Cookhouse is across the bay from Eureka. In 1996 it is open to the public as a unique restaurant that still follows logging camp menus with everyone eating at long tables.

For salvaging what it could from the hulk, the Navy let a contract to the Northwestern Pacific Railroad to build a trestle over the beach and tidewater to the side of the ship. The cruiser was stripped of its guns, everything that could be removed, then the hulk was abandoned.

Camp Milwaukee was built on the sand dune to house salvage workers and the guard detachment of sailors and marines who protected the wreck from vandals and overly enthusiastic beachcombers.

In the months that passed, the Navy made a valiant effort to salvage everything from the cruiser it could dismantle but also left behind some valuables like $5,000 worth of cables abandoned in the water. An emergency "village" called Camp Milwaukee was built behind the line of dunes near the beach. The shacks included a warehouse, a cook shack with mess hall in addition to sleeping quarters. The Northwestern Pacific Railroad was contracted to build a standard railroad trestle from the beach out to the wrecked cruiser. From its earlier terminal at Samoa, a short line of track was laid to the beach, then over the trestle to the side of the ship. A derrick was hoisted aboard the wreck and placed at the rail. From here, the heaviest of salvage, including the big guns, were lowered by the derrick directly into waiting railroad cars.

After the Navy finished its salvage efforts, the Marines were sent to occupy Camp Milwaukee. Their orders were to do guard duty on the beach and on the wreck to keep vandals, and the many "aggressive beachcombers" who appeared, at bay.

Toward the end, when the pounding breakers made occupancy on the cruiser too dangerous as the ship was then coming apart, the Navy ordered a stop to salvage efforts and left the great fighting ship, cheated out of a place in the First World War* to the elements.

About 1919, the Navy and the Marines pulled out after the remains of a once great ship were sold to a salvager for just $3,000. What this entrepreneur took off the ship must have been trivial.

Still later, when the scrap metal drive opened after the start of World War-II, a firm boarded the wreck to salvage bronze and scrap iron.

Parts of the ship could be seen from the shore during low tide as late as the mid-1980's. On October 29, 1995, nothing was visible at a 3.0-foot low tide, but local residents claim there are still the edges of bulkheads visible on minus-tide days. One resident told the authors that her toddler son always wants to go

---

* The First World War had been in progress in Europe since 1914 but the United States Congress did not declare war on Germany until April 6, 1917. This was just 80 days after the loss of the USS Milwaukee. The fortunes of war being what they are, those Marines doing beach guard duty on Samoa Spit, missed the deadly action in the trenches of Europe.

Life ring from the cruiser is shown by volunteer from the Humboldt Bay Maritime Museum. The museum contains the "mother lode" of artifacts from many nearby shipwrecks.

to the beach to see the "sharks," as he calls the edges of the old rusty bulkheads that appear just above the water on those days.

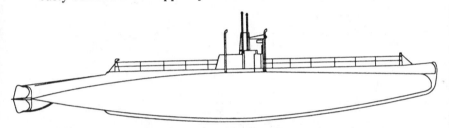

The *Garfish – H-3* was of sleek design, carried eight torpedoes but no guns. No one slept aboard, the crew going to the tender at night. Today's submarines are twice the size. —AUTOCAD drawing by Richard E. Webber

In the meantime, what about submarine *H-3*? It was decided no further efforts would be made to pull the vessel off the beach by the Navy, so the earlier bid of Mercer-Fraser was accepted after all. The principal of the task was a simple one. Just move it overland in the same manner the firm moved huge redwood logs. They placed logs alongside the hull, then passed wirerope cable underneath the vessel, now about six-feet deep in the beach, then with jacks, lifted the stranded "diver" out of its sand trap. With 12 x 12 timbers under the vessel and the side-protecting logs, a steam donkey engine pulled the weird looking load on a skid-road about 3/4-mile across Samoa Spit and into Humboldt Bay. The *Garfish* was finally towed to Mare Island Navy Yard for a refit.

The design of the *H*-class subs was determined to be much too small for use in the fighting in First World War so the three

Sailor, with .45 Colt on his belt, stands guard at the *H-3*. (LOWER) **The sub during salvage, is slowly pulled on skids by donkey engine (not shown) across Samoa Spit and into Humboldt Bay. See page 98.**

vessels were assigned to the training command. □

AUTHORS NOTE: The *Seawolf* (*H-1* - S-28) grounded and sank in Magdalena Bay, Mexico on March 24, 1920. The *Nautilus* (*H-2* - S-29) was decommissioned October 23, 1922 then stricken from the Navy list on December 18, 1930 and sold for scrap in September 1931. The *Garfish* (*H-3* - S-30) was decommissioned October 23, 1922 stricken on December 18, 1930, then sold for scrap on September 14, 1931.

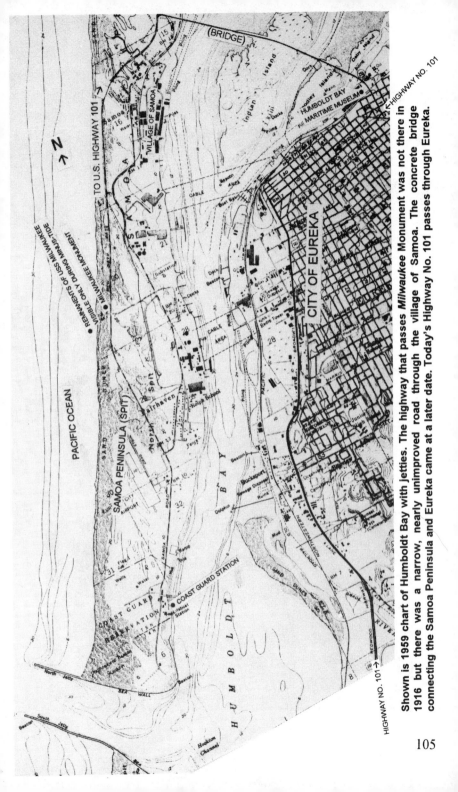

Shown is 1959 chart of Humboldt Bay with jetties. The highway that passes *Milwaukee* Monument was not there in 1916 but there was a narrow, nearly unimproved road through the village of Samoa. The concrete bridge connecting the Samoa Peninsula and Eureka came at a later date. Today's Highway No. 101 passes through Eureka.

Scene on Samoa Spit near location of stranding of the *H-3* and the *Milwaukee* as viewed during low tide on October 29, 1995 by authors. (LOWER) Monument to *USS Milwaukee* is easily found. See chart on page 105

—25—
Many Die as *Alaska* Sinks; Tug Saves 166
Stranded on Blunts Reef August 6, 1921 –sank

The final Morse code message from the steamer *Alaska* was:

.-- .   .- .-. .   ... .. -. -.-. .. -. --.

W E   A R E   S I N K I N G

As the 327-foot long liner slipped off its rock and plunged into deep water, Captain Harry Hobey, in refusing a life jacket or a place in a boat declared:

> I prefer to go down with my ship. My place is on this bridge until the last man and woman are safely afloat.

It was the foggy summer night of August 6, 1921 – Thursday. There were 211 persons on the *Alaska* – 131 passengers and 80 crew. The sea was calm. In the salon, there was a dance orchestra providing the entertainment. Just about 9 o'clock, the music came to a stop as the ship suddenly quivered from stem to stern. Then there was a jolt that caused even the most casual traveler to sit upright and wonder what catastrophe was happening. In seconds, everyone knew his life was in imminent danger.

XTRA!

Humboldt Standard

EUREKA, HUMBOLDT CO., CALIFORNIA, SUNDAY, AUGUST 12

12 DEAD, 171 SAVED, WRECK TOLL
LIFE SAVERS BRING BODIES TO EUREKA

EXHAUSTED MEN AIDED EACH OTHER AS HAND OF DEATH WAS NEAR

Nine of Dead Identified In Morgues Here

Alaska One Of Largest Steamers In Coast Trade Formerly Kansas City; Had Crew Of Seventy Men

CRUSHED, MAIMED AND OIL SOAKED MEN AND WOMEN REACH EUREKA

Wife, Husband and Babe Were Reunited On Deck of Boat

ONE WOMAN SERIOUSLY HURT

Betty Jean Sanders, But Four Years of Age; Drifted On Sea for Seven Hours; She Is Saved

—Humboldt Bay Maritime Mus.

The ship had hit a rock at an infamous "Port of Lost Ships," Blunts Reef.

Deck officers were shouting to passengers to get into the cork life jackets and report to their lifeboat stations –pronto. They were adamant there was no time to go to one's cabin to pick up anything. The radio operator was pounding his brass key with SOS messages seeking to reach any ship hearing the dots and dashes. The *Anyox*, a Canadian steamer, was just 15 miles away. It pushed its engine to FULL SPEED and headed for the tortured ship. The Table Bluff Wireless Station was also close by but it was "on the air" with other traffic (messages) so did not hear the SOS. But radio waves do strange things and often times messages are heard hundred of miles away. And so it was that the station at North Head, Washington, near the Columbia River, read everything that was being sent from the *Alaska*. North Head Radio relayed the SOS to Eureka. At daybreak, the *Ranger*, the bar tug on Humboldt Bay, set out for the wreck site. In the meantime, the *Anyox* got a message through to Table Bluff Radio.

> STEAMER ALASKA ON BLUNTS REEF LISTED HEAVILY TO STARBOARD AND SANK WITHIN 15 MINUTES OF STRIKING. THE LOSS OF LIFE IS HEAVY...

108

Ship's name plate is exhibited at Humboldt Bay Maritime Museum

After the crash, crewmen from the engine room rushed on deck declaring that the vessel was taking water very fast. Captain Hobey, without a moment's hesitation, ordered the boats be readied for lowering. Lowering boats is always a dangerous business even under the best of conditions. And conditions were absolutely under-organized as boats lowered away without proper loading and with insufficient crews. The first boat over the side was swamped, then its occupants crushed against the steel side of the ship. Boats No. 2 and No. 3 to be let away did all right but the fourth was swamped and lost many of its passengers in the sea.

The ship's lights slowly blinked out as the generators in the engine room were flooded throwing the scene into an uneasy darkness. By now, the last of the summer day had just fallen into the night. The oarsmen, and some oars were being handled by women, in the lifeboats that made it, had a difficult time because of the crashing breakers at the reef. Those in the boats lacked direction of where to go other than to put distance between themselves and the stranded vessel.

It was all over in a hurry. The *Alaska,* as if to tip her hat, slid off the reef starboard side first then hissing steam from the engine room and twisting in the current, plunged into its deep water grave. All this activity from the moment of impact: 15 minutes.

The *Anyox* first on the scene, was being hampered because of a barge in tow. It took about one hour to reach the scene where the first lifeboat was spotted. Everyone in it was oil-covered, a number were hysterical on seeing the rescuers and all were in various degrees of shock. Thirty more survivors were plucked from the oil-covered sea by sailors from the *Anyox* who were using the lifeboat from the *Alaska.* The night's search-and-rescue by several boats and the tug, brought a total of 166 passengers and crew out of the water.

By daylight, the *Ranger* appeared from Humboldt Bay then with the *Anyox* still towing its barge, the convoy made for port.

At the dock in Eureka, the Red Cross was waiting as were other volunteers. The hospitals were instantly overwhelmed with emergency patients, most of which needed at least a hot bath. Some with oil clinging in their hair, elected to have hair-cuts.

When the Coroner's Jury convened on August 9th, there were 17 unidentified bodies in the city morgue. But many others were unaccounted for. The jury declared the deaths had been caused by the *Alaska's* having struck the reef then sank "precipitating passengers and crew into the sea...." There were 42 dead or missing.

As in many such cases, there were arguments trying to place blame. Some survivors blamed the ship's officers. Others just cried – could blame no one. Some wanted to send a "Thank You" to the crew of the *Anyox* for working far beyond their normal call to duty. With the *Alaska* on the bottom of the sea, there would be no salvage. □

—26—
Humboldt Bar Claims Steamer *Brooklyn*
Her back was broken crossing the bar November 8, 1931 —sank

The Humboldt Bar was having one of its worst days when heavy breakers, coupled with a madly howling wind from the ocean, crashed the outbound *Brooklyn* so severely that the force, as she crossed the bar, broke her back.

The damaged ship, with a load of dimension lumber, drifted seaward only to sink. And it happened just that quickly. Eighteen died. One survived only because he, and the piece of wreckage he clung to, was fetched from the open sea by a passing ship days later. This lone survivor was the *Brooklyn's* Second Mate.

The disaster struck so quickly there were no boats lowered. The storm was of such severity that the Coast Guard could not respond due to the perils of the bar. The following day, in calmer circumstances, the 36-foot motor life boat with its Coast Guardsmen aboard, could only cruise among the floating wreckage that had once been a proud lumber schooner. No bodies were recovered. But sea-soaked lumber was fetched from the surf and from the sands by beachcombers for many weeks afterward. □

The cannon is a remnant of the _Shark_.

—27—
Loss of the United States Naval Sloop _Shark_
Stranded September 10, 1846 —sank

> "The first United States flag to wave over undisputed and purely American territory of Oregon" came from the 184-ton sloop that was lost while outbound on the Columbia bar on September 10, 1846.

Baker's Bay, Columbia River
December 1, 1846

Dear Governor [George Abernethy]: One of the few articles preserved from the shipwreck of the late United States schooner <u>Shark</u> was her stand of colors. To display this national emblem, and cheer our citizens in this distant territory by its presence, was a principle [sic] object of the <u>Shark's</u> visit to the Columbia; and it appears to me, therefore, highly proper that it should henceforth remain with you, as a memento of paternal regard from the general government.

With the fullest confidence that it will be received and duly appreciated as such by our countrymen here, I do myself the honor of transmitting the flags (an ensign and union-jack) to your address; nor can I omit the occasion to express by gratification and price that this relic of my late command should be emphatically the first United States flag to wave over undisputed and purely American territory of Oregon.

With consideration of high respect, I remain your obedient servant,

Neil M. Howison
Lieutenant Commanding United States Navy

Governor Abernethy sent a courteous reply which included

these words remembering it was only recently that the British flag had been a common sight:

...sincerely hoping that the 'star-spangled banner' may ever wave over this portion on the United States.

The *Shark* (Captain Scheneck) had been sent to the northwest coast, and particularly to the Columbia River for several reasons, some still debated by professors of history. For one, the navigation charts of the Columbia bar and its approaches on both sides were vague. There had been ships lost and the people wanted a safe river and believed the crossing of the bar would be improved if it was properly and completely surveyed. While Lt. Neil Howison, United States Navy, was in the Oregon City area, he visited with Methodist missionary Jason Lee which gave rise to some speculation, by the British, that Howison's collaboration with Lee was to get a report from Lee about the conditions there and the British (Hudson's Bay Company) influence.

Others expanded on this by claiming that Lee was a pawn of the U. S. government and had been funded to settle in the Willamette Valley and Howison was there for Lee's "report."

Still others believed that the flag-waving American naval vessel was there to show the British that the American government was ready to fight if need be, right there in Oregon; that the so-called "survey mission" was just a cover for possible battle action.

(The British had a much larger ship with more guns parked at Fort Vancouver on the Columbia River. The officers of both ships partied together and got along fine.) Speculation never ceases!

The validation of poor navigation charts at the river's entrance was proven when the *Shark* landed on a sand bar on its way in. It was July 1, 1846. As the bar was smooth that day, the ship was refloated on the incoming tide then proceeded on its way.

The *Shark's* crew was very glad to see dry land after many months being cooped up in the ship, A considerable number of them deserted. Advertising was sent out offering rewards for their capture and return to no avail. And, no local men would not sign on as replacements.

The ship left the river on September 10 and started its crossing of the rugged bar. This time the bar was rough. The vessel was too far to the south, was in shallow water, then suddenly jammed itself on Clatsop Spit in a flurry of rapidly crashing breakers.

Captain Scheneck immediately ordered the ship lightened. The cannons were pushed overboard and the masts were cut down. But the *Shark* was already well-embedded in the sand and the breakers were causing havoc with the wooden ship. It quickly broke up. The crew took to the boats and landed safely to be taken in by the settlers. The crew was eventually given passage to San Francisco on the *Cadboro,* a ship chartered for the purpose from the Hudson's Bay Company.

The wreck of the *Shark* is remembered in several ways. Among them is "Shark Rock" a stone with original engraving and its historical marker on an Astoria street, and a unique happenstance. A piece of the ship's deck, with one of the non-jettisoned cannons mounted on it (along with a capstan which may not have been from the *Shark*), landed on the beach south of Tillamook Head near Arch Cape. The nearly 8-mile long beach was named Cannon Beach because of this. A community near the north end of the beach, called Elk Creek, was founded but the name was changed to Cannon Beach and this became the city known today.

For many years, the cannon was mounted as a monument near where it landed but in 1989, it, and the capstan, was moved to Astoria by the Clatsop County Historical Society. □

—28—
Bark *Oriole* Sinks
Takes Parts For New Lighthouse to Bottom
Stranded September 18, 1853 —sank

The loss of the *Oriole* (Captain Lewis H. Lentz) and her cargo set back improved navigation in northwest coast waters by about two years because the bark carried lighthouse parts and construction workers.

The bark had been standing off the Columbia River bar for a week awaiting a break in the weather after a voyage of 22 days from San Francisco. The bar pilot, Captain Flavel, came aboard then with a suitable wind blowing, the ship started her trip over the bar on an outflowing tide. All went well for the next two hours then, as the wind quit, the ship was at the mercy of the currents. The drifting vessel, anchor out and not catching, was soon dragging her bottom on the sand. Then the vessel was caught on a reef and could not float free due to her heavy load of freight. The ship, inside Clatsop Spit, started to come apart.

Water was coming in as the hull came loose from the frame. As the ship started to settle, the rudder post pushed through the deck. There was no doubt in the minds of the two captains aboard, they were losing the ship.

As night came on, two lifeboats were put over the side and lashed together and all 32 men got in. The weather was turning miserable and everyone, thoroughly wet, spent the night in the open boats. In the meantime, the *Oriole* slid off the reef, rolled over, then sank in about 100-feet of water.

Near dawn, the *California,* the pilot boat, came along looking for the *Oriole* but instead found the men in the boats. All were taken aboard.

The sea broke the *Oriole's* hull into two pieces. The portion carrying the mizzen mast and the cargo of cans of paint, building blocks and other parts, beached near the entrance of Netarts Bay. Many of these parts, along with iron salvaged from the *Shark*, were used in the construction of the *Morning Star*. ☐

—29—
Wreck and Salvage of the *Bawnmore*
Stranded August 28, 1895 —sank

The lumber company surveyor-agent crawled from his bedroll, dressed (which included the usual knee-length laced boots), then he put together some easy-to-prepare breakfast while his coffee perked on his little pressurized distillate (gasoline) stove.

His first task of this day, Wednesday, August 28, 1895, was to take the short walk over the nearby sand dune to the beach to take his regular reading from his tide gauge. On climbing the dune, one can imaging his surprise when he saw a steamship stranded only about 700 feet off shore. The ship was about op-

Bawnmore **hard aground just off the beach at Floras Lake in August 1895. Although everyone was rescued and much cargo was salvaged, much more had to be abandoned. The ship eventually broke in two then it sank during winter storms. White lines in picture are scratches, not a sleet storm.**

posite his tide gauge on this very foggy morning. With his pocket telescope, the observer saw that the anchor had been dropped seaward but the ship seemed unable to pull itself off the beach. This was exciting.

The *Bawnmore* (Capt. Alexander Woodside) was a 279-foot long steamer of British registry and was nearly new. It had been completed in 1889. This 1,430-ton freighter had 30 people on board a few being passengers. The ship had stopped at a couple of ports on Vancouver Island, in British Columbia, and was carrying general cargo for Peru.

There was no doubt about it: This ship was hard aground.

The surveyor chose a large, fairly flat weather-beaten piece of driftwood that was white with age. Then finding apiece of partially burns driftwood, he fashioned the words

WILL SEND HELP

in large letters with the charcoal. In the meantime, he had been spotted from the ship so when he held up the sign, which was read with a spy glass, the skipper on the steamer answered with a short blast of the whistle.

The surveyor trudged back to his camp where he saddled his horse then headed though the brush and trees to the Denmark store. There, he told of the tragedy and had the postmaster locate someone to ride as quickly as possible the nearly twenty miles to the United states Life Saving Station at Bandon. The rider was the only means of communication as this was before telegraph or telephone lines existed here. The surveyor returned to the beach.

In the meantime, the ship's captain ordered the ship's whistle sounded at intervals in the event there were other ships in the vicinity. He received no answers. But a ship's whistle can be heard for miles thus over a dozen farmers, who wondered about the blasts, headed for the beach. Others, summoned by the rider on his way to Bandon, soon joined. The fog was still hovering now just above the masts of the ship.

Two of the crew were trying to swim ashore with a codfish line tied around their waists but the alongshore current carried them south so others on the vessel had to pull them back. The breakers became quite strong as did the undertow.

Next, a small boat was launched bearing an officer and two men. This craft capsized as it went through the breakers but some of those on shore, who were anticipating such a situation, and with lines around their waists, ran into the surf to assist the men who were clinging to the swamped boat. One from the ship apparently was suffering some broken ribs when he was thrown against the edge of the boat. It was a close call. Had this first landing effort failed, the rest of the crew would have had to stay on the *Bawnmore* until the Life Saving Station men arrived. When they did it was nearly nightfall.

When the skipper of the ship saw his party ashore, he had men attach heavier lines, to the end of the lighter line which was then pulled ashore and secured to sand anchors which had been prepared on the beach. A sand anchor is made of the heaviest driftwood which has been buried in the sand one behind the other thus the anchor becomes formidability strong and could withstand considerable strain. To these anchors, life-lines and surf-lines were fastened with a round turn from one log to the next thereby equalizing the pull on them all.

As quickly as possible, the ship's large lifeboat was lowered into the sea with each end secured by pulley wheels on the line that would keep the boat from turning broadside while running toward the beach through he surf. Using this method, the boat's crew was able to pull the boat to the shore along the line and did not use any oars.

It didn't take long before the lifeboat was on the beach but, as anticipated, all in it got a through drenching. Mrs. Woodside, the captain's wife, came in this boat and brought her pet parrot in its cage. While this drama unfolded, some of the volunteers on shore had set up a wind break of driftwood and started some fires behind it to keep people warm – particularly those who had been drenched by the sea – which was most of them.

Following the tradition of the sea, Captain Woodside was the last man to leave the *Bawnmore*.

Just before the last of the crew disembarked, they released a number of prize cattle which had been sheltered in a special stall on the steamer's deck. The idea was for the cattle to swim to shore as the animals were lowered over the side of the ship on the shore side. But the animals did not understand any of this and most of them just swam in circles, a few heading to the open sea. The current carried some on a southerly course toward Blacklock Point. But a couple of hefty bulls made it to shore. Some of the volunteer farmers chased the animals and tried to attach short ropes around their necks but this venture was unsuccessful as the animals were scared, absolutely terrorized and ran off the beach into the woods and disappeared.

> Just where the bulls from the *Bawnmore* sheltered themselves does not seem to be recorded however, the evidence of a lot of new calves being born during the next year appears to indicate the bulls had a field day along the dairy cows. One source claims these offspring were dubbed the "*Bawnmore* breed."

The rider, who had been dispatched to fetch the Life Savers, arrived back at the Floras Lake beach rescue camp about noon.

He announced that the crew was on the way but had to travel along the beach with a team of horses hauling a lifeboat, their line-shooting gun and all the usual rescue paraphernalia. This

THURSDAY, AUGUST 29, 1895.

ASHORE NEAR BANDON

British Tank Steamer Bawnmore Reported to Be a Total Wreck.

SHE RAN ON THE BEACH IN A FOG

One Sailor Was Washed Ashore, and the Life-Saving Crew Is Present to Rescue the Rest.

BANDON, Or., Aug. 28.—A messenger has just arrived here bringing word that the British steamer Bawnmore is ashore ten miles down the coast. One sailor, a Japanese, reached shore in an injured condition; but he could give no particulars of the accident.' It is supposed the steamer ran ashore in the fog. When the messenger left the place, 30 or 30 persons could be seen on the deck. The sea was breaking heavily about the vessel. The messenger says that the Bawnmore is breaking up, and will prove a total loss. The sailor who was washed ashore probably jumped from the steamer when she struck. Captain Scott, of the lifesaving service, left for the scene of the accident with his crew and apparatus as soon as the word came, and is now on the ground.

Description of the Bawnmore.

The Bawnmore was on her way from Comox to Tampico. She was in Portland a short time ago, bringing a part cargo of petroleum. She loaded 500 tons of flour for Central American points, and then went to Comox to coal for the trip down the coast, sailing from the latter port last Sunday. The steamer arrived here August 14, and sailed August 18. Her oil was discharged at the gas works, and she took on the flour at Columbia dock and the flouring mills.

The vessel was what is known as a tank steamer, being arranged expressly for carrying petroleum. She was in command of Captain Woodside, a brother of the owner. The captain's wife was also on board. The steamer, which registered 2633 tons, sailed from Belfast, and was a first-class English cargo boat. Mr. Campbell was first mate, and Mr. McKerchie chief engineer.

On her trip up the coast from Payta, Peru, where the oilfields are located, the Bawnmore stopped at San Francisco and discharged the greater part of her cargo. Then she took on a miscellaneous lot of freight for Mexico and Central and South America, and finished here. She had a cumbersome deckload, including a quantity of lumber, a dozen street-cars for La Libertad, two steam launches, and three coffee lighters. In her hold, in addition to the flour, were building materials, lumber, wine, cement, kerosene, beer, rice, livestock, carriages, coke, lime, machinery, furniture, etc.

The Bawnmore's lower hold was divided by fore and aft athwartship steel bulkheads, made into tanks for carrying petroleum. These tanks, at the hatchways, extend through the 'tweendecks to the upper deck. When loading, the tanks are filled to about two-thirds up from the 'tweendecks to the top of the hatch, so that whatever position the vessel is in at sea, the lower hold is always full of oil.

The steamer had the reputation of being a fast sailer, and was one of the staunchest vessels afloat, but nothing could withstand the breakers on an exposed coast. The steamer was owned by Grace & Co., of San Francisco, and was the first of a direct line of oil steamers to ply between Payta and northern ports.

LOSS OF THE BAWNMORE.

Scene of the Wreck Ten Miles South of Brandon, Or.

ONE LIFE KNOWN TO HAVE BEEN SACRIFICED.

SAN FRANCISCO, Aug. 29.—The steamer Bawnmore is a total loss. The crew has been saved. J. W. Gracy & Co. received this brief message from the north to-day, and the sea-faring public was much relieved to learn that Captain Woodside and his wife are safe. They are sorry, however, to be told of the total loss of the Bawnmore.

The steamer went ashore near Bandon, Oregon. Captain Scott of the United States Life-Saving Service and a crew of men went to the rescue. A good deal of nervousness is felt in this city for the safety of Captain Woodside and his wife, who are on board the steamer, and news from the stranded vessel is eagerly awaited.

A mail carrier who arrived at Marshfield this morning, reports that the body of a Japanese sailor was washed ashore. Another seaman, badly injured, was cast up by the breakers on the beach.

The scene of the wreck is ten miles south of Bandon, and the steamer went on the beach broadside and her deckload was soon washed overboard.

A dense fog prevailed and the vessel's crew could not see 500 yards ahead of them. Captain Woodside acted with great coolness when the steamer struck, and advised his men to stand by the craft and not attempt to reach shore. It is reported that two of the Japanese crew disobeyed the Captain's orders and tried to reach the shore. One was drowned.

The Bawnmore is a steel tank steamer of 1,436 tons burden. She carried a crew of thirty men. She recently left this port with a cargo of goods for Central America. She went to Portland, Oregon, to secure a cargo of flour.

The vessel and cargo are valued at $125,000, partly insured.

Sacramento Union
Sacramento, Cal.
Page 1, Col. 5
Aug. 30, 1895

119

would take a lot of time as the trudge on sand was about 3 to maybe 4 miles in an hour. The rescuers arrived at the beach camp about supper time. On learning that the people from the ship were safely ashore, some of the life savers set up camp for the night on shore while others interviewed the ships' officer for the official report. A faulty compass was blamed for the stranding of the ship.

The captain revealed that he and his brother were the principal owners of the steamer. They had been to Portland where they took on the general cargo then were bound for Peru by way of Central American ports. The heavy fog caused the ship to get too close in-shore which caused the accident. The vessel, he said, was strongly built of steel and was fitted out as an oil tanker having been in that trade previously .

A couple of days later, the Captain realized there was nothing that could be done to save his ship so he and his wife and the crew left for San Francisco.

In due time, tug boats and salvage ships arrived off the beach from San Francisco. The sea turned rough as if to protect the beached vessel, therefore the tugs could not get close. They went back to port. On the basis of the reports from the salvage men, the underwriters put the ship and cargo out for bid.

The lumber company's surveyor, the man who had first sighted then reported the stranded steamer, was the sole bidder at just $500 for everything – vessel and all its freight. He won. No one else wanted to take the chance but none had visited the scene except the tug and salvage boat people who had turned in their unsatisfactory reports.

There was little joy in realizing that the ship and cargo had been won. Money had to be found to pay off the underwriters – the $500 – before anyone could step on board. There was also the realization that if the cargo was successfully landed, there was no transportation available to haul any of it to market. The dilemma hardened when a sudden severe storm broke the ship in two.

There was a cargo valued at nearly a quarter of a million dollars in the two sections of the ship. As a rule, nearly all stranded ships as close to shore as the *Bawnmore*, will break in two sooner or later is the surf pounds hard enough. When a ship

Loss of The Bawnmore.

The British steamer Bawnmore, which went ashore about 15 miles below Bandon, last Wednesday morning will be a total wreck, judging from the latest news received from the scene. The passengers and crew were landed safely, and it is probable that some of the cargo has been saved.

The following regarding the Bawnmore is from the Oregonian of Aug 29th: "The Bawnmore was on her way from Comox to Tampico. She was in Portland a short time ago, bringing a part cargo of petroleum. She loaded 500 tons of flour for Central American points, and then went to Comox to coal for the trip down the coast, sailing from the latter port last Sunday. The steamer arrived here August 15, and sailed August 18. Her oil was discharged at the gas works, and she took on the flour at Columbia dock and the flouring mills:

The vessel was what is known as a tank steamer, being arranged expressly for carrying petroleum. She was in command of Captain Woodside, a brother of the owner. The captain's wife was also on board. The steamer, which registered 1438 tons, hailed from Belfast, and was a firstclass English cargo boat. Mr. Campbell was first mate, and Mr. McKerchie chief engineer.

On her trip up the coast from Payta, Peru, where the oilfields are located, the Bawnmore stopped at San Francisco and discharged the greater part of her cargo. Then she took on a miscellaneous lot of freight for Mexico and Central and South America, and finished here. She had a cumbersome deckload, including a quantity of lumber, a dozen street-cars for La Liberted, two steam launches, and three coffee lighters. In her hold, in addition to the flour, were building materials, lumber, wine, cement, kerosene, beer, rice, livestock, carriages, coke, lime, machinery, furniture, etc.

Coos Bay News
Marshfield, Oreg.
Wed. Sept. 4, 1895

The Bawnmore's lower hold was divided by fore and aft athwartship steel bulkheads, made into tanks for carrying petroleum. These tanks, at the hatchways, extend through the 'tweendecks to the upper deck. When loading, the tanks are filled to about two-thirds up from the 'tweendecks to the top of the hatch, so that whatever position the vessel is in at sea the lower hold is always full of oil.

The steamer had the reputation of being a fast sailer, and was one of the staunchest vessels afloat, but nothing could withstand the breakers on an exposed coast. The steamer was owned by Grace & Co., of San Francisco, and was the first of a direct line of oil steamers to ply between Payta and northern ports.

STEAMER BAWNMORE.

Fire Completes the Wreck of the Stranded Vessel.

SAN FRANCISCO, Sept. 2.—Fire completed the destruction of the tank steamer Bawnmore, which was wrecked ten miles below Bandon, Or., on the 28th of August. Twelve hours after she went ashore the waves beat her down to starboard and the water rushed into the cabin and forecastle and got into the tanks. In the after tank there was a large quantity of lime, and as soon as the water reached in the flames broke out. From tank to tank the flames spread, and soon the hull and iron decks were red-hot. The street cars, lumber and boats were soon in flames, and although each succeeding sea that broke over the ship would put out the fire, it was only temporary. The heat of the hull was sufficient to start it again, and in a short space of time every bit of woodwork about the steamer was burned out.

When the tug Monarch reached the stranded vessel there was nothing to do but leave her to break up. Her machinery is still intact, and, with proper appliances, it may be saved. She was insured for only half her value. As she was engaged in carrying oil the rate of insurance was very high, so Captain Woodside took half the risk himself. The cargo will be a total loss. The steamer went ashore in the sand, and is now firmly imbedded in it. Every sea makes a clean sweep of her, and she is going ashore piecemeal.

Sacramento Union
Sacramento, Cal.
Page 1, Col. 1
Sept. 3, 1895

The descriptive narrative of the grounding and salvage of cargo on *Bawnmore* varies considerably with several newspaper accounts of the time. Even the newspaper stories do not agree. The narrative does not mention a fire but one paper lists lime, in cargo, as cause, another says "the coal cargo" was afire. If the ship was substantially burned out within five days of grounding, as one story claims, how could salvage be conducted for about nine months as detailed in the narrative? The number of street cars varies from two to a dozen depending on where one reads.

is broadside of a beach, the undertow sucks the sand out from under the bow and at the stern leaving the vessel supported only amidships. In this condition, considering the weight of the ship and its cargo, the only expectation is that the hull will break.

The Rumor

Rumors start from no where but seem to go every where with the speed of greased lightning. The wreck of the *Bawnmore* was no exception. The man who discovered the stranded ship, the surveyor, had never revealed why he was there. Accordingly, the rumor reached him that he had searched for a desolate place where the ship could be grounded then for him, in collusion with the owners, to claim the cargo at a ridiculously low price. The gossips were very good. They even said he had placed his tide gauge in that certain place as a marker where a ship was to be stranded. Every one on the beach could see this marker just a short distance from the fore end of the vessel. The tide gauge was also right there on the beach for all to wonder about. At any rate, guessing as to why he was there seemed to be satisfied even though there was no truth in it. But this idle chatter reached the underwriters and caused considerable delay in paying the owners their just claims.

With salvage rights in hand, consideration as to methods for unloading the *Bawnmore* became top priority. It would take a lot of strong and fearless men. If a profit was to be realized, the work needed to be done quickly because of expected storms. The work would be dangerous. The vessel was a total loss thus a lone tugboat that suddenly appeared left quickly as there was no tow possible.

It would be good to get seasoned stevedores for the work but none were available. Also, there were no sailors accustomed to working on a heaving sea.

With no other choice, it was necessary to advertise in the nearest newspapers for men and offering exceptionally high pay. This amounted to $1.50 *an hour* on the basis that all wages would be taken in merchandise salvaged. There would be no cash wages. To establish value, the current price of the goods would be established then that price reduced by half.

The usual wages for working in town and on some farm jobs, were only $1 or $2 a day with board. But the rate offered for this work did not consider the usual 10 to 12 hour day. This work could only be accomplished at low tide which meant two to four hours a day and this would be mostly at night. On the days when the sea was too rough, even at low tide, there would be no work. But the operator would still have to provide free room and board. Suitable beachside quarters would have to be erected as the men would be constantly wet, very tired and there was no way to town.

The first task, once some men responded to the advertisements, was to build a fair size shed. This would serve as bunkhouse, cookhouse, dining room as well as warehouse for salvaged goods. This was constructed with salvaged lumber and corrugated iron taken from the ship. Some of the posts were large driftlogs that were already strewn around the beach.

The vessel was unloaded with carriages made of strong wood frames, 6 x 10 feet, interlaced with heavy rope netting making 6-inch mesh. Each of these carriages was suspended from four pulley wheels on two parallel wire cables running to the ship. These materials had been salvaged from the abandoned old sandstone operation on nearby Blacklock Point.

Transport from the beach to the ship was by the lifeboat that had been used when the crew escaped from the ship on the day the ship stranded. The men in the first boat to the *Bawnmore* pulled wire ropes with them. On the vessel, one rope was tied to the foremast and the other to the after end through more pulleys. When operations started, a carriage of goods, shore-bound, passed an empty carriage going in the opposite direction on the second rope. To get the apparatus to move, a team of heavy horses and a driver were hired to pull, on the beach, when the signal was received from the ship.

To a new man, it appeared rather dangerous to go back and forth to the ship in the dangling carriages. Wreck salvaging is always dangerous at best and the safety of these men had to be considered. When sending men to the wreck, they were told to hold on fast and to sit down putting their legs through the large meshes of the rope netting. The carriages would sometimes be struck by incoming breakers, as the long wires would unavoidably sag down in the middle because of the length and the heavy load. However, courageous men will take much risk for high pay.

The first job a new man to the job was assigned was on the ship. This quickly provided a measurement as to the man's ability as well as his stamina for this work. Some dreaded the water and left the same day. Others, once on the ship, would size up the job and come back to shore on the next carriage unwilling to accept the job. Great credit is due those who stuck it out. Some seemed to realize if their valiant leader would take the chance, so would they.

Having received a list of the vessel's cargo from the Custom House in Portland, it was finally possible to know what was on board and to try to set priorities as to what to take off first, remembering that every day there was risk that the ship might break further and all efforts would have to be abandoned. Until now, all work, as to goods and values, had been pure speculation. True, some deck cargo had been identified but that was about all. The inventory was extensive. Because of the deal for setting fair value, a Montgomery Ward Mail Order Catalog was used for this purpose. There was no trouble with the workers over the arrangement and pay and, under the circumstances, the work progressed.

Some of the ship's goods were:

Flour, 900 pounds in sacks	Canned paint – yellow
Potatoes, several hundred tons	1 grand piano in hermetically
Dried beans in sacks	sealed case
Rice in sacks	Canned goods
General hardware items	Various other goods
Several electric trolley cars	

The piano was immediately purchased by the keepers at the Cape Blanco lighthouse. According to the local people, this was the first grand piano in the country for miles around.

Water will only penetrate a sack of flour for a fraction of an inch thus making an airtight covering of hard caked dough that will preserve the rest of the flour in the sack a long time. This salvaged flour first sold for $15 per ton but as everyone took a few sacks and there was still tons more, the price dropped to only $5/ton. At that price, nearby farmers came to the beach and paid cash. Even so, there was a great lot of flour and potatoes and some other foods, so arrangements were made for some hog farmers to build a corral of driftwood close by to the lake. Into this enclosure they drove their hogs to be fattened on sea-water soaked spuds, bloated beans, swollen rice and the flour. Much of this was spoiled for humans to eat but the hogs took right to it.

About the paint in the cargo.

This was in iron drums from Pacific Rubber Paint Company. Some had been punctured and were leaking but with a rubber base, there was little damage. These drums quickly sold for 30¢ a gallon. All of it was bright yellow! Some other paint colors were in small cans and these sold equally as well.

It became a sight in that part of Curry County to ride along and observe a great many buildings painted all the same color – bright yellow!

A story passed around related to a salesman from out of the area talking with a person in town asked why so many buildings were the same color? Because the key person to all this extravaganza was present, he was pointed out with an accusing finger and admonition: "Ask him"! Thus the story was told.

No technical description of the electric trolley cars has ever been found. It was reported there were 12 of them but the number was never confirmed. These were off-loaded by some unidentified means, then were reported to have been sold to farmers to use as out-buildings. This was unique for Curry County, which never had a public railroad, but it now had trolley cars.*

The salvaging of the *Bawnmore's* cargo continued through the winter, weather permitting, but the method was slow and only about one-quarter of the goods ever reached shore.

* When the authors were diligently researching for their book on Lakeport (see bibliography) in the mid-1980's, nearly 100 years after the wreck of the *Bawnmore*, they could not find any trace of the street cars or locate anyone who knew about them.

After the ship broke, which was during a very rough but typical northwest coastal storm, the two parts of the ship separated by about 20 feet. A length of wire rope was stretched across this gap with the mesh to walk on. But the crashing waves surging back and forth made of the men seasick while crossing the gap – one did not dare to look down. The crashing of the breakers on the hulks was so strong it knocked off many of the ship's steel plates.

On one day some 12 men were on the foredeck and about the same number on the after deck when heavy breakers rolled up and knocked down the stack. This was on the night shift and the meager lighting was instantly put out as the breaker crashed over the entire deck taking all that was not secured with it. On the ship, signals were sent to the beach then the men hounded into the carriage to be brought ashore.

Alas, the second line that would have brought the other carriage to the stern snapped at the same time the huge wave broke the rope mesh bridge between the two sections and that bridge was instantly lost. This stranded those men who were on the aft of the vessel.

It would have been plausible for those men to climb into the mast's rigging to avoid being grabbed by the waves but to have to stay up there until the next low tide was unthinkable. The thought came to mind that it might be necessary to send for the Life Saving men from Bandon.

The wind was from the north, it was winter and to add to the general discomfort it was raining. As the wire sagged into the sea, then rose up again, it collected a large amount of seaweed. All work was at a standstill. The days, never long enough, were gray and absolutely everything was wet either from the crashing seas or from the rain. The men could not get warm. With the windchill, the temperature was probably about freezing. There seemed to be no relief. To be exposed to these conditions did not make for happy feelings and was downright dangerous.

It was decided to rescue the men on the hulk one at a time. A man would be tied tightly to a clevis (shackle) attached to the 700-foot long rope that ran to the beach. Although the men were cautioned about leaving the wreck too close together for to do so would cause the line to sag, the first fellow got stuck out in the middle of the line on accumulated seaweed. This cause a blockage on the line as the other men, slipping along the rope, ran into him. The wire, in its center now developed the sag as had been predicted so it and the men on it were frequently under water.

Men, in these conditions tend to either cuss wildly or totally shut up. These several stuck on the rope were some of each. One who had just slid down the wire to the stopping point, pulled out his large sheath knife. This was passed, carefully, to the first man who then hacked away the seaweed. It was not an easy or quick job but eventually the wire was cleared then all the men on the wire, roared down the line toward the beach arriving their in a heap. The courage, toughness and stamina under these conditions was what separates men from boys. Some decided, on getting to the beach, that this life and work was way more than they bargained for – decided life was too short for this kind of work and went home. But the majority stayed.

If there was personal discomfort, it was from boils that most of the men developed. Whether it was from too much fat pork in the dinners, or the constant saltwater baths, with no fresh water for a rinse, was not studied at the time.

Of constant annoyance on board the ship, was the oil from the bunkers that floated to the top and got into everything. It made some of them quite ill when they accidentally swallowed some it when they got dunked while working.

Nearly nine months later, and after there was a tremendous pile of salvage sitting on the beach, it was discovered there was no longer any market. The main sales came from local people who knew about the wreck and the salvage operations. Much of the goods were consigned to the men as wages. Yet there was more. To get any of the goods to the nearest population center, Port Orford, was an out-of-pocket $16-ton payable at the time of the haul. Only the lightest and most valuable articles would be sent this way because all the potential profits from the venture could easily be eaten up in freight costs. To overcome this obstacle, it was decided to hold a public auction right on the beach.

An auctioneer in Marshfield (that town later renamed Coos Bay) was commissioned to advertise the sale in the Bandon and

Marshfield newspapers. Interest was intense and the crowd was fairly large considering this country was sparsely settled and roads were nearly non-existent.

Everything went cheap. There were the ship's winches, usually $1,000 each, went for a top bid of only $18. This was the price of scrap iron less freight. A 1,000 pound kedge anchor was finally sold for just $1.

The Top-selling Item From the Wreck

If there was a comic break from this awful affair, it had to do with a large number of unlabeled tins. They were about 5-gallon size. When the lids were pried open, the contents looked like paste. It was brown colored and with a peculiar very strong aroma. These sold very fast and at good prices with everyone guessing what it was. The guesses were pretty wild with everything suggested from sheep-dip to opium. Some said it must be paint or "boiler compound" or was it a medical concoction? The answer, which was kept secret, taken from the Custom House manifest, revealed these cans to be filled with gingerbread cookies. Not being waterproof, the cans had taken on saltwater and oil. As they sloshed back and forth with the wave action in the hulk's hold, the contents had become thoroughly mixed to the brown mush. On the day of sale, these cans were the top seller.

The sale went well but that night there was an unexpected occurrence. The watchdog became restless and growled long and low then broke into a challenging bark and tugged wildly at his chain. Several men had been observed during the day poking through the salvage but had never made any bids. Much that was sold was still on the beach awaiting the new owners to arrange for hauling. It was assumed the prowlers were looking for whatever they might sneak off with, but there was also concern for the stash of money that had been taken in. The cabin, which was near the warehouse shed, was barricaded.

The best protection was the dog's noise. The moon was out that night so the figures moving about the goods were clearly seen. No one in the cabin said anything above a whisper and no lights were lit. Eventually, after stealing a few hand-size articles, the intruders departed. But no one slept for the rest of that night.

The next morning, several of the men set out along the beach and along the trail around Floras Lake toward Denmark looking for the strangers. No one was seen. On another occasion, night-stalkers picked up flotsam from the wreck and silently entered the camp to steal whatever they could carry. Once someone stole a splendid coupe (buggy) that had been freight on the *Bawnmore*. A search indicated no tracks from the wheels but later it was determined that after pushing the buggy to the lake, someone had returned and covered the tracks. By use of a small boat, the buggy had been taken to a distant arm of the lake and hidden in the underbrush. But not well enough. After extensive searching, it was discovered then returned to the beach.

After the auction, work on the ship stopped. The rigging had been damaged in the storms and both ends of the ship seemed to be slipping from the roost on the sand bar. There was very little of the salvage remaining on the beach and what was there had little value. What was still on the ship's two hulks, would have to be abandoned. Items on the beach but not sold were stored in the barn of a farmer in the area until some further disposal could be arranged. Just about everyone in northern Curry County and southern Coos County had something from the *Bawnmore*.

By now, nearly ten months had elapsed since the fateful foggy day when the ship stranded off the beach.

The surveyor departed for San Francisco on a ship out of Eureka. Later, he went into the ship salvage business. ☐

END NOTE: What was a surveyor doing camped on this desolate stretch of the beach in the first place? He was there looking at the feasibility of digging a canal between the ocean and Floras Lake, the distance between the two waters being less than a quarter-mile. Real estate promoters envisioned a great city at this new "seaport." The town of Lakeport was founded here, grew to become the largest city in northern Curry County with a 3-story hotel, weekly newspaper, and a United States postoffice. But it all came apart when it was revealed that the lake, slightly higher than sea level, would he drained if a canal was dug thus the real estate scam was exposed and everyone moved out. The Coast Guard occupied the remnants during World War II with a heavily armed Beach Patrol headquarters as that stretch of beach had been determined to be "ideal" for an expected invasion by the Japanese. Refer to *Lakeport* in bibliography.

—30—
The Two *Yaquinas*:
Yaquina City – *Yaquina Bay*

Yaquina City stranded December 4, 1887 —abandoned
Yaquina Bay stranded December 9, 1888 —abandoned

The two *Yaquinas* each piled up on the beach nearly at the same place and within five days of being exactly one year apart.

The Oregon Development Company was working hard to make a major seaport at Yaquina City, about 7 miles up the Yaquina River from the bar, by bringing commerce from San Francisco to its port instead of ships having to sail farther north to the Columbia River, manage to get over its dangerous bar, then sail another 100 miles upriver to Portland. At Yaquina City*, there was the Oregon Pacific Railroad ready to carry goods to Portland with convenient stops at Corvallis and other way-points. The steamer *Yaquina City* (formerly named the *Western Texas*, was the initial key to this business.

On December 4th, 1887, the *Yaquina City* stood off the bar ready for entering the bay. Was it an act of commercial sabotage perpetrated by rival commercial interests in Portland? Or was it just bad luck that set back the development company's plans?

While crossing the bar, the ship lost her rudder cable and stranded on the beach at the entrance of the river. Everyone on board got off without difficulty but not so the vessel. This was before the jetties were built. Salvage efforts were frustrated by storms and crashing breakers pounding on the ship. It took only eight days before the vessel broke apart.

The promoters of the company definitely wanted to get a piece of that lucrative Columbia River business so, with the insurance money from their wrecked ship, they set out to buy another vessel. They bought a bigger one, the 6-year old *Caracas*, renamed it *Yaquina Bay* (Captain Lord), and reopened for business. With the new 1,200-ton ship, that was more-than-the-ordinary for passenger comfort, she sailed out of San Francisco on her maiden

---

* Yaquina City has all but disappeared within the City of Toledo with the earlier village of Newport, on the north shore of Yaquina Bay, presently the major city and port of Lincoln County.

voyage for Yaquina City. She never made it. At the bar, on December 9th, the ship was taken in tow by a tugboat as a precautionary measure. All went well until the towing line snapped under pressure, which caused the vessel to be caught in the breakers that slammed the *Yaquina Bay* on the sand almost in the same place the earlier ship had been wrecked just one year ago.

As before, everyone aboard was assisted off the 257-foot long ship. As before, the ship became a total wreck in a matter of days.

The company's officers, disillusioned at the twin events, quit the passenger business. ☐

—31—
Lupata Crashes at Deadman's Cove – Sinks
(Officially registered as *Lupata* aka: *Lupatia*)
Sank January 3, 1881

The Captain of record, Captain Irvin, died at sea shortly after this 1,400-ton bark left Antwerp for Japan by way of Portland, so the First Mate B. H. Ravan assumed command.

When off the Oregon Coast, a typical winter storm was howling and churning up the sea all along the northwest coast. The night was dark. The vessel was ploughing along opposite Tillamook Head just 1-mile to the east. About 8 o'clock in the evening, the *Lupata* slid by Tillamook Rock so close that the men working there, preparing the final stages for putting the brand new lighthouse in operation, could detect the creaking of the ship as it passed. On hearing a barked command from the ship, "Hard aport" the men on the rock lit all of their lanterns, set off powder blasts, then built a bonfire from what refuse was available to provide a homemade beacon for the ship. Then all was quiet except for the constant crashing of waves around the rock.

When dawn came, the workers looked toward shore through the mist and in the distance saw what was left of a once fine ship. There, among floating wreckage, sticking out of the sea was the mizzen mast breaking the watery grave. This was near the base of Tillamook Head. At the bottom of the steep cliff is a small shallow cove that is inundated at high tide. Local's say this is called

Deadman's Cove because of the wreck of the *Lupata* there.

The *Lupata* had driven head-on into the small off-shore reef that faces the cliff. With a holed hull, the vessel probably sank within minutes. The crew, 16 in all, drowned. Most of the corpses were recovered.

The anti-climax of the *Lupata* catastrophe is that only 19 days later, famous Tillamook Rock Lighthouse,* 1-mile offshore (45°56'N - 124°1'W), was ready for service. Its 1st Order Fresnel beam could be seen up to 18 miles and its fog horns, jokesters claim, were such that even the seals on the lower rocks could not sleep. □

—32—
Tragedy at Sea for *Alaskan*
Sank at sea May 12, 1889

The steel-hulled, side-wheel steamer was bound from Portland to San Francisco without its normal load of passengers as she was headed for dry-docking and routine overhaul. The ship, *Alaskan* (Captain R. E. Howes), had crossed a smooth Columbia River bar while a light west wind was blowing about 11:30 in the morning. He ordered the helmsman to turn to the south at the whistling buoy. The *Alaskan* was doing 9 knots. All activities aboard seemed normal and relaxed.

By 11:30 p.m., the ship's lookout called out that Foulweather's light house beam (Yaquina Head lighthouse – visible up to 19 miles) was 14 miles bearing east by northeast.

The wind seemed typical for this position being from the south. The ship was passing through rain showers but the baro-

---

* The construction of the lighthouse was an engineering triumph completed under the most trying conditions. What many do not realize, is that the natural round top of the rock had to be blasted off then a flat platform developed before the lighthouse could be built. The light is 133 feet above the sea and often, too often for the well-being of the keepers who lived there, the ocean in its winter frenzy, crashed over the top sometimes injuring the men, knocking the light out of service and causing severe damage. The lighthouse was discontinued in 1957. For the entire amazing story, see bibliography for *"Terrible Tilly," Tillamook Rock Lighthouse, The Biography of a Lighthouse.*

meter was steady at 29.85 (29.92 normal). Their position was 43°5'N and they were moving right along being 18 miles off shore on Sunday the 12th.

The skipper trimmed his ship at 3 in the afternoon by setting the main trysail to keep the bow headed into the wind due to a drastic change in the weather. The sea was beginning to get nasty. Water started coming over the rail so the captain ordered speed reduced to DEAD SLOW. The ship had never been intended for the open sea having seen much duty in Puget Sound and in the Columbia River.

At 4 o'clock, the guard on the port side started to break and the afterhouse started to pull loose allowing seawater to enter easily. The crew tried to keep up with the growing troubles by stuffing bedding into holes but all this would soon prove useless.

At 6 p.m. the port guard, just forward of the wheel, gave way taking with it the covering board and bursting an upper plate.

The pumps continued to work well. The captain wrote in the ship's log:

By stuffing the rents with blankets we had great hopes of saving the ship, if it [weather] moderated at all but it did not, wind and sea increased and the ship's upper works gradually west to pieces, water pouring in on all sides, pumps working to their fullest capacity but the water increasing rapidly.

Captain Howes headed his ship into the wind at 11 p.m. as the engine stopped due to sea water in the fire boxes. His next order was to launch all four lifeboats which was accomplished without trouble. But one broke up before anyone got in.

All of the crew did not want to get into the small boats in the raging sea believing their chances were better if they stayed on the broken ship. The boats trailed behind.

> At 1 o'clock on Monday morning a vessel's lights were seen to the north. Although rockets were fired and torches were burned there was no response.

The *Alaskan's* bow went up out of the water then the vessel sank stern first breaking in two as she went at 2:15 a.m. The men watched from the lifeboats. The captain, engineer and about 10 of the crew were still with her.

Captain Howes jumped off the ship at the last moment. He made for a piece of floating deck and managed to get on it. The engineer was seen hanging on to another bit of deck. With only their hands for paddles, they made for each other. The pilot house, with three men on it, drifted within hailing distance when the engineer decided to paddle to that wreckage. He was knocked off his piece of the deck by a large wave and was not seen again.

Captain Edward McCoy, aboard his tugboat *Vigilant*, towing a Bowers dredge, discovered the mass of wreckage floating on the sea when he passed by so he started an immediate search for survivors of what he thought might be the result of a disaster. His thought was verified when, shortly thereafter, he picked up a dead body. Then he found three men still perched on the pilothouse and Captain Howes on his still floating piece of the deck. Later, in full daylight, the tug's lookout, who had climbed atop the mast, called out that he saw a man was on a bit of wreckage.

The tug gingerly approached and fetched up the sunken ship's first mate after he had floated for 33 hours. Then another piece of wreckage was sighted from which the ship's quartermaster was rescued. He was in poor shape with gashes to one of his legs caused when he was hit by the ship's propeller. He died of shock and loss of blood. Along with the other corpse that had been taken aboard, the two were buried at sea.

A lifeboat with 10 survivors made it through the surf and beached itself near the Siuslaw River.

In the meantime, the *Vigilant* with survivors aboard, still pulling its tow, slowly made its way to the Columbia River. Off the bar, the few men picked from the sea were put on board the steamer *Columbia* for the voyage upriver to Portland.

The voyage of the 260-foot long *Alaskan*, to a dry-dock and refit, that started so peacefully but ended in tragedy off Cape Blanco, cost 31 lives. Of the 47 on board at departure, only 16 lived to tell about it. □

—33—
Stranded *Baroda* Refloated
Stranded (no date) 1894 –refloated

When tough weather forced the 1,417-ton *Baroda* on to the beach near the Coquille River in 1894, the picturesque abandoned lighthouse, that tourists now flock to for photography and artists can't resist the temptation to paint, was still two years away from reality. Had the lighthouse been available, there is likelihood that its 4th Order beam, which was visible up to 12½ miles, would have warned the ship away.

One could have uttered: "No lighthouse warning –we ended up on the beach."

For about one month, there was evidence that the British bark would have a permanent resting place right where she landed. But an enterprising salvage crew got her back into deep water during a high tide.

When an owner determined he could make more money with the ship as a barge, the vessel was cut down, the deck was pealed off and all excess fittings in the hold were removed. Once, in her barge days, while hauling a load of coal, the barge, on fire partially sank in 1910 at Esquimalt. But she survived even that ordeal to be repaired and returned to service. As a barge, the *Baroda,* even possibly with a new name, may still be around. □

> **Baroda, anchored, with tug *Flyer* in 1902.**
> —Curry County Historical Society

—34—
South Portland Captain Loses License
Stranded October 19, 1903 —sank

A Coroner's Jury, convened to investigate the deaths of 18 people who had been killed as a result of the wreck of the steamer *South Portland*, found:

Captain J. B. McIntyre was criminally negligent in abandoning the wrecked steamer before seeing to the safety of passengers and crew.

Captain McIntyre's license was revoked.

The *South Portland* left Portland with a load of grain for San Francisco and, in foggy weather, crashed on Blanco Reef. The reef extends 1½ miles southwest from Cape Blanco and consists of numerous rocks and ledges. Only a few rocks of the reef are visible. These are Black Rock, 1.2 miles southwest of Cape Blanco Lighthouse (42°50'2"N - 124°33'8"W) and Pyramid Rock that is 1 mile west of the light. In clear weather, small vessels, mainly fish boats, whose masters are aware of the hazards, sometimes run between Blanco and Orford Reefs. But larger vessels are warned to stay away.

Why the lookout on the *South Portland* did not hear the fog horn or spy the beam from the lighthouse is unaccounted for.

The ship carried a crew of 25 and had a passenger list of 14. The vessel had been steady at 7 knots and struck the rocks bow-on with a resulting shock that knocked everyone who was standing to the deck. Into the resulting hole in the ship, sea water poured in a great gush. Confusion reigned and the skipper almost immediately ordered everyone to abandon the ship. The crew put two boats, filled with both passengers and some of the crew, over the side. The captain was in one boat. Both turned over and all the occupants struggled in the sea.

The Chief Mate, Charles Bruce, had stayed with the ship. As there was some steam still showing on the gauges, he set the ship in REVERSE and was successful in backing the *South Portland* off the reef. Then he moved the ship ahead slowly to the base of the bluff, fortunately missing more rocks, where, on entering shallow water the vessel stopped. There was no salvage effort made on the vessel. Just to both the north and south sides of the end of the cape there are beaches. It was on one of these that a lifeboat managed to put ashore.

There was argument during the hearing by the Coroner as to why the mate was left on the vessel and the captain abandoned his command taking the first boat away? The mate, who had been successful in moving the vessel, testified that it was he who recommended the skipper be in command of the first lifeboat. But that did not seem to have any affect on the jury that considered the tradition of the sea that a captain is always the last to abandon a disabled ship.

The name plate of the ship drifted northward on the Davidson Current that winter and was beachcombed by Boy Scout's from nearby Camp Meriwether. □

—35—
Furious Storm Takes *Western Home*
Stranded November 13, 1904 —abandoned

The 135-ton schooner *Western Home* stranded on the beach north of the Coquille River, during a furious early-winter storm, then broke up where she lay. □

—36—
The *C.A. Klose* and the *Advance*
Klose stranded November 12, 1904 —refloated
Advance stranded November 1, 1904 —refloated
Advance stranded December 29, 1905 —refloated

Two vessels were stranded in nearly the same place in less than two weeks. Then a year later, one of the two revisited for another try. The same rescue teams and vessels worked these incidents and with success.

The three-masted schooner, *C. A. Klose,* stranded November 12, 1904 within a stone's throw of the Coquille River Lighthouse. She was hove to off the entrance of the river at 10 in the morning. Then picking up a slight wind, she tried to cross the unsteady bar but the breeze was too slight so her sail went limp. The river is

The *C.A. Klose* cuddles with the Coquille River Lighthouse.
—James A. Gibbs col.

narrow for maneuvering there being no room to turn around. Observed from the U. S. Life Saving Station, the life-savers pondered whether to stay home and be needed later–too late–or to put their boat into the water then not be needed. The commander decided to get into the water with full gear just in case.

By the time the lifesavers reached the ship, the *Klose* was already hard aground. Pulling up to her side, a line was passed over then rowed out to the bar tug *Triumph,* that had come upon the scene, ready to try to muscle the schooner off her perch.

The lighthouse keepers were surprised, in looking out a window, to see the tall ship immobile and virtually at the base of the fog signal house. Keeper Frederick Amundsen noted that the masts of the *Klose* rose higher in the air than did the dome of his lighthouse.

With the line secure and her boiler hot, the tug, puffing steam, exerted her total horsepower in an effort to free the stuck schooner. The ship did not budge. More power was needed. The schooner's donkey engine was started but there was not enough line of sufficient strength to use for such a task.

While the *Triumph* pulled for all its worth, the surfboat crew went back to Bandon to get another hawser. This, secured to the south jetty, gave the donkey engine the extra purchase it needed to do the trick. With both the *Triumph* and the donkey engine straining themselves, the *Klose* was gradually pulled free. Underwater obstructions, however, took their toll and the hull was badly damaged as the ship scraped clear. Without the best efforts of

Captain Robert Johnson and his surfmen, the *C. A. Klose* would have become another of the many casualties that occurred at the Coquille gateway. (Several months later, the repaired schooner almost went to Davy Jones locker in a storm off the Columbia River. Beaching herself like a dying whale, the *C. A. Klose* was later declared a total loss).

—0—

The other ship that appeared attracted to the Coquille River Lighthouse was the schooner *Advance*. A frequent visitor to the river, she often encountered trouble on the bar. It was only 11 days before the stranding of the *Klose* that the *Advance* ran aground (November 1, 1904) at the north side of the river.

Captain Johnson and his life saving crew were on hand then to perform a similar act as was done for the *Klose*. On that occasion the first effort of the bar tug to pull the *Advance* free was successful.

Then on December 29, 1905, seeming to have a will of its own, the *Advance* decided to get chummier with the lighthouse. Inbound with a cargo of hay, general cargo and explosives, the vessel ran out of wind on the bar and once again took up residence near the north jetty. This time it was 12:40 in the afternoon. There was even greater urgency now, on the part of the life-savers and the bar tug, for these rescuers believed their was risk that wave action might cause the explosives to ignite.

The strain on the tow line between the *Advance* and the *Triumph* caused the line to snap. The surfboat made the now customary mad dash to obtain a replacement tow line. This time the tug managed to pull the *Advance* into the channel only to have the second hawser part under the strain. The runaway schooner next waltzed her way to the sandy beach close to the lighthouse.

The beacon was not due to go on until sunset, but if turned on early, its shaft of light would give aid and comfort to the tired crew of the stranded schooner. All the while, with little relief, the surfmen kept a close eye on the vessel for fear the hull would split. Should this occur, it would demand immediate rescue efforts.

The nautical almanac revealed there would be an exceptionally high tide at 8.5-feet on January 8 just 10 days away.

JANUARY. 1906

Day of—		Time and Height of High and Low Water.			
W.	Mo.				
M	1	5:32 7.6	11:58 2.8	17:30 6.4	23:49 1.5
Tu	2	6:20 7.6	12:52 2.8	18:32 6.0	. . .
W	3	0:39 2.1	7:10 7.6	13:55 2.7	19:43 5.8
Th	4	1:38 2.7	8:00 7.5	14:59 2.3	20:55 5.6
F	5	2:40 3.2	8:51 7.7	15:56 1.7	22:02 5.7
S	6	3:40 3.5	9:43 7.9	16:45 1.1	22:58 6.0
S	7	4:33 3.6	10:27 8.2	17:28 0.4	23:45 6.3
M	⑧	5:23 3.6	11:08 8.5	18:07 —0.1	. . .
Tu	9	0:28 6.6	6:08 3.6	11:47 8.8	18:43 —0.6
W	10	1:07 6.9	6:47 3.5	12:25 8.9	19:18 —0.8
Th	11	1:44 7.2	7:27 3.4	13:05 9.0	19:55 —0.9
F	12	2:22 7.5	8:07 3.2	13:45 8.9	20:33 —0.8
S	13	3:00 7.7	8:50 2.9	14:30 8.7	21:11 —0.5
S	14	3:36 7.9	9:37 2.7	15:15 8.3	21:51 0.0
M	15	4:16 8.1	10:20 2.6	16:08 7.7	22:33 0.6
Tu	16	5:01 8.2	11:15 2.4	17:07 7.0	23:20 1.3
W	17	5:50 8.1	12:18 2.2	18:17 6.4	. . .
Th	18	0:18 2.1	6:45 8.1	13:32 1.9	19:37 6.0
F	19	1:22 2.7	7:47 8.2	14:48 1.4	21:02 5.8
S	20	2:33 3.2	8:50 8.4	16:00 0.7	22:19 6.0
S	21	3:45 3.4	9:49 8.7	17:02 0.0	23:22 6.4
M	22	4:53 3.4	10:45 9.0	17:55 —0.6	. . .
Tu	23	0:15 6.8	5:51 3.3	11:37 9.2	18:40 —0.9
W	24	1:00 7.2	6:43 3.1	12:25 9.3	19:23 —1.1
Th	25	1:40 7.5	7:29 2.9	13:10 9.2	20:03 —1.0
F	26	2:18 7.7	8:13 2.7	13:53 8.9	20:40 —0.6
S	27	2:55 7.8	8:57 2.6	14:35 8.4	21:15 —0.1
S	28	3:30 7.9	9:40 2.5	15:17 7.9	21:50 0.5
M	29	4:06 7.9	10:20 2.5	16:00 7.3	22:23 1.2
Tu	30	4:40 7.9	11:05 2.5	16:48 6.7	22:57 1.8
W	31	5:20 7.7	11:54 2.5	17:42 6.1	23:43 2.5

Could plans be made in that time? General cargo was first taken off to lighten the burden on the beached hull. Then the cases of explosives were removed with great care. Finally, steel hawsers were run to the beach, set up and pulled taut to await high tide.

The old but dependable tug boat, *Triumph*, arrived. The surf-men were in reserve. As the crest of the tide approached, the *Triumph* started her pull. To the cheers of all those on the vessels, the schooner finally began to slide from the beach into the water. The tug continued the tow all the way across the bar. Of all the ships that stranded on the bar before and after this event, none were able to get as close to the Coquille River Lighthouse as the *Advance* and the *C. A. Klose*. Both were pulled to safety. □

141

—37—
Local Ship *Onward* High on Beach
Beached February 25, 1905 —dismantled

The Coquille River bar claimed the three-masted schooner *Onward* at the end of her voyage from San Francisco to Bandon when she attempted to enter the river on February 25, 1905. The vessel stranded just south of the river. High on the beach at low tide, the crew climbed over the rail and set their feet on *terra firma*. After stripping valuables from the *Onward*, it was abandoned where she lay. The ship had beeen built at nearby Parkersberg, on the river, just four years earlier. □

—38—
Peter Iredale Becomes Oregon Landmark
Beached October 25, 1906 –abandoned

About 100 miles south of the Columbia River, the bark *Peter Iredale* headed into a dense fog, but Captain Lawrence was of the opinion that by the time the vessel reached the river's mouth, the fog would have lifted. On clear days, the four-masted ship, when in full canvas, was always a beautiful sight.

The ship sailed past Tillamook Rock which was obscured in the fog. There does not seem to be any reports of anyone on the ship hearing the lighthouse's fog horn.

On the morning of the 25th of October, 1906, the wind was a gale force with a zero visibility. The vessel was on the way to Portland from Salina Cruz in Mexico.

When the lookout shouted there were breakers being heard, an immediate effort was made to bring the ship about. But with the momentum of the vessel, the force of the breakers, and the short distance to the beach, the *Peter Iredale* stranded on the sand with a lurch and a list to port. She hit hard enough to snap the mizzen mast followed by the fore and main masts. The skipper passed word among the crew to prepare to abandon the ship. Although a lifeboat was prepared, the crew observed that if a boat was lowered, it would drop directly into the breakers. With very little

The bark *Peter Iredale,* became a permanent tourist attraction on a popular beach to be enjoyed by millions during the decades following the 1906 stranding.

discussion, everyone remained on board.

Fortunately, help was not far away or long in getting there. One of the members of the crew from the U. S. Life Saving Service at Point Adams had been on the morning beach patrol when, through the fog, he observed and heard the creaking hull of a ship. But he had over two miles to run back to the station and alert the rest of the men. Once on the scene, a breeches buoy was rigged to the vessel then the sailors was taken off one at a time. The men were given food and temporary housing in a barracks at nearby Fort Stevens.

> **Captain Lawrence, lamenting the loss of his ship, when brought ashore is reported to have carried just three items:**
>> **The ship's log**
>> **The ship's sextant**
>> **A demijohn of whiskey**

The skipper and the first mate occupied a temporary shelter on the beach near the vessel to maintain a guard as well as to be at hand if there were salvage experts who wanted to talk about saving the ship.

143

The easily accessible *Peter Iredale* is part of Fort Stevens State Park.

The stranded ship was a spectacle to behold and an immediate attraction. The nearby school dismissed early so everyone could go see the ship. When it was determined that the vessel could not be pulled off the sand, special Sunday passenger excursions trains from Portland brought many hundreds of the curious public who inundated the quiet village of Warranton, through which the folks walked to the beach. But a tough pre-winter storm soon lashed the northwest coast. Its huge breakers picked up the *Peter Iredale* and moved her even higher on the beach where she was destined to stay to the present time. With this repositioning of the vessel, all hopes of saving the ship vanished.

Because the ship was built of steel and the hull kept her integrity (didn't leak) nearly all of her worthwhile fittings – the instruments, and other contents – were taken off during periods of low tide.

During World War II, the beach on which the hulk rests was one of those considered by military authorities to be a potential invasion site for the Japanese. Accordingly, the *Peter Iredale,* and all of the beach in that area, was guarded by soldiers from "B" Battery of the 249th Coast Artillery. The wreck also received a wrapping of barbed wire to keep everyone off, especially invading Japanese who never did show up.*

The bones of the *Peter Ireland* have been visited by hundreds of thousands of people during the past decades. But folks who return time and again are noticing that there is not much left. ☐

---

* The wartime activities at Fort Stevens, with the *Peter Ireland* sitting in its "front yard," and the excitement when the Japanese Navy shelled Fort Stevens in June of 1942, are covered in detail in *Silent Siege-III; Japanese Attacks on North America in World War II.* See bibliography.

Flywheel and crankshaft from *Washcalore* is in the sand on Myers Creek Beach but it has not been seen for several years. —Walter Schroeder photo. Ship's bell is exhibited at Curry County Historical Society Museum in Gold Beach.

—39—
Crew Survives but *Washcalore* is Lost
Struck reed May 21, 1911 —foundered

The 140-foot *Washcalore* ran into a small bare reef a little south of the entrance to the Rogue River on May 21, 1911. After drifting off the rock, the wooden-hulled ship, which had been built in 1905 on Coos Bay, broke in two and stranded near Hunter Creek which is approximately half way between Cape Sebastian and the Rogue River. The skipper of the vessel and his crew survived. □

—Curry County Hist. Soc.

—40—
Czarina Wrecked – One Survives
Stranded on Coos Bay Bar January 12, 1910 —sank

A severe winter sea struck the Southern Pacific Railway Company's *Czarina* (Captain Charles Dugan) when the ship was on the bar at Coos Bay on January 12, 1910. One of many huge breakers crushed the bridge causing the crew to seek refuge elsewhere as the ship went out of control. The 1,045-ton 216-foot long vessel was forced onto the south spit with its cargo of coal, sacked cement and lumber. It was locked firmly in the grip of the storm. Then, with anchors down for an attempt at stability, the vessel was dragged to the north spit. Everyone on board climbed the rigging to try to escape the furious breakers which were crashing over the entire vessel. People who had gathered on the shore, including the powerless lifesaving crew, braved a gale force wind. It was impossible to do anything but watch the 25 officers and men and a passenger, the captain among them, drop into the sea one at a time. Only one person survived. □

—41—
Condor Lost, Crew of 3 Saved
Stranded November 17, 1912 —abandoned

The next morning's headlines in the *Oregonian* newspaper out of Portland, told the story in few words.

CONDOR DRIVEN ON ROCKS; CREW SAVED

Sloop Drops Propeller at Yaquina's Mouth.

LIFESAVERS' WORK IS DARING

Schooner Mirene Gets Line to Craft, but Seas Part It.

BOAT'S DAMAGE IS GREAT

It May Be Possible to Save Part of Cargo of Merchandise and Machinery When Water Becomes More Calm.

NEWPORT, Or. Nov 17— (Special)— The gas sloop Condor was wrecked here early today when in attempting to enter the harbor, she lost her propeller and was driven against the rocks at the end of the north jetty. Her crew of three, W. H. Dority, master; George Waddell, engineer, and george Mustoe, mate, were daringly rescued by the Government lifesavers, who battled their way through heavy seas to the sloop's side.

The ship was a sloop-rigged schooner built just six years earlier at Astoria. The *Condor* (Captain W. H. Dority) was in the process of crossing the Yaquina bar when she dropped her propeller then, in a flash, the current whipped the 60-ton vessel onto the rocks of the north jetty. The three crewmen got off all right, rescued by the lifesavers, but the ship was quickly smashed by the sea beyond recognition.

The *Condor* and the *Mirene* (Captain Mays) had been waiting outside the bar for the weather to improve before entering the harbor. Both ships had left Yaquina the day before, carrying cargo for Alsea Bay merchants. The bar at Alsea Bay was running dangerously heavy so the ships turned around to return to Yaquina. They arrived off the Yaquina bar at 7 a.m.

By agreement, the *Mirene* and the *Condor* decided to cross the bar running fairly close together. All was going well until the *Condor's* propeller fell off. The crew tried to get a sail up, which was not possible in the wind and thrashing sea, then they tried to drop the anchor but before this could be done, the vessel was on the rocks. The mast broke on impact.

Considerable wreckage and assorted cargo washed ashore which was gathered and kept at the lifesaving station. □

—42—
Randolph Upside Down, Stranded
Stranded April 15, 1915 —sank

The 60-foot long schooner with a wooden hull displaced but 42-tons. It did a good job in its limited size and was easy to handle. At the south entrance of the Coquille River, the *Randolph* hit rocks and was partially swamped in a storm. The crew managed to beach the vessel where it remained for awhile, then after some gigantic breakers, the ship floated off the beach and rolled upside-down. Next, it floated back on the next wave to be stranded in the surf inside the breakers.

Rescuers making a daring move, mounted the slippery bottom and chopped a hole large enough to extract the injured ship's engineer. Three others died. □

The *Randolph* landed on the beach (TOP) **during a storm then was lifted off only to be rolled upside down** (LOWER) **by big breaker. Men on hull are sawing a hole through which a crewman was rescued.**

Santa Clara in the surf (TOP) was eventually pounded to pieces by breakers. –Curry County Historical Society (LOWER) Boarding the wreck at low tide.

—43—
Santa Clara Sinks at Coos Bay Bar
Stranded November 15, 1915 —sank

When the *Santa Clara* (Captain August Lofstedt) hit an uncharted shoal on the Coos Bay bar's south entrance, her wood hull opened causing the engine room to flood. It was November 15, 1915. The ship, 1,588-tons, with about 60 passengers and crew, could not be backed off the bar. One of the six boats lowered upset but the others made shore. Sixteen perished. □

—44—
Fifield Loses Propeller, Stuck on Jetty
Stranded February 21, 1916 —abandoned

Captain C. Bakeman lost his venerable 173 foot 6-inch long steam schooner near the end of his run from San Francisco. He was headed to Bandon, just over the bar of the Coquille River, on February 21, 1916. During the night, he was caught by a heavy gale blowing from the south so he waited at sea for daylight before attempting to cross the bar. The *Brooklyn* also awaited the dawn then she made it over the bar but with considerable stress to all aboard as the vessel bounced around like a cork.

The *Fifield* followed the *Brooklyn* by a few minutes. With strong currents, as well as the stiff wind tugging at the *Fifield,* the helmsman had difficulty holding his course. Under these conditions, the little ship, with 22 in the crew and 4 passengers, wrecked her propeller on the rocks. Now out of control, a huge swell lifted the ship then the *Fifield* was slammed down breaking planks on deck, as well as steam pipes in the engine room, and cracking the hull. The crew, busy every minute during the disaster, tied a stout line to rocks protruding from the jetty then helped everyone get off the ship.

Regardless whether the catastrophy was observed on shore by the U. S. Life Saving Service or someone notified the station, the lifesavers made their way to the stranded *Fifield*. At the site, they found most of the passsengers already landed.

A salvage effort was made immediately using some sealed oil

drums to provide extra buoyancy. The idea was to float the vessel away from the jetty. The attempt was a valiant one and the *Fifield* was moved about 100 feet when the tow lines had to be dropped in the face of the increasing storm.

The 634-ton *Fifield,* only eight years old, was stuck on the south jetty at the entrance of the river. After the storm settled, and when the tide was out, the ship was a favorite subject of folks with their box cameras as well as for scavengers. This was a winter storm therefore lots of the spilled lumber was carried to the beaches to the north on the Davidson Current. □

—45—
The Forlorn Life of the *Bandon*
Stranded plausibly in 1909 —refloated
Stranded September 1, 1916 —refloated

This vessel, a steam schooner with an exciting but luckless history of losing her way, banged against the jetty and settled on its rocky foundation at the Coquille bar about 1909. When this happened she was almost new just two years out of the yard at North Bend. The 642-ton, 172-foot long combination passenger and cargo carrier's guests in the 1909 stranding got off all right.

On September 1, 1916, the ship went aground near Port Orford but was again pulled free and returned to service.

For a period of time, the *Bandon* was tied up at Bandon on the Coquille River then she was sold to Mexican shippers.

Her next history is not clear. In winter of 1941, whether still is U. S. registry or by then Mexican, the ship (renamed *Atrevedo*) lost an argument with the rocks at Trinidad Head, California. After that, the underwriters declared her a total loss. She was converted to a barge and may still be operating. □

—46—
Sinaloa: Her Crew Saved but Ship is Lost
Grounded June 15, 1917 —abandoned

The 1,648 ton *Sinaloa* (Captain James Sannaes), a gasoline schooner, grounded near Blacklock Point, about 3 miles south from where the *Bawnmore* beached herself in 1895. This is between Cape Blanco and Floras Lake. The *Sinaloa* was on a voyage from San Francisco to Astoria when, in heavy fog, it hit offshore rocks. Whether the vessel was purposely beached nearby or drifted there due to loss of power has not been discovered. The crew got off, but the vessel and cargo were lost. □

—Curry County Hist. Soc.

—47—

Rustler Had Active Life

Stranded on beach plausibly in December 1917 —refloated
Burned at sea in 1918 —abandoned

An undated newspaper clipping reveals that the *Rustler* (Captain David Colvin) loaded with Christmas merchandise, was awaited by local people who had gathered on Gauntlett's Point to watch for her. About 50 persons witnessed the near tragedy. Apparently, as the 61-foot boat came in, she rolled taking water into the engine room which stopped the gasoline engine. Unable to control his powerless craft, the skipper had no choice but to watch his ship beach herself near Doyle Rock.

During low tide, Mr. D. M. Moore hired a team and wagon to unload the freight which never got wet.

By the time high tide arrived, a tugboat from the Umpqua River pulled the vessel off the beach apparently with no damage.

In another incident, the *Rustler* (Captain Knite) in 1918, caught fire off Cape Blanco and burned to the water line. The skipper and his crew rowed to Port Orford in the small lifeboat. □

EDITOR'S NOTE: Neither Gauntlett's Point nor Doyle Rock are listed in *Pacific Coast Pilot*.   —Photograph from Curry County Historical Society

J. A. *Chanslor* Lost in Fog, Strikes Reef

Position at sea 45°50'17"N - 124°32'2"W December 18, 1919 —sank

The J. A. *Chanslor* (Captain A. A. Sawyer) was a 4,900-ton Associated Oil Company tanker carrying 30,000 barrels of bulk

The Davidson Current and Its Affect on Things That Float*

During the winter months, the Davidson Current, a counter-current, is the predominant along-shore current running from south to north. The Davidson upwells off Baja and runs the coastline to about the Straits of Juan de Fuca when it makes a U-turn, <u>under</u> the surface, to return to the south. The south-bound Davidson Current is not a surface current.

When anything that floats gets into the Davidson Current, be they pretty glass Japanese fishnet floats – even big ships – these various objects stand a better-than-average chance of beaching somewhere along the northwest coast. This appears especially true when the wind is strong from the west or northwest or even sometimes from the north for a sustained amount of time.

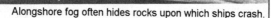

Alongshore fog often hides rocks upon which ships crash.

Some say that ships were sailing too close to the coastline during fogs when they lost their way and landed on rocks or on a beach, and should set their course farther at sea to have leeway due to compass variations. Or perhaps, did ships become wrecked due to some navigators not being mindful of the effect of the Davidson Current and the sharp northwest winds in spite of compass differences and magnetic variations?

---

* The phenomena of the Davidson Current, with a chart, is in Chapter 2: "Glass Balls and Oceanography" in *I'd Rather Be Beachcombing*. See also *Between Pacific Tides*. Refer to bibliography.

Associated Oil Company tanker *J. A. Chanslor* stranded then broke polluting the beach with oil. (LOWER) The portable fog horn from the *Chanslor* can be seen in the Curry County Historical Society Museum in Gold Beach. Mildred Metzgus, a museum volunteer, demonstrates the horn's operation. Pull the handle one direction expanded a bellows, in reserved direction honks horn. After the wreck, this fog horn was used on a nearby ranch to call field hands to meals.

oil when it lost its way, close to shore, between Cape Blanco and the mouth of the Sixes River. It was December 18, 1919. The fog was heavy and the sea was rough when the loaded ship ran up on the off-shore rocks.

When the tanker went on the rocks, she was within sight of Cape Blanco's lighthouse being about 400-feet off the steep cliff and $1/8$-mile north.

Just as quickly as the ship hit, the furious sea snarled over the deck with crashing waves that broke the ship into two parts – the cargo of oil suddenly unleashed from its tanks spilled into the sea. The officers and crew, 39 in all, were swept off the ship into the tumultuous sea. Only the skipper and two others surfaced then luckily found a bobbing lifeboat into which they struggled. They drifted for 34 hours, tossed around like a cork, until the breakers heaved the boat at the shore where the men were thrown out then they washed up, fighting for breath, onto the beach. The other 36 of the crew drowned with only some of the bodies recovered.

For many weeks, the front half of the vessel stuck on the rock for all to see. But the real testimony of the catastrophe was the blackened nearby beach sand and dead oil-soaked birds and fish that were cast up on the tideline. □

—49—
Acme on the Beach, Crew Saved
Stranded October 31, 1924 —abandoned

Nicknamed the "Flying Dutchman" due to her fine sea qualities and ability to keep schedules, the *Acme* (Captain Miller) lost its bout with the breakers near the Coquille bar on Halloween 1924. The 416-ton wooden ship, standing off the river's mouth, awaited for the sea to moderate before attempting to enter it. As the wait would be awhile, the skipper turned the helm over to his mate, Mr. Hoffman, then he went to bed. What caused Hoffman to let the ship slip into the breakers does not seem to be known, nevertheless, four miles north of the river, the breakers caught the *Acme*. In the emergency, the mate called the captain out of his sleep. On realizing the predicament, Captain Miller pointed his vessel at the beach and immediately ordered that FULL SPEED be given.

In the meantime, five of the crew lowered a boat but in getting into it, the boat upset and all of the men took a dunking. The scene was fairly close to the beach so the men thrashed their way through the last line of breakers and gained the safety of the beach.

When this experience started, observed by spy-glass from the Coquille River Lighthouse, the man on watch called out the life-savers. When the Coast Guard got to the beach, the first 5 of the ship's crewmen were already there. The rescuers hooked up a breeches buoy and brought the remaining men ashore.

The *Acme* was on the beach above a "normal" high tide line so in the days that followed, her cargo was unloaded. Regrettably, all efforts to refloat the ship, which had no hull damage, failed. To mitigate the loss, everything that could be removed from the vessel was dismantled and hauled away to be sold. After the insurance people decided nothing more could be done, the hull was set ablaze. □

—50—
South Coast Sinks, All Hands Lost
Lost at sea approximately 42°44'N - 124°36'5"W September 18, 1930

The 43-year old steam powered schooner left Crescent City bound for Coos Bay with a full load of cedar logs. The crew of 19, headed by Captain Stanley Sorenson, apparently ran on to Port Orford Reef, broke up and promptly sank with all hands.

When the *Tejon*, a tanker, was passing through the general area later, the lookout spied the *South Coast's* deckhouse floating in the water off Port Orford. There were further reports from vessels southwest from Cape Blanco of many logs in the water. There was also an empty lifeboat observed. Exactly what happened to the *South Coast* has not been determined. □

USCG *Yaquina* and the *Melba*
3 Coast Guardsmen Die in Rescue Effort

Yaquina swamped February 20, 1935 —sank
Melba swamped February 20, 1935 —sank

When the Coast Guard motor lifeboat *Yaquina* answered the call of duty to assist the disabled dredge *Melba,* that was in the breakers at the Yaquina Bay bar, both vessels were swamped by a gigantic wave. Five men were drowned. Because of the position of the dredge and the danger from the pounding sea, it took quite some time for the *Yaquina* to make a useful approach.

Once on the lee of the *Melba*, a huge wave broke over both vessels. Three Coast Guardsmen, George Elkins, George Meadows and William Stults, were washed overboard and drowned by the breaker. Their boat was severely damaged. Two men from the dredge were also drowned.

Some witnesses on land estimated the seas at the bar were, at times, more than forty feet high. □

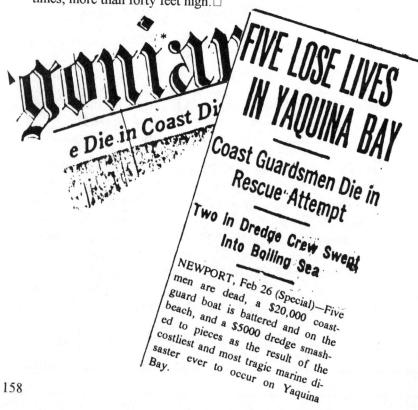

gonian

e Die in Coast Di

FIVE LOSE LIVES IN YAQUINA BAY
Coast Guardsmen Die in Rescue Attempt
Two In Dredge Crew Swept Into Boiling Sea

NEWPORT, Feb 26 (Special)—Five men are dead, a $20,000 coast-guard boat is battered and on the beach, and a $5000 dredge smashed to pieces as the result of the costliest and most tragic marine disaster ever to occur on Yaquina Bay.

Phyllis

159

Cargo being off-loaded on the 1¼-mile long high-line from the *Phyllis*

—52—
Crew Saved but *Phyllis* is Lost
Beached March 9, 1936 —abandoned

The 215-foot long Phyllis (Captain Victor Jacobsen), started to leak in heavy weather which caused the skipper to run his vessel up on the beach in order to keep her from sinking. The stranding occurred about 2½-miles south of Port Orford and about 1 mile north of Humbug Mountain. All the crew was saved but the ship became a total loss. To salvage the cargo, a rig was set up to handle a 1¼-mile long high-line between the vessel and the shore. On this line the general cargo was successfully off-loaded but it took awhile. The *Phyllis* eventually broke up. □

—53—
Wreck of the *Cottoneva*
Stranded February 10, 1937 —abandoned

The *Cottoneva* (Captain E. Stahlbaun) was docked at Port Orford for a load of lumber when the skipper decided to put to sea as a severe winter storm roared in. This was on the night of

Port Orford's bay and beach at low tide on a sunny day in February 1995. Humbug mountain in center-rear. Battle Rock on right. (CENTER) *Cottoneva* came ashore near Humbug Mountain then drifted north (LOWER) where it broke up.

—Lower pictures from Curry County Historical Society

WRECK OF THE COTTONEVA

ON FEB. 10, 1937 WINDS OVER 75 M.P.H. CAUSED
THE 190- FOOT STREAM SCHOONER "COTTONEVA"
TO RUN AGROUND AT BATTLE ROCK. IT WAS IN
PORT ORFORD LOADING LUMBER. THE CAPTAIN
AND ALL 26 SEAMEN WERE RESCUED BY THE
COAST GUARD CREW USING A BREECHES BUOY.
THE COTTONEVA WAS CONSTRUCTED IN 1917 AND
ORIGINALLY CHRISTENED THE "FRANK D. STOUT.
ONLY THE PROPELLER REMAINS.

(TOP) **Propeller and shaft from** *Cottoneva* **exhibited at Battle Rock Park,
Port Orford.** (CENTER) **The ship's engine block, once a beach fixture,
washed out to sea during a storm years ago.** —Walter Schroeder collection.
Life ring (LOWER) **is exhibited at Curry County Historical Society Museum.**

162

February 10, 1937. The ship plausibly did not have full steam power up when the vessel was cast off for the *Cottoneva*, 1,113-tons and 190-feet long, was unable to get to sea before being driven back into the harbor by a 75-mile-an-hour gale. The vessel ran aground north of Humbug Mountain. When daylight came, the Coast Guard from the local port rigged a breeches buoy and took off the crew of 26.

On an unobserved later date, the wreck drifted northward until it was a few hundred feet south of Battle Rock. Here it broke in two sections with the bow resting at the high tide line. The aft part wallowed in the surf eventually breaking up.

The *Cottoneva*, built in St. Helens, Oregon in 1917 for the McCormick Lumber Company, was then named the *Frank D. Stout*. The vessel had been sold just a week before the disaster to Charles R. Ayers who ran the Stelltree Line.

Although the encrusted mount for the 600-horse power engine, which had been in the surf for many years, disappeared in the 1970's, other remnants can be seen at the present time. The aft length of shaft with the propeller attached is exhibited on a concrete slab in Battle Rock Park. In the Curry County Historical Society Museum at Gold Beach is a cork life ring. □

—54—
Feltre Raised From Columbia River Bottom
She Becomes the *Clevedon*

Feltre: Sunk February 15, 1937 —rebuilt
Clevedon: Exploded January 13, 1942 —sank

It turned out to be a bad day for Captain Mario Ranieri of the 450-foot long Italian motorship *Feltre*. He was cruising slowly in the Columbia River about six miles east of Longview when his ship was suddenly rammed by the *Edward Luckenbach*. And just as quickly, the holds filled with river water and Captain Ranieri's mount settled in the mud on the bottom.

The cargo-passenger liner's steel hull crumbled like paper when the 10,000-ton freighter, in the same displacement class as the battleship *Oregon*, crashed into her. (The *Luckenbach* sus-

The steamship *Feltre* is shown (TOP) sitting on the bottom of the shallow Columbia River after collision. (RIGHT) The bill to repair and modernize her came to $300,000 after which she was re-christened the *Clevedon* (ABOVE).

tained nothing much more than a dented nose.) With the *Feltre* secure on the river bottom, and excess crew taken ashore, the first part of the salvage was carried out just four days later with a certain amount of secrecy. This was due to the fact that $185,000 in silver bars was in the broken hold and divers were commissioned to go down into the flooded ship to retrieve it.

Because of reports of the divers as to the conditions found under water, and the fact that this was a major vessel that should be repaired, a decision was made to raise the vessel. The salvage of this very big ship took a full month to the day when the *Feltre* was raised to her water line. But the joy was stifled when seemingly only minuets later, the ship lost its buoyancy and sat her bottom back into the mud. Determined to succeed, the salvagers brought in more pumps and went back at the task of raising the 450-foot long ship. With a crash mat secured over the gaping hole, tugboats lashed to the ship as well as others standing by, the vessel was slowly raised. Then, with clearance for right-of-way, the strange flotilla of tugs escorting what resembled a wounded monster, the fleet went upriver to Portland where on April 18th, the damaged *Feltre* went into dry-dock.

In the meantime there were charges and counter-charges as to which ship was at fault. In the end, it was decided the trouble had occurred over misinterpretation of whistle signals.

In the dry-dock, careful inspections were made to find out what it would cost to rebuild the ship to its original integrity. This took time. What turned out to be a more serious matter was the huge bill the salvage company had accrued against the ship for all its work. The salvagers prepared and filed a claim against the *Feltre* for $200,000. As the claim could not be met, the ship was ordered, on June 1st, to be auctioned, as is, where is, to the highest bidder.

When bids were opened June 9th, the *MS Feltre* was sold to Pacific American Fisheries Company of Bellingham, Washington. Fisheries got it for a mere $55,000, a pittance of the true value of the vessel. The thought was to use the vessel in Alaskan waters.

PAF decided their investment was such that they could afford to spend real money for a major overhaul so awarded a rebuilding contract worth $300,000. To that date, this was the largest ship repair job the city of Portland had ever had. The work took one year and one week to complete. The ship was re-registered in the United States with the name *Clevedon*.

In 1938, when the federal government finally decided to seriously look into building up the defenses in Alaska, there was a need for ships that would double as troop transports and also handle cargo. The *Clevedon* met the specifications. Sometime afterwards, the ship was leased to the U. S. Army as a transport. The Army in turn, contracted with the Alaska Steamship Company to operate it.

The author's first knowledge that the *Clevedon* existed, was on July 11, 1941 – five months before the Japanese attack on Pearl Harbor – when he and several hundred other GI's were bussed from the staging area at Fort Lawton, to the Alaska Steamship's docks on the Seattle waterfront.

"As your name is called, answer with your serial number and step aboard," was the 1st Sergeant's bark. And so, the men boarded the ship by walking up the gang-plank one-at-a-time.

The ship had retained all of its staterooms and the original configuration of two bunks in a room. The Signal, Medical and Quartermaster troops, to be off-loaded at Kodiak, were assigned the staterooms. The troops for Unalaska (Dutch Harbor) would live in a hold where steel frame bunks, 4 high, with canvas stretched between the rails to sleep on, had been installed. We of the Kodiak troops had lucked out. But it was an official plan as Kodiak would be the first major port-of-call and off-loading from the staterooms would be faster and easier. (The *Clevedon* went non-stop from Seattle to Seward – five days – but only a handful of military passengers left the ship at Seward.)

The stop at Kodiak Island, two days later, was at Woman's Bay, at the Naval Air Station's dock. On leaving Woman's Bay, the *Clevedon* rounded Chiniak Point then set course for Unalaska.

The cruise across the Gulf of Alaska had been uneventful. It was summer. The good food was plentiful and current phonograph records were played over the ships intercom system.

The Alaska Steamship Company offered the state-room troops the amenities it offered its earlier civilian passengers. A surprise awaited the stateroom occupants that first night, when the ship was still in the Straits of Juan de Fuca, and continued every night as far as Seward. This was a special inter-com announcement by the ship's Steward at 9 p.m. that proclaimed it was "time to report on deck for cold cuts and French bread."*

The *Clevedon* continued in her role as an Army transport hauling passengers and cargo until she met her sudden end on

---

* From the recollections of the author who was in the Army Signal Corps on the *Clevedon* for that voyage to Kodiak. Once the war started, there was great secrecy about all troop and ship movements, but for the *Clevedon's* departure from Seattle that July day in 1941, there were many guests on the pier. Some were tearful sweethearts watching the ship leave with their honey's.

January 13, 1942. On that day, the ship was at the dock at Yakutat when fire broke out. The ship was carrying a load of ammunition. In haste, the steamer *Taku* steamed to her side, tossed a line to the burning ship then quickly towed the ship away from the pier and beached the *Clevedon* then the *Taku* dropped the tow line and retreated to a safe distance. It seemed just minutes later, but it was probably longer, that the *Clevedon,* with her crew removed, suddenly exploded. □

—55—
'Christmas Ship' *Mauna Ala* Stranded on
Clatsop Beach Due to Blackout
Stranded December 10, 1941 —abandoned

When the west coast of the United States, the closest part of the continental U.S.A. to Japan, struggled to get into gear to fight a war, it was a surprise to find out just three days after the attack on Pearl Harbor that the first landing on the northwest coast was not a Japanese invasion force, but an American freighter that had lost her way because of the new blackout.

This was the 6,256-tons, 420-feet long Matson Navigation Company steamship *Mauna Ala* (Captain C. W. Saunders, Jr.).

The first ship of the Matson fleet to be lost in World War II was not a victim of enemy action, but was wrecked because of circumstances and conditions attributable to the war. The *Mauna Ala* was bound for Honolulu when word came that Peal Harbor had been bombed. Because of the dangers on the route to Honolulu, the *Mauna Ala* was ordered to proceed to Portland, Oregon. Since the West Coast was under complete blackout, all navigational lights had been doused, and the ship went ashore on December 10, 1941, as it attempted to find the mouth of the Columbia River. The ship broke up on the beach and the vessel and cargo were a total loss.   —*Ships in Gray; The Story of Matson in World War II*

Clatsop Spit, just south of the mouth of the Columbia River, for generations one of the great beaches for shipwrecks along the northwest coast, claimed another victim when the *Mauna Ala* was stranded there because of the blackout.

Soon after the stranding, a Notice to Mariners was posted:

The blackout of navigation aids, lights, and the silencing of radio beacons at the mouth of the Columbia river under wartime restrictions caused the wreck of the *Mauna Ala*, which stranded on Clatsop Spit, December 10, 1941.

As breakers smashed the *Mauna Ala* the cargo spilled into the sea to be hurled upon the beach. Investigators sent to look at the damages decided the cargo was a total loss.

It was at 6 p.m. on Wednesday when the ship grounded. Just prior to that time, the skipper, Captain Saunders, had been told that a blinker light message apparently reading H A L T had been witnessed, then the captain ordered the vessel to DEAD SLOW speed. As nothing further occurred, the ship was again brought to FULL SPEED with the anticipation that the beam from the *Columbia River Lightship* would be seen. In what seemed to be only moments later, the vessel lurched to a sickening stop just 700 yards off the beach. The ship's radioman sent an SOS to the fact that the ship was aground.

Although the ship hit head-on, the incoming breakers twisted the ship so it was parallel with the beach then commenced its fury of destructive force to pound the vessel into junk.

Within a very short time, two things happened:

1) The Coast Guard from Point Adams Station sent their 52-foot motor lifeboat the *Triumph* to investigate. With a series of trips, the *Triumph* took off the 35-man crew without mishap, the men being rescued never wet their feet.

2) A host of salvage boats and tugboats arrived to refloat the freighter. None would get the job.

Mauna Ala

There was something special about the *Mauna Ala*. It was the "Christmas Ship" on which Honolulu's merchants waited. The vessel carried 60,000 Christmas Trees, a huge cargo of frozen turkeys, 50-pound gunny sacks filled with mixed nuts, nearly a ton of fruit cakes, hundreds of cases of butter, along with seasonal goods of all kinds. All this was now strewn along the beaches of Clatsop Spit and along the North Beach peninsula on the north side of the Columbia River. There was no formal salvage, but towns-folk, as well as soldiers from Fort Stevens just a few hundred yards away from the wreck, and folks on the Washington side, scrounged the beaches for unspoiled edibles and anything else considered worthy enough to be carried away.

The site of this stranding was just south of the remains of the *Peter Iredale*.

In the days that followed, the ferocious winter storms totally broke up the *Mauna Ala* to where, in just a couple of years, there was no longer any trace of her. ▢

—56—
Sergeant Rude and the Coast Guard Intruders
The Wreck of the 36-Boat
Wrecked about November 15, 1942 —abandoned

Pulling duty at the 249th Coast Artillery's "B" Battery outpost named "White Evelyn," at the base of the south jetty at the Columbia River, during World War II, was no picnic – unless it

1st Sergeant Lawrence Rude was a spit-and-polish soldier.

was summer time. In winter there were the stormy, wet, bone-chilling days and nights. But summer duty at the outpost was like being on an extended overnight camping trip and getting paid for being there.

The 249th was an Oregon National Guard outfit whose members, except for the draftees who had been forced into the outfit, were mostly comfortable home-town boys who had done their annual two-week summer drills together at the various stations at Fort Stevens Harbor Defense post for years. When 1st Sergeant Larry Rude spoke – barked was a better word – everyone jumped. He ran "B" Battery with a very tight fist.

His battery was designated the "Outpost Battery." This meant that Rude's men were strung out all over the periphery of Fort Stevens. There were machine gun nests at several places along the beach and facing the Columbia River. One of the .30 caliber Browning water-cooled First World War machine guns was in the beach grass just above the remains of the old *Peter Iredale*. Anther was near "White Evelyn."

Sergeant Rude often went with the Sergeant of the Guard at night, but always with no advance notice, to make certain that his men were awake and "doing their duty." The duty was mostly to stay awake. Also, to be alert, and report any odd occurrences to

"White Evelyn" command post was inside the abandoned water tank.

the message center using the hand-cranked field telephone system.

Some of his best and most experienced "old-timer" members were at "White Evelyn." This assignment was the pick-of-the-duty when it came to being sent to an outpost. The "office" of the White Evelyn observation post was in what looked like an abandoned railroad water tower, there having been a railroad there in earlier days for the construction of the jetty. Near the tower was a French 75mm howitzer that was fired occasionally at fishboats as they came into the river. If the skipper of the fishboat did not show the proper recognition signal, or forgot to signal, he got a prompt reminder in the form of a shell placed over his bow from this "challenge gun" at the jetty.

On the night in question, a 36-foot motor lifeboat of the Coast Guard was doing bar patrol. These patrols were west of the bar with the usual cruising route running from the west end of Peacock Spit, on the Washington side, to a mid-point between Tillamook Rock and the south jetty at the river on the Oregon side. This night, when it was time to go back to Point Adams Station, the boat missed the mouth of the river and going full tilt, rammed the south side of the south jetty. It had a crew of five. The motor lifeboat was smashed. Two of the men were thrown forward on impact, their bodies crashing on the rocks resulting in severe injuries which included one broken leg. The other three Coast

The Coast Guard's 36-foot self-righting motor lifeboat was the so-called "standard" response craft for search and rescue work for many years.

Guardsmen were badly shaken but their injuries, by comparison, were slight. The two sailors who were hurt could not be moved without extra help. It was decided that one of the three less injured would stay with the two hurt men and the other two would walk the jetty to seek help.

The night was very foggy. It would be difficult to find one's way even on level ground let alone walking over jagged rocks of the jetty for over one mile before they reached the spit. They set out in the dark. Making their way over the jetty rocks took over two hours. Finally, they came in struggling through the barbed wire near "White Evelyn," climbed the dune behind the outpost and passed two machine gun nests. They were finally on one of the paved streets of Fort Stevens, when a roving unlighted guard patrol, in a ¼-ton Dodge weapons carrier, stopped them with the command: "Advance to be recognized"!

The bedraggled, cold, and thoroughly worn out, as well as injured sailors, told their tale to the guard. He was skeptical but took the Coast Guardsmen directly to the Guard House for interrogation. There, the Office-of-the-Day listened, then he called Point Adams Station to verify that there was indeed a 36-boat wandering around in the dark, and was told that the boat was missing. The two wet sailors insisted on having a patrol go out on the jetty for a rescue mission. Then, in another truck, they were taken to Point Adams Station. Just as quickly, the "hot-phone" on the floor at Sergeant Rude's bedside jangled as only a phone can jangle in the middle of the night.

Rude, instantly awake, answered. Then he was quiet as the

Officer-of-the-Day told him what was going on. Rude was ordered to form a search party "forthwith" and get the patrol out on the jetty and "find those man" – and to keep in mind that a blackout was in effect.

The search patrol eventually located the injured men, stretcher-carried them back over the jetty to a waiting Army ambulance and a Coast Guard sedan that had been sent to "White Evelyn" to await their arrival. The rest is history. But events of that night will never be forgotten by members of "B" Battery until each man's dying day.

The next morning, veteran 1st Sergeant Lawrence Rude called for a formation in front of the barracks of all men not at the outposts. The men were seldom in parade formation during wartime as nearly every man had a job thus there were never many men hanging around the barracks. But this time, all non-essential outpost duty personnel were rounded up and brought in for the Sergeants "important announcement."

With the men standing at stiff attention, every one of them was put through personal inspection of the picky, nitty-gritty kind. Then Rude exploded in his very best Top-Sergeant GI Army profanity about how could the members of *his* outpost battery allow strangers, especially lowly Coast Guard swabbies, prowl through all *his* perimeter defenses and not get caught? He was adamant. He demanded to know. No one stirred and no one dared to offer an answer. He harped on this in his loudest voice for nearly 40 minutes until he was hoarse. Next he restricted all passes off the post for one month. Then be dismissed his troops. □

—57—
Beautiful Ship *Erria* Afire
Stranded December 20, 1951 —salvaged

The Danish 8,786-ton passenger-freighter *Erria,* with 114 passengers and crew, was waiting at anchor off Tongue Point for a calmer Columbia River bar before passing outbound when, around 2 in the morning of December 20, 1951, she caught fire.

Trapped by heavy smoke, fumes and flames amidships, eleven persons (eight passengers - three crew) were burned to death.

Not a good day for the *Erria*

The skipper's first order was to abandon the ship. But this can be confusing in the middle of the night as passengers tried to grab important belongings then find boat stations.

Responding to emergency messages radioed ashore, the Coast Guard removed the people and, with other vessels, pushed the 450-foot long *Erria* (Captain Neils Agee) onto the mud flats to keep her from plausibly sinking in the shipping channel. After quenching the stubborn fire, which took days, and had been started by a short-circuit, the ship was towed to Portland for inspection then await a decision as to what o do. The underwriters decided that except for a little cargo, the *Erria* was a total loss.

The Danish East Asiatic Company, Ltd., owners, decided to tow the wreck to Rotterdam for rebuilding so they sent the big tug *Zwarte Zee* to tow the hulk home – 8,900 miles. The tow left on May 16, 1952 taking 51 days. The *Erria* became a sleek cargo-only freighter. □

—58—
Oliver Olson Stuck on Jetty Forever
Stranded November 3, 1953 —abandoned

While crossing inbound on the Coquille River bar, the *Oliver Olson* (Captain Carl Hubner) was caught in a sudden cross current. The ship grounded at the west end of the south jetty with damage to her propeller and rudder. There were also some jagged holes in her starboard side well below the water line which caused flooding in the engine room and in two holds. The Coast Guard cutter *Bonham* came along as did the tugboat *Port of Bandon*. They were going to try to work the ship off the rocks but the weather did not moderate enough to attempt this.

The *SS Oliver Olson* ran into the end of the south jetty on November 3, 1953. After various methods to pull her off failed, the ship was left where it rested and the hull was filled with rock to form a part of the jetty. Today, on a quiet, non-stormy day, one might risk a hike to see part of the ship protruding from its rocky grave.

A Coast Guard breeches buoy had been set up earlier but now, with refloating the ship impossible, the crew of 29 was brought ashore. As the *Oliver Olson*, 307-foot long, which was supposed to take on a load of lumber at Bandon, continued to take on water, the underwriters, largely Lloyds of London, decided to cash out the 35-year old ship that was now classed as a wreck.

Salvagers bid on the work of dismantling the vessel and a firm from Napa, California won the award. All of the deck equipment, and much of the interior fittings were taken off. In less than one month, winter storms set in that prohibited further salvage. There had been plans to use cutting torches to salvage the steel plates of the hull but this plan was abandoned.

For some time, officials in Bandon had been trying to get the south jetty's run-down condition restored. The U. S. Army Corps of Engineers, which had been observing the situation from the sidelines, stepped into the picture. The plan was to extend the south jetty by 450 feet and the 307-foot hull of the vessel was in the right place to become part of the work. With little discussion, the Corps took ownership of the hull then awarded a contract to have the hull filled with heavy jetty rock. When the work was finished by the summer of 1954, the hull of the *Oliver Olson* had became a permanent part of the jetty. □

—59—
Marjean Beached, Buried by Bulldozer
Stranded December 15, 1973 —buried

The new ferro-concrete 48-foot schooner *Marjean* probably had about the shortest life at sea on record. From the time she left the dock, then entered the Pacific Ocean, until she was hopelessly stranded on the beach was estimated at less than one hour.

The vessel was on her maiden voyage. She had sailed from the small dock at Taft on Siletz Bay, which is now a neighborhood at the south end of Lincoln City. The skipper-owner set his course for the ocean and entered the channel *on an incoming tide*. Just over the bar his small engine quit. He did everything he could do to get it restarted as his ship slowly drifted toward the surf.

MARJEAN

He was still furiously trying to get the gasoline engine going when *Marjean* entered the breaker line where the heavy seas forced the now helpless yacht toward the beach. One of the next breakers picked up the yacht, as if it was a cork, and heaved it with a thud onto the beach. This bad landing, along with huge telephone pole-size drift logs hitting the hull on the next waves, cracked her hull. Between waves, the occupants stepped off their vessel and walked to the nearest house to telephone for help.

The official name where the vessel beached is Siletz Spit. But many Oregonians know it best for its nickname "Salishan Spit." The vessel had not been there long before the tides created an embayment around the vessel. This caused the state to worry about the *Marjean* laying on its beach because that area is considered very fragile and subject to coastal erosion especially during winter's stormy months.

There are dozens of palatial homes on the spit, the spit and its houses getting much publicity because of coastal erosion. During one particularly vicious winter storm, one writer declared, "King Neptune wants his sand back," so the breakers chewed at the foredune, on which most of the houses rest, chewed out sand under

One might find some of the *Marjean's* reinforcing wire protruding from the sand.

one building while a newspaper cameraman stood by and photographed a building is it slid down the 20-foot high dune and crashed on the beach below. The next breakers smashed the house beyond recognition within less than one week.*

The owners, of the *Marjean,* who had envisioned sailing around the world, stayed home. Marine inspectors looked at the wreck and reported the loss of the vessel at $100,000.

The incoming high tides seem to have especially picked the Salishan Spit beach as a great place to heave huge logs. The logs come on one tide, and may be washed back out to sea on the next tide. These waves rapidly washed away much sand from around the grounded vessel which worried authorities who feared the washout might work its way along the beach. Accordingly, the *Marjean's* owners were emphatically directed to get the wrecked boat off the beach and do so right away.

The concrete hull was cracked. The vessel was deemed unrepairable. Apparently the only way to move the ship off the spit was to bury it. At low tide, a bulldozer dug a huge grave then after smashing the ship into small pieces, pushed all of the pieces into the hole – buried it.

Sometimes, if one walks on the beach to that certain spot toward the end of the spit a little northwest of the last house, one might find some of the *Marjean's* reinforcing wire protruding from the sand. □

* Coastal erosion has caused the entire town of Bayocean, on Tillamook County's Tillamook Spit, to be eaten away and there has been severe damage to other spits such as Nestucca Spit which lost its entire end. In Washington, the once beautiful Cape Shoalwater is totally under the sea yet the erosion continues to the present time dropping buildings, including a postoffice and a lighthouse over the edge almost on a schedule. Salishan Spit, already washed over with crashing waves that flowed over the top of the dune and ended in Siletz Bay, is so precarious, observers claim, that it and its million-dollar houses could be totally eliminated by a severe winter storm. A State Geologist said a few years back, "I would not build a house there." For the fascinating story of Salishan's troubles see the chapter in *Bayocean, The Oregon Town That Fell into the Sea.* See bibliography.

—60—
Capsized *Que Sera* Now Alive and Well
Capsized December 13, 1973 —sank —salvaged

When the 60-foot long one-of-a-kind Dutch-built ketch the *Que Sera* capsized then sank off Waldport on December 13, 1973, she went down with, among other things, a souvenir collection of gold coins valued at $24,000.

The owners and crew of the boat, Mr. and Mrs. Joe Browning of El Cajon, California, were rescued by Coast Guard swimmers after fighting to keep their boat afloat for 48-hours in a winter storm.

Coast Guard divers retrieved the sack of gold coins when they dived on the ketch after the boat foundered. The souvenirs were part of the Brownings' life savings as was their investment in the uninsured *Que Sera* which was valued at $150,000. They made no effort to salvage the boat but sold it "as is - where is" for $1,000 to Ken Dye and Kent Cochran from Portland. The Brownings, who had planned a long ocean voyage in their boat, went back to Southern California on the train.

The *Que Sera* was salvaged from the surf on May 15, 1974, five months after the mishap by Dye and Cochran who were professional divers. (An earlier effort had been made to beach the craft in January, but rough seas prohibited it.) After moving the boat to the Bay Shore Beach Club, temporary repairs were made then the ketch was trucked to Oregon City for rebuilding. The 45-ton ketch had 12-foot beam and was 13-feet high with its fold-down masts.

Rebuilt *Que Sera* viewed on Nov. 25, 1995. New fore-mast is 62-feet tall.

Dye soon bought out his partner. One day when he was pumping sand out of the hull, he discovered "sunken treasure" – jewelry boxes that had belonged to Mrs. Browning. These were sent to her.

Dye posted a sign requesting beachcombers to kindly return items "mistakenly taken" from the ketch but he never got them back. These included the ship's wheel, small boat, a winch and other items all requiring effort to take them.

Ken Dye spent 17 years and $130,000 in parts and equipment in his part-time rebuilding project and has now made two trips to Alaska in his vessel, the once-sunk *Que Sera*. The home port is Sportscraft Marina on the Willamette River at Oregon City. □

—61—
Despite Daring Efforts *Shaun* Sinks
Collision November 10, 1981 —sank

The fishboat *Shaun* plunged to the bottom of the sea on November 10, 1981 and apparently took three lives with it. The 50-foot bottom-fishing vessel may have collided with the barge *Bandon,* about 2 p.m. under tow by the Sause Brothers tugboat

A Coast Guard rescue helicopter from North Bend Air Station stands by while a Coast Guard lifesaver investigates the floating stern of the fishboat *Shaun*.

Mary Catherine in relatively clear conditions – high over-cast, 10 miles visibility and winds blowing about 30-knots.

The accident was about two miles west of Cape Arago. The Coast Guard reported that the missing people were Franklin T. Lanegan, operator, Daniel Nicholas and Kenny Hultin, crew.

The end for the *Shaun* came about 8:45 p.m. two miles north of the Coos Bay bar entrance buoy in between 84 to 150 feet of water, while the boat was being towed by the fishboat *Bernadette.* When the end came, the wreck was being kept afloat presumably by air trapped in the stern with only the stern above water.

The chances of the men being alive in the air bubble in the stern were "pretty, pretty slim," remarked commercial diver Bill Shires who with diver Pat Miller were at the scene with the Coast Guard.

The Coast Guard summoned its outboard gasoline-powered 17-foot rubber raft, piloted by Chief Roger Russell, from Charleston Station to bring extra equipment to the scene in one of several daring efforts to rescue the missing men.

In one effort, Petty Officer Tom Rainy, Shires, and Miller were lowered from a helicopter by cable to the boat soon after the *Shaun* turned over. They rapped on the hull but heard no sounds to indicate there was anyone therein alive.

When the Coast Guard responded to the first call for assistance in the afternoon, a line was passed to the fishboat and a tow started by a Coast Guard motor lifeboat. The tow was transferred to the *Bernadette* then, apparently, the line got caught in the lifeboat's propeller. The first lifeboat had to call a second motor lifeboat for help because of the disabled prop.

A helicopter searched a 2-mile circular pattern around the sinking *Shaun* looking for survivors but found none. □

—62—
Captain Didn't Speak English
Blue Magpie Sinks
Crashed jetty November 19, 1983 —sank

Knowing how to communicate would have been the key to safety for Captain Kim Gab Bong on the night of November 19, 1983 when he and the U. S. Coast Guard exchanged words about his ship, the *Blue Magpie,* and where he wanted to go in it.

The Japanese flag Korean-manned ship was hugging the shore getting ready to put in to Yaquina Bay when it missed the channel and rammed the north jetty. The vessel's navigation lights had been spotted from Cleft of the Rock Lighthouse, at the base of Cape Perpetua, when the vessel was proceeding northward in the darkness a few hours earlier.

The Coast Guard was talking to the ship pointing out that the *Blue Magpie* should not attempt to cross the Yaquina bar. The difficulty was that Captain Bong understood so little English that the warning went unheeded. His lack of knowledge of the language cost him his ship.

The *Blue Magpie* was badly holed when it struck the outer side of the north jetty. It healed over in the water then it broke up. In an amazing rescue, the Coast Guard helicopter, using flood lights in the middle of the night, picked up all 19 Korean crew members from the sinking ship and handed them on terra firma. □

Death throes of the *Blue Magpie* off the end of the north jetty at Yaquina Bay. —U.S. Coast Guard

—63—
Disaster Strikes the *Kingfish*
Capsized January 4, 1984 —sank

Ples Matthews, 38, a commercial fisherman, with a string of crab pots in the ocean outside the Coos Bay bar, had finished working his pots and was ready to head for home. On the *Kingfish* with him were his girlfriend, Kathleen Dolan, 31, and his father Ples Matthews, Sr., 62. Ms. Dolan regularly helped on the boat. Matthews Sr., was from out of town and was visiting his son for the first time in a number years.

About 4:30 p.m., the three observed a fast forming fog. Matthews said they had been delayed in working with the pots and now he knew he could not get back inside the bar without being overtaken by the fog. Trying to get back to port, he said that the marker buoys were invisible in the fog but he spotted foam on the surface of the water indicating to him he was near a rock jetty.

Realizing he was lost on the bar, he turned around and headed back to sea. In front of him, a huge wave loomed so he yelled into his radio, knowing the Coast Guard monitored the frequency: "We're on the Coos Bay bar and we're in big trouble."

Matthews recalled that when the breaker crashed on his boat,

Night on sea buoy keeps death away

it knocked the cabin roof off and flipped the boat upside-down. He said the three were swimming and trapped in the cabin. But he suddenly popped to the surface sputtering for air with the thought flashing in his mind he was the only one to get out. He was immediately concerned with the fear that his dad and Kathleen were still trapped. But they surfaced also. Kathleen was struggling to hold on to an 18 x 36-inch wood fish box. She was able to climb on the large box as Matthews, holding one of the rope handles, tried to paddle in the direction of his Dad's calls but his father was not heard again.

Huge swells forced Matthews, still desperately holding the box's handle, under the surface many times as be searched for a sanctity – anything solid. He paddled with one hand against great odds of making any headway in the angry sea. Apparently Kathleen was also able to paddle. She called out that she thought she saw a buoy so they paddled in that direction. At the buoy, he had to relinquish his hold on the box to gain the top of the steel buoy. On top, he turned to Kathleen, but she, and the box, was nowhere to be seen. She just drifted away in the fog in those few seconds. He called but there was no reply. Had she fallen off the box?

He climbed up into the buoy's cage leaving the barnacled hull below him. This was the Baltimore Rock bell buoy. Every time a wave hit the hull of the buoy and tilted the cage, one of the clappers hit the gong. He tied off two clappers with his belt and wedged his legs against the other two. This way, without the clanging, he could listen for any passing vessels. In the foggy dark, he apparently didn't recognize the buoy or it's position.

> Baltimore Rock (43°21'25" N -- 124°23' W) is covered with eleven feet of water but usually breaks in swells, is .6 of a mile northwest of Cape Arago Lighthouse. The bell buoy is 450 yards north of the rock. This "9 x 20" buoy is 9-ft diameter at waterline with overall length 20-feet mostly under water.

He also realized he had lost both his dad and his mate, Kathleen. He said as he sat there in the bone chilling cold, he did a lot of thinking. He was dressed only in a T-shirt, wool socks and jeans. During the night, no boats passed near the buoy.

With the arrival of dawn, three Coast Guard boats on patrol appeared in the distance because a friend had called the Coast Guard serving notice that the *Kingfish* had not returned to port. But the lifeboats moved away from the buoy and never saw Matthews waving his arms. It was learned later that the Coast Guard never received the emergency radio call for help the evening before.

Hours later, a charter boat, with whale-watchers on board, cruised slowly into Matthew's vision. He made his way up throught the buoy's framework to the top and frantically waved his arms. The skipper on the boat, the *Cabrilla*, Duane Farrer, said he though the flapping on top of the buoy was birds, but being unsure, he turned to some of his passengers and asked them what they thought? Was it a person? They thought so therefore, with everyone on the boat waving toward the buoy, the *Cabrilla* was turned in that direction.

The weather had never really settled down from the earlier storm thus Farrer, because of high waves, could not bring his boat close enough to the buoy to remove Matthews without risk of collision with his boat.

The skipper, realizing the need for a helicopter to reach down and fetch the man off the buoy, raised Coast Guard Radio Coos Bay and alerted them that he had found a missing fisherman clinging to the Baltimore Rock buoy. A helicopter at the North Bend Air Station was already being readied for the search for the missing fishboat so took to the air at once.

On the scene, the flyers lowered a litter basket to within Matthews' reach. He climbed in, was hoisted aloft then flown to a hospital for examination.

Later he said:

Once I realized that you had found me the loss of Dad and Kathleen hit me. But I was so glad you found me. I prayed to Jesus all night. I asked God to send somebody there to get me. I should have waited out the fog. I thought of all this on the buoy. It's just a lot of should-ofs, you know.

I know what it takes to survive. You just have to reach a little deeper and find the strength. You can't give up.

After looking at the wreckage of the fishboat *Kingfish*, a Coast Guard spokesman said the boat "looked like somebody took a bulldozer and broke it apart."* □

---

* Material, and photograph by Jim Warner, © Southwestern Oregon Publishing Co. 1984, used with permission of Coos Bay *World*.

St. Nicholas and the Natives:

Timothy Tarakanof, a Survivor of the Russian Ship _St. Nicholas;_
His Adventures, Sufferings and Escape From the Natives
Drifted on reef near Quillayute River September 1808 —sank

The Russian trading ship _St. Nicholas_ (Captain Nikolai Bulagin) had been at New Archangel (Sitka), then set out on September 8, 1808 on a cruise to the south to improve their navigation charts and to do some trading with the natives. Near Detruction Island, the ship lost headway due to a lack of wind and drifted shoreward. Near today's LaPush, Washington, the ship became stranded on offshore rocks. With no hope of refloating, the captain ordered the crew, along with his wife who had hoped to enjoy the cruise, to make for shore. They succeeded but that was only the beginning of a long series of challenges for everyone in the party.

> Narrative prepared from the written testimony of Timothy Tarakanof, a survivor of the _St. Nicholas_. His papers are in the Alaska State Library. This is the earliest documented shipwreck along the northwest coast.

Although all sorts of supplies and light equipment had been salvaged from the ship, even one cannon, encounters with natives were not long in coming. The survivors put up a small shelter and made great efforts to keeping the captain's wife, Anna Petrovna, as comfortable as possible. As the days passed, the men could only watch the ferocious pounding breakers crush their ship little at a time.

The men faced the situation without much enthusiasm. They could stay where they were and face harassment from the Indians, which was happening, or try to hike to Grays Harbor. Along the way they were again attacked by natives during which encounters men on both sides were killed. The sailors had hard going for they were not mountain men, had no equipment for such a venture and worst of all, everyone was hungry. Their rendezvous with so-called friendly natives proved a fiasco when the Indians turned on them. In desperation, because in one encounter the captain's wife had been kidnapped, Captain Bulagin relieved himself of command turning over authority to Timothy Tarakanof. Everyone was soaked and what few supplies they had, especially gun powder, was wet.

The crew, without Anna, set up a small building of logs that was very cramped, but of such size everyone could get in to it. At this location in the woods, they spent the winter. In the spring of 1809, the party again set out trying to reach Grays Harbor but further encounters with the natives prohibited their progress. In a bold effort, Tarakanof and his men attacked an Indian village, captured two Indian girls as hostages to use as barter for Anna Petrovna. The ruse didn't work and before long all the Russians were prisoners of the natives. The prisoners were then separated. A local chief took Tarakanof to a village near Cape Flattery. Anna died in captivity. On learning this, Captain Bulagin lost the incentive to live and died a few months later. In 1810, what remained of the prisoners were taken to a village on the Strait of Juan de Fuca. In 1811, the *Lydia* (Captain Brown) an American brigantine, came along and while trading with the natives, word reached Tarakanof of the ship's presence. He managed his escape from captivity, went to the ship and was taken aboard.

Captain Brown agreed to seek the other Russians and to ransom them if possible. The task proved difficult but in the end all of the Russian sailors – three plus Tarakanof – who were in the area, were produced by the natives who extracted severely large quantities of booty in exchange. Some of the Russians had been traded among tribes and could not be located. Another was ransomed on the Columbia River when the ship *Mercury* stopped. But many of the Russians were never located. Of about 26 men of the original crew, seven were known to have died while prisoners of the Indians. Anna was dead. So was the ship's captain. Only thirteen got back to New Archangel in 1811 nearly three years after they had sailed on the *St. Nicholas*. □

Indians near Cape Flattery, Washington discover three stranded and nearly dead Japanese survivors of trans-pacific drift.
—Courtesy of Astoria Public Library

—65—

Hyojun Maru; Amazing Adventures of the Japanese Waifs and Dr. McLoughlin

Stranded Near Cape Flattery in 1833 —abandoned

The strange tale of the Japanese sailors whose junk stranded near Cape Flattery in 1833, became far more than an isolated shipwreck that occurred in a land inhabited by unfriendly natives.

The *Hyojun Maru* was on a voyage between Yedo (Tokyo) and Toba, a distance of about 220 miles. A storm caused the junk to lose its mast and rudder and to be swept out to sea. Entering the North Pacific Drift, the drifting junk finally grounded just south of Cape Flattery in the "Oregon Country."

One might suspect when sailors were stranded at sea in a junk with a cargo largely of rice, they would have plenty to eat. Yet during the drift from Japan to the coast of North America, which took slightly over one year, the rice, with the fish they caught, proved a deadly diet. The crew came down with beriberi because of the lack of fresh food for so long a time.

Of the crew of 14, there were but three survivors: Iwakichi, 28; Kyukichi, 15; Otokichi, 14. They were in poor physical con-

189

dition when their junk grounded. At this time, the Edict Period in Japanese history, Japanese mariners were forbidden to visit foreign lands on the promise of death on their return if they did. The Shogun of Japan also forbid all foreign vessels from calling at all Japanese ports with a single exception: The Dutch were permitted to maintain a presence in Nagasaki and the Dutch annual supply ship from Holland was allowed.

Along the northwest coast, the natives also had a tough policy on strangers but there does not appear to be any incident other than the present one when the Indians enforced it. Accordingly, when the castaways were discovered on the beach, the natives promptly enslaved them. But there was a "jungle telegraph." It took only about two months for word of the strangers at Cape Flattery to reach the potentate of the Hudson's Bay Company, Chief Factor Dr. John McLoughlin, at Fort Vancouver on the Columbia River. The fur trading company had a policy of being friendly but firm with the Indians because both sides enjoyed a lively trade as a result.

The "message" reaching Dr. McLoughlin was a crude drawing on a piece of "China paper." The picture illustrated three people on a beach with a wrecked ship on the nearby rocks and Indians busy taking goods from the ship. Dr. McLoughlin was known as a benevolent person and was always anxious to offer help regardless of who needed it. He also wondered how the Indians were treating their uninvited visitors?

McLoughlin had his frontiersman, Thomas McKay, organize a search and rescue party of thirty men to proceed along the coast in the direction of the Strait of Juan De Fuca to see what they could find out, and to ransom the shipwrecked sailors if need be.

It was still early in the year – March – when McKay started on this venture. Regrettably, he ran into the normal severe weather as he proceeded up the coast. He had no choice but to abandon the mission and go back to the fort empty handed.

Dr. McLoughlin was disappointed, but he realized the situation and determined to try again. The next effort was to commission his ship the *Llama* (Captain Wm. McNeil), which was stationed at the fort, to sail north along the coast to try to reach these men. McNeill took trade goods to properly pay the Indians if it proved true that the Indians had subjugated the waifs. Mc-Neill found the Indian village and it was true, the survivors of the wreck were there. Captain McNeill bought their freedom, also traded for some of the goods that had been on the junk, then he and his guests boarded the *Llama* and went back to Fort Vancouver.

As the Japanese guests could not speak or write English and could only try to communicate their basic needs with barely definable hand signals, McLoughlin directed they be entered in the small school. This was the first school in the Pacific Northwest.

> ## The School's Uniqueness
>
> Fort Vancouver's school was taught by an American Missionary from Oregon who was teaching Japanese sailors in a British school in what became the State of Washington.

This school was taught by Cyrus Shepard of the Methodist Mission to Oregon. The verification that this happened in taken from a letter written by Shepard in 1835 in which he declared, "I also have three Japanese under instruction, remarkably studious, very rapid improvement."

Dr. McLoughlin had no plans to sent the waifs back to Japan. Instead he but them on the ship *Eagle* bound for London with a load of furs. He sent an account of where these strange looking men came from, their rescue and schooling – they now spoke English – and suggested that the Hudson's Bay Company use the survivors as a means to get the Japanese government to open trade. In London, while this meeting was going on – several days – the waifs were held virtual prisoners on the *Eagle*.

The "Honourable Company" wanted no part of it, shipped the waifs to China and charged Dr. McLoughlin's personal account with all their expenses. But another uniqueness surfaced. The day before the ship (not the *Eagle*) left The Thames, the waifs were allowed to roam the streets of London on a sight-seeing venture thus they became the first Japanese to ever set foot on "jolly old England."

The story of what happened to the three Japanese survivors of the wrecked junk in 1833, and to other waifs rescued from other wrecked junks (but no others landed on the northwest coast), could fill another book. Let us conclude the incident by stating that all three found work in China including being Japanese/English interpreters.

Years later, after shipping restrictions in Japan were slightly relaxed, when the Japanese boarded a foreign vessel on one occasion, the boarding party amazed the captain when the captain was confronted by a Japanese person who spoke fluent English and who was dressed in western style clothing. It was Otokichi. □

—66—
The Collision of the *Pacific* and the *Orpheus*
Pacific: Collision November 4, 1875 —sank
Orpheus: Stranded November 4, 1875 —abandoned

The collision of these vessels, the *Pacific*, a side-wheeler, and the *Orpheus*, a full-rigged ship, made newspaper headlines to rival the sinking of the *Titanic* years later.

The 875-ton steamer *Pacific* (Captain J. D. Howell), with about 275 passengers and crew, departed in the middle of the morning from Victoria, B.C. headed for San Francisco on November 4, 1875. The side-wheeler left the Strait of Juan de Fuca and rounded Cape Flattery in the late afternoon in a very routine manner. The ship was rolling in heavy swells with a southwest wind and had dropped speed considerably as darkness came.

About 10 o'clock that night, the *Pacific* rocked with a shock that caused passengers to be knocked from their bunks. In minutes, the ship sank. A few passengers grabbed at wreckage when they found themselves in the water. Of all those who had sailed, only two would survive. Henry Jelley, who later died probably due to exposure, and Neil Henley, a quartermaster.

Henley hung on to a bit of wreckage until he was spied from the *Oliver Wolcott,* a Revenue Cutter. At the Court of Inquiry, he made these statements:

I was off watch and about 10 p.m. was awakened by a crash and getting out of my bunk I found water rushing into the hold at a furious rate. On reaching deck, all was confusion. I looked on the starboard beam and saw a large vessel under sail, which they said had struck the steamer. When I first distinguished her she was showing a green light. The captain and officers of the steamer were trying to lower boats but the passengers crowded in against their commands, making their efforts useless. None of the lifeboats had plugs in them. There were fifteen women and six men in the boat with me, but she struck the ship and filled instantly, and when I came up I caught hold of the skylight which soon capsized.

I then swam to a part of the hurricane deck, which had eight persons on it. When I looked around, the steamer had disappeared....

In a little while it was all over ... and we were alone on the raft, the part of the deck on which was the wheelhouse. Besides myself, the raft supported the captain, second mate, cook and four passengers, one of them a young lady. At 1 a.m., the sea was making a clean breach over us, carrying away the captain, second mate and the lady and another passenger, leaving four of us on the raft. At 9 a.m. the cook died and rolled off into the sea. At 4 p.m. the mist cleared away and we saw land about 15 miles off. We also saw a piece of wreckage with 2 men on it. At 5 p.m. another man expired and early the next morning the other one died leaving me alone. Soon after the death of the last man I caught a box and I dragged it on the raft. It kept the wind off [me] and during the day I slept. Early on the morning of the 8th [of November] I was rescued by the *Wolcott*.

Henry Jelley, and four others, managed to grab hold of an upside-down lifeboat but only Jelley survived the waves that were breaking over them. He dangled in the water for 48 hours but was seen by the lookout on the *Messenger* and was taken aboard.

The currents caused many of the corpses to float into the Strait of Juan de Fuca all of which were picked up as they came to notice.

In the meantime, when word reached Victoria, the city went into mourning. The *Colonist* newspaper eulogized on its editorial page:

We have no heart today to dwell on the disaster that had hurried into eternity so many of our fellow citizens with whom only a few brief hours ago we mingled on the streets or met in the social circle, as full of life, hope and energy as any who may read the *Colonist* today. The catastrophe is so far-reaching that scarcely a household in Victoria had not lost one of its members, or must strike from its list of living friends the face and form that found ever a warm greeting within their circle. A bolt out of the blue could not have caused more widespread consternation that the awful tidings spread far and near yesterday. In some cases, entire families have been swept away, in others fond wives returning from a visit to their childhood homes to meet husbands and younger children in San Francisco have gone down to an early grave. In others, the joyous, happy maiden, the sweet, innocent, prattling babe, the banker, the merchant, the miner, the public officer – all have found a common grave in a dreadful and tumultuous home, wide opening and loud roaring still for more.

Whether the catastrophe was one that human skill could have averted we cannot now say. All we do know is that a steamship carrying a cargo of precious lives has gone down and that do far as is known only one man, out of 275 persons on board, has been saved. We can only express the hope that the vessels now flying like ministering angels to the scene will return with glad tidings of great joy for some of the hearts that are now bowed down with grief.

When the "rescue" ships returned empty handed, there was no joy.

The Cargo Loss
—SS Pacific—
November 4, 1875

In addition to the loss of life,
the *Pacific* also carried:
- $79,220 in a safe
- 2,000 sacks of oats
- 280 tons of coal
- 261 hides
- 31 barrels of cranberries
- 18 tons of general goods
- 11 casks of furs
- 10 tons sundry items
- 10 cords of bolts
- 6 horses
- 2 buggies
- 2 cases opium

The *Orpheus*, 1,100-tons, which had been heading for Nanaimo, B.C. in ballast for a load of coal, did not pick up any of the people thrown into the sea by the crash. Why not? When the captain testified before the Coroner's Jury he declared:

The *Orpheus* was steering north, keeping close into the land, with the wind from the southward, and blowing fresh with fine rain, the ship going about 12 knots. Her head yards square, thus leaving the ship in such a position that she could be hauled offshore on a moment's notice, if anything came into view.

At 9:30 p.m., I left the deck in charge of the second mate, Allen, with orders if he saw anything, to starboard the wheel and keep her head to the northwest offshore. I went below to consult the chart with my oil clothes on, looking at the chart, when I heard the second mate tell the man at the wheel to starboard the helm. I looked up at the compass over my head and saw that the ship's head was rapidly coming up toward the northwest. I immediately went on deck and asked the officer what was the matter, and he said there was a light on the starboard bow.

I let the ship come up in the wind until she headed to the southward of west, and the after sails aback. My ship was comparatively at a standstill, in just such a position as I would be if I were going to take a pilot aboard. This brought the steamer's light a little forward the starboard beam. I stood looking at her with my glasses. I did not then think there was going to be a collision, but I said to the second mate, "She will be into us," I though I did not think she would, for I thought she would see us and keep off. I made up my mind that she would hit us, and shortly afterward she blew her whistle, and immediately struck us on the starboard side in the wake of the main hatch. The blow was a slight one. She had evidently stopped her engines and was backing and gave us a glancing blow, for she bounded off and again struck us at the main topmast back stays, breaking the chain plates. She then bounded off and struck us at the mizzen topmast chain plates, carrying away the back stays and bumpkin, main topsail braces, leaving me comparatively a wreck on the starboard side.

Before she blew her whistle my wife came on deck and stood by my side. We could plainly see her deck from the pilot house to her bows and not a soul was to be seen there as she passed the stern. I hailed her [the ship] and asked her to stand by me, but she made no reply. My wife attempted to jump on board her, and would, had I not grabbed her. We [the ships] drifted apart and I gave my attention to my ship and gave orders to the mate to cut the lashings on the [life] boats and to the carpenter to sound the pumps. My rail was broken from the fore rigging to the main rigging. The first report the carpenter made was that the ship was half full of water. I told him to take a light and go down the fore hatch to see.

In the meantime I found there was no water in the hold. I gave orders to the mate to never mind the boats, but to take all hands and secure the back stays and repair damages. All my starboard braces had been carried away with the blocks, etc. Now, while I was attending to the condition of the ship, it certainly took from ten to fifteen minutes, and during that time I never looked after the steamer, neither did anyone else that I know of. We were all busy attending to our own necessities. When, after I found I was not seriously damaged, I looked for the steamer, I just saw a light on our starboard quarters, and when I looked again it was gone.

There has been a great deal said about crying and screaming of the women and children on the steamer. Not one sound was heard from her by anyone of my ship, neither was anyone seen on board her. Neither did any one on my ship think for a moment that any injury of any kind had happened to the steamer, for at 1:30 a.m., as the sailors were furling the spanker, they commenced to growl, as sailors will, about the steamer, after running us down, to go off and leave us in that shape, without stopping to inquire whether we were injured or not.

The sailors on the *Orpheus* made repairs that allowed the ship to proceed, but her adventures of the night were not over. Within a few hours, the ship had a second collision, this time with rocks near Cape

Beale. Although the crew got off, the vessel was a total loss.

The navigation error that caused the second collision was because the charts on the *Orpheus* did not show Cape Beale lighthouse which was relatively new. The sailing directions being followed stated that the Cape Flattery lighthouse was the most northerly. * ☐

—67—
Ferndale and Mrs. White's Determination
Stranded January 29, 1892 —sank

The *Ferndale* was about 50 miles off the Columbia River when clouded in heavy fog, the decision was made not to try to cross the bar under such unfavorable conditions. While awaiting the weather to clear, the offshore Davidson Current, in which the vessel thought she was standing still, was actually causing the *Ferndale* to drift north. When the vessel was about 15 miles north of Grays Harbor, she crunched to a stop near the beach at 3:30 on the morning of January 29, 1892.

It occurs that later that morning, Edward White and his wife were strolling on the beach near their home at about today's Copalis Beach. During a brief respite from the fog that was hugging the ground, they were amazed to see before them the outline of an ocean liner. By agreement, Mrs. White was to stay there as a lookout and her husband started his foot-after-foot jog for help.

No sooner was he out of sight, than she thought she saw the outline of a person being tumbled in the breakers. Without any thought for her own safety, she dashed into the surf, grabbed the man and pulled him out of the water onto the beach. Looking up, she saw another form barely managing to keep his footing as he walked through the breakers. She rushed to the stranger and also managed to get him to the safety of the beach.

It seemed only seconds later that she saw still another figure struggling in the water. This was a very big man, very strong, but in a state of frenzy, unable to understand help was at hand so he

---

* Cape Beale lighthouse (48°48'N - 125°13'), is the southeast entrance to Barkley Sound in British Columbia. It is the site of the only lighthouse (completed in 1874) until 1891 thus was the only aid to navigation on the sea coast side of Vancouver Island at the time of these disasters. Cape Flattery lighthouse is on Tatoosh Island (48°24'N - 124°44'W). It was established in 1857.

fought her off. All this in the surf, when an incoming wave knocked both of them down into the water. Against great odds, she was able to maintain a tight grip on the man's clothing and with super-human strength and determination, she withstood the attacks on her by the delirious sailor. All the while she was working her charge toward the beach.

When the rescue crew arrived with her husband, there were the three men this housewife saved from the sea, these men the lone survivors of a crew of 21.

The news of the disaster and of the valiant rescuer was quick to reach London as the *Ferndale* was of British registry. The British awarded a gold lifesaving medal to Mrs. White for her tenacity in saving the men. Then there was a purse collected for her by the people around Grays Harbor. In her unpretentious way she thanked her well-wishers by saying, "I'd gladly do the whole thing over if I thought I could save a life." □

—68—
The Disinterrment of the *Nora Harkins*
Stranded October 16, 1894 —abandoned

When old-timers around Grays Harbor studied the hulk that had dis-interred itself from the sandy beach on Point Chehalis, they concluded it was that of the *Nora Harkins*. The ship ran aground on Tuesday, October 16, 1894.

According to an old undated newspaper clipping believed from the *Daily World* in nearby Aberdeen, the gentlemen were not merely guessing.

Millard Peterson, Westport, and John Ferrier, Aberdeen, have definite recollections. Peterson, the son of Frank Peterson and the grandson of Glenn Peterson were all pioneers who lived at Peterson's Point. This was an early name for Point Chehalis. As a teenager, he recalls playing on the hulk of the *Nora Harkins*.

John Ferrier recalled the wreck in the early 1890's when he first arrived in town. Both men specifically remember the location of the old hulk they once played on as kids and the location of the recent resurrection of whatever-it-is in the same place.

This is the wreck of the *Nora Harkins* which piled up on Point Chehalis October 16, 1894. One life was lost. The hulk was dis-interred from the beach due to coastal erosion on an unknown date. The specifications of the *Nora Harkins* closely resembles those of this hulk, both being two-masted centerboard schooners. Date of the photograph unknown.

—Don McArthur collection

The *American Shipping Register* for 1892 lists the *Nora Harkins* as a 199-ton schooner of two masts, 121-feet long with a 32-feet 4-inches beam that had been built at Parkersburg, Oregon in 1882. Thomas Harkins was her master and owner. The last survey was in December 1885 at Port Townsend.

The newspaper clipping states when the vessel stranded, there was one life lost. □

—69—

Point Loma Stranded – All Survive
Stranded February 28, 1896 —abandoned

The wind was at gale force, the sea was rough when the *Point Loma* (Captain Conway) developed a leak in the hull that flooded the engines about midnight of February 27th, 1896. By daybreak the next morning, the tide and wind drove the disabled vessel toward the beach near Seaview, Washington on the North Beach peninsula.

The vessel had left Grays Harbor with a load of dimension lumber bound for San Francisco.

When the fire in the boiler was drowned by the incoming sea water, Captain Conway fired distress flares from the bridge. These were seen by people on the shore. The U. S. Life Saving Service turned out to do whatever it could. It is always a test of stamina and strength to launch a row boat, regardless of its size and number of oarsmen, into the face of crashing breakers.

Although these trained men tried, several times, they could not breech the breakers with the boat but were driven ashore every time. As an alternative, they shot a line to the vessel. This line was used as a guideline when the men launched a raft and pulled their way to the beach along the line. All survived. As traditional with ship strandings on beaches and on rocks along the northwest coast, the *Point Loma* was ground to waste by the incessant pounding of the breakers. □

—Don McArthur collection

—70—
Bones of *Kate & Ann* Scrutinized
Stranded approximately 1885-1886 —abandoned

"It's my distinct recollection that the *Kate & Ann* was lost in the storm that drove her ashore in 1885 or 1886 at or near the spot where she has been found 64 years later [1959-60]," declared 90-year old James B. Kesterson.

Mr. Kesterson was referring to the hulk that was discovered as sand eroded more of Point Chehalis, near Westport, and revealed what was left of the old vessel. He also was quick to correct his listeners when they referred to "Point Chehalis" which he said was really "Point of Chehalis."

Newspaper reporters, responding to the hulk's sudden appearance between the Coast Guard lookout tower and the beach, said the discovery "confounded history and maritime experts alike."

A study of the ship's bones present this discussion:

The craft was heavily constructed and probably 60 feet long. It measured a 20-foot beam and has about 6-feet draw. As the craft has a centerboard well, this supposedly dates the vessel as probably one of the earliest on Grays Harbor. The ship is nearly flat bottomed and has a molded bow. The stern is missing.

Does anyone have a better identification? ☐

Columbia River Lightship No. 50 slipped her moorage at sea during a storm and was driven ashore near McKenzie Head on Cape Disappointment. *No. 50's* salvage was not by the usual method, but house movers jacked her up and hauled her over land for half-a-mile then launched her into Baker Bay.
(LEFT) **The lightship ready for launching into Baker Bay after lengthy salvage operations.** (LOWER) **Hard aground before overland trek.** —James A. Gibbs col.

—71—
Overland Trek of *Lightship No. 50*
Stranded November 29, 1899 —refloated

The voyage of this lightship, which is supposed to be on a specific position at sea, <u>over land</u>, can hardly be imagined until one learns of the factors that precipitated it.

The mariners who frequented the Columbia River were jubilant when news spread that the government would build a lightship and station it off the mouth of the Columbia River. The contract was let in 1891 to the Union Iron Works of San Francisco, the same yard that had built the famous battleship *Oregon* a few years earlier.

The assigned position for the Columbia River Lightship when the service was inaugurated in 1892, was 8½ miles southwest of Cape Disappointment. With changes in the aids to navigation over the years, which includes jetty construction, *Lightship No. 50* is shown in the 1934 *Light List* at 46°11'N - 124°11'W that being 5.3 miles southwest of the end of the south jetty on the Main Channel Range Line. (The lightship was discontinued in 1979.)

The mariners grew to depend on the lightship and especially its bellowing fog horn which blew in desperately foggy weather. But its strong beam and its horn went silent at 6:30 in the evening of November 28, 1899 when her anchor cables parted in a raging storm dislocating the lightship from its designated position. In a valiant effort to keep the now drifting ship at sea, the crew got a sail up but in short order, the ferocious wind ripped it apart. The lightship was left to drift with the storm.

When dawn arrived, the lighthouse tender *Manzanita* and the tugboats *Wallula* and the *Escort* were on the way to assist the wallowing lightship. The crew of the rescue ships got an "E for Effort" that day as each was successful in getting tow lines aboard, but the sea was too tough to conquer and under the strain, the lines, except for line to the light-weight tug, *Escort,* parted.

The *Escort* remained with the lightship as she drifted helplessly toward shore. It did not take long before the lightship was in the breaker line off Cape Disappointment where the *Escort* was forced to drop her line and to stand off for her own safety. In short order, the ship was driven onto the beach near McKenzie Head which lies between North Head and Cape Disappointment.

The U. S. Life Saving Service crew at Cape Disappointment responded to the call of help. And they were not alone. Troops of the Army's Battery M, Third Coast Artillery, that were stationed at Fort Canby, right next door, were ordered to the beach to be available if manpower was needed. Civilians from the area also turned out to see the spectacle of a lightship sitting on the beach.

By 7:30 in the morning, the lifesavers had set up their Lyle gun and tried to shoot a line to the lightship but the first shot fell short. The next shot made it but the line became fouled and it was not until 11:20 that the first sailor was brought to shore in a breeches buoy. All 7 of the crew, some with injuries resulting from being tossed by the storm, as well as Captain Joseph H. Harriman, were landed safely.

The vessel had been very tightly constructed and to the amazement of many observers, it withstood continuing winter onslaughts. Thoughts of salvaging the ship now became actual plans. The tug boats went to the scene in January, got lines aboard and with teamwork, started their pull. No luck. The Lighthouse District's Portland office called for bids to salvage the lightship. There was an award to salvager Captain Robert McIntosh on January 9th to free the vessel from the beach. He did his level best in the face of the continuing severe northwest coast winter storms. In the next 60 days, he actually moved the lightship 40 feet, had her afloat but as there was no standby tugboat, the next tide put the lightship even higher on the beach.

On a very high tide in April, Captain McIntosh tried again. It looked like be might be successful but, regrettably, the cable snapped. In June, impressed at the lack of results in salvaging the vessel, the 13th Lighthouse District canceled the contract. New bids were advertised.

All this time there was no lightship off the mouth of the Columbia River to the consternation of mariners.

A number of bids came from various salvage outfits with propositions for "hook-up-a-rope-and-pull-it-off-the-beach" technique. But there were several from outfits that wanted to drag the vessel over land and into Baker Bay.

When the bids were opened in Washington, D. C., a bid was accepted although Captain McIntosh's offer was lower cost, from Wolff & Zwicker Iron Works in Portland. The firm set up a camp and moved in many men and heavy equipment. By August 13th, with anchors in place, the firm had tugboats at sea, cables in place and anchors ready, the lightship would not move due to a severe sand buildup around her. The contractor sent a plea to Washington D. C. explaining the cause for delay and was granted an extension to October 25th. The saying "time nor tide tarrieth no man"* proved to be true for the deadline came and went without success.

In near desperation, the Lighthouse District called for a 3rd set of bids. But this time there was a twist: The method of salvage must be over land. When the opening occurred on January 19, 1901 – *Lightship No. 50* had now been out-of-service since November of 1899 – the offers ranged from $14,650 to $25,000. But an ordinary house moving firm in Portland won the contract for only $17,500.

The idea of salvaging a shipwreck with a house mover seemed too much for the imagination and questions quickly arose. Further, the bidder declared he could have the ship floating in Baker Bay in a maximum of 33 working days!

Many shipwreck salvage stereotypes were to be broken.

Normally, such work was a daylight job as one needed to see what he was doing. Fine. The contractor moved a portable light plant to the scene and ran flood lights for use in dark hours. He installed railroad ties under the vessel thereby permitting the ship to be lifted as if moving a house – jackscrews. When April 3rd came, the vessel was several feet off the beach and a cradle was being built. This was a new approach to salvaging a ship and all this took time – too much time. There was a penalty of $100 a day if the work was not timely. With the risk that the work would have to be stopped and the contractor would "pick up his marbles and go home," the government, appreciating what it was viewing, dropped the penalty clause thus the work continued.

On huge rollers, the vessel started moving "over-the-hill-and-through-the woods" by April 12th. The uniqueness of the operation was not lost on the Astoria newspaper which promoted the venture. In short order, an excursion boat went into service charging a fare of $1 per ticket to the Baker Bay side of the spit where picnickers went to watch the progress.

When the salvage contractor got the lightship out of its sand trap and well off the beach so a close inspection of her bottom could be made, he provided a detailed report of what he found and what he didn't find. For one, the rudder had apparently been lost

---

* Robert Green in *Disputation*. (1592)

presumably in the stormy sea. The sternpost was gone as was her keel. There had been copper sheathing torn off and lost in the storm and part of the starboard bilge keel was also missing.

While the vessel was being slowly rolled toward Baker Bay, the contractor received a letter containing an additional contact to fix the damage while the ship was out of the water and still on his rollers. This would be fine at such time as he could locate competent carpenters. This took about two weeks. But no time was lost for during this interim, the launching ways were built into Baker Bay.

With a throng of onlookers and well-wishers, *Lightship No. 50* was launched into Baker Bay at 11:45 p.m. June 2, 1901 as that was the hour of the high tide. The vessel was towed across the wide Columbia River to Astoria by the steamer *Callender*. On arrival on June 4th, there were whistle salutes from small and large craft gathered to escort the vessels into port. The crowds on the waterfront were very large.

It took the dry-dock in Portland until August 12 to put final touches on the lightship and to make a final inspection then get her back to the operating base at Tongue Point.

After only three days more of waiting, mariners approaching the lightship's position found the beam blazing in the night and the bellowing fog horn had re-awakened to welcome them. □

—72—
The 3,000-ton Burden in the *Alice*
Stranded January 15, 1909 —sank

The French 2,500 ton full-rigged *Alice* (Captain Aubert), was discovered about 300 yards offshore near Ocean Park, Washington by a boy and his dog about 7:45 o'clock on Friday, January 15, 1909.

The boy, seeing the ship leaning heavily to starboard, recognized trouble so trotted off to find help. The Klipsan Lifesaving Station with its beach apparatus responded at once. The team that normally pulled the cart, with the apparatus and surfboat, spooked in the soft sand and could not be persuaded to haul the load.

With the ship carrying 3,000 tons of dead weight – cement –
when the hull cracked the only direction the ship could go was ↓

Captain Conick, the commander at the station, was a man who did not give up so he unloaded the surfboat where they were, put it into the water and the crew rowed the boat four miles to the stricken ship. By the time they arrived, all the crew from the *Alice* was ashore having used the ship's small boat.

The January storm was still raging and only nine of the crew of 24, along with Captain Aubert, would risk a trip back to the vessel to retrieve personal property.

The cargo on the ship was mostly cement – 3,000-tons of it. When the steel hull cracked under the pounding of the breakers, and sea water met the cement, the cement quickly set up into an impenetrable mass. Deadweight. As there was no way to salvage the ship, she was abandoned and considered a total loss after spending 176 days at sea. Her run had been from London by way of Australia with final destination the Columbia River. The ship stranded on the beach about 15 miles shy of the goal. □

Checkered Life of the *Rosecrans* Ends
Stranded January 13, 1913 —sank

The *Rosecrans* (Captain L. F. Johnson), was running before a gale as she crossed the Columbia River bar. In a heavy fog, the ship heaved as if in a death gasp then crashed head-on into Peacock Spit. At 5:15 in the morning, the radio operator at Cape Disappointment U. S. Life Saving Station was startled as his ears listened to the clicks of Morse code:

STEAMER ROSECRANS ON BAR SEND ASSISTANCE SHIP BREAKING UP FAST CAN STAY AT MY STATION NO LONGER

When the breakers on the Columbia River bar seem to go mad in storms, there seems little leeway between life or death to anyone caught in a ship of any size there.

The *Rosecrans* was on a run from San Francisco with 20,000 barrels of crude oil. As she piled up on the spit, the seas crashed over the ship carrying away everything that had not been secured. About 8 o'clock that morning, the ship broke in two spilling crude oil in the sea as men desperately climbed into the rigging in an effort to save themselves.

The lifesavers from Point Adams Station managed to get their oversize rowboat to the wreck seeing only a mast arising above the sea. Of all the crew of 36, the lifesavers could only see four still clinging for their lives. On viewing their rescuers, one of them jumped into the water and tried to swim to the lifeboat. He did not live to tell about it as he died in the water, the lifesavers having only his dead body to haul aboard. The others stayed where they were until the boat got in closer. The three were saved.

```
Rescued:
Erick Lindmark, carpenter
Joseph Lenning, quartermaster
 (Mr.)  Peters
```

But the lifeboat could not cross over the bar to the safety of the bay so the tired oarsmen rowed out to sea to the Columbia River Lightship.

At the lightship, a heavy swell caught the lifeboat and the

corpse in the boat was unshipped into the sea to disappear.

Speculative stories ran in the newspapers as to how Captain Johnson had lost his ship. A plausible explanation was that he had mistaken North Head lighthouse for that of the lightship therefore throwing off his bearings. Both lights emit white beams. He apparantly did not see the Cape Disappointment light as it emits red and white light. ☐

Author's note: The *Rosecrans* was launched in Glasgow, Scotland in 1883 as the *Methven Castle*. She was renamed *Columbia* and transferred to United States registry. The vessel was chartered by the U. S. Army as a troop transport for the Spanish-American War with the name *Rosecrans*. After the use of the ship was discontinued by the Army due to excessive operating costs, she was sent to the Pacific Coast for conversion to a tanker for Associated Oil Company.

The *Rosecrans'* troubles: The ship ran aground north of Santa Barbara where two of the crew drowned. Within a few months, the ship was totally gutted by fire at Gaviota while loading oil. Then the ship was lost at the Columbia River.

An item to be observed about the three wrecks which are in common is the fact that Captain L. F. Johnson was in command off Santa Barbara, at Gaviota and when the ship crashed into Peacock Spit and was lost.

—74—
Short Life of the *Janet Carruthers*
Stranded January 22, 1919 —abandoned

The picturesque 240-foot long, 2-year old, 5-masted schooner *Janet Carruthers,* landed on the beach about 4-miles north of Grays Harbor north jetty on January 22, 1919. Six of the crew drowned in their haste to abandon the ship when the lifeboat swamped. At low tide somewhat later, other crew walked ashore.

Although salvage work started promptly by dumping fuel oil into the sea (the ship had twin-screws and an oil-burning engine), the Washington State Department of Fisheries halted the work because the state claimed there would be irrecoverable damage to clams. With their hands tied, owners of the vessel abandoned salvage efforts and the *Janet Carruthers* quickly broke up.

This incident was said to be due to the skipper's mistaking Grays Harbor light for North Head light. ☐

Lighthouse characteristics:	
Grays Harbor light:	**North Head light:**
Alternate flash *red and white* every 30 seconds	Group occulting flashes *white* every 30 seconds
Visibility 17 miles in clear weather	Visibility 20 miles in clear weather
Installed in 1898	Installed in 1898
	—U.S. Dept. Commerce *Light List 1934*

H. F. *Alexander's* Broken Nose
Collision August 7, 1922 —salvaged

When the passenger liner *SS H. F. Alexander* crashed on Cake Rock off the Washington coast on August 7, 1922, she had to be running at a very good speed in order to do the severe damage to the bow that cost $210,000 to fix. That was very big money in 1922. The bow was wrinkled back to the foremast.

After sending an sos reporting the ship's position and situation, the *Admiral Schley* came alongside and transferred 317 passengers and 135 of the crew leaving only a skeleton crew on the ship. There were no casualties other than wrinkled nerves and headaches due to the sudden impact. The collision bulkheads were closed thus water imported at the bow went nowhere.

Cake Rock is 2-miles northwest of James Island. A lighthouse on the island (47°54'3"N - 124°38'8"W) was opened two years later. Cake Rock is not considered difficult to see as it stands 116 feet above sea level.

The *H. F. Alexander* went in to Seattle to the dry-dock under her own power and was greeted by a host of eager photographers and reporters. ☐

—76—

The Mysterious *Ryo Yei Maru*
Derelict at sea October 31, 1927 —cremated

A lookout on the bow of the merchant ship *Margaret Dollar* (Captain H. T. Payne) reported he was looking at a small vessel off their starboard bow. The steamer was off the northwest coast of Washington headed to the Strait of Jan de Fuca on her way to Seattle.

Captain Payne focused his binoculars on a strange little craft and suddenly ordered his ship to change course and make for the vessel. In a few minutes he ordered his steamer STOP, then drifted in for a closer look. The strange craft had a narrow hull reaching forward to an overhanging sampan-type bow. A wooden taff rail

Ryo Yei Maru (foreground) and *SS Margaret Dollar* at Seattle dock.

around the stern was supported by carved stanchions like those of old sailing ships.

Shredded canvas hung limp from two battered masts. Yellowed, once-white paint peeled from the rust-streaked deckhouse and hull. As the eerie craft rolled in the ground swell, the men on the steamer could see a crust of barnacles below the water line with seaweed streamers several feet long.

The deck was a litter of wreckage amid which human bones, bleached and clean-picked, gleamed white. Faded black lettering on the transom bore the wording

RYO YEI MARU - MISAKI

As soon as the Captain ordered a boat lowered from the steamer, crew members pulled to the wallowing mystery craft. The men cautiously hauled themselves over the bulwark. The only sound that greeted them was a clatter of loose gear banging in the rigging as the vessel rolled.

The men picked their way forward, forced open hatches and peered into holds. Empty. They crept into the pilot house and found only an unmanned helm and musty litter.

When they pried open the engine-room hatch, they observed a rusting, partially dismantled two-cylinder gasoline engine. As the vessel rolled, oily bilge water sloshed over the engine scattering tools and parts over the floorboards.

When the investigators reached the crew quarters, a certain feeling of tenseness gripped them. When the door was forced open, an escaping wave of stinking foul air all but turned their stomachs. They inched down a ladder with handkerchiefs covering their noses. At the bottom was a little galley. In a corroded kettle on a rusty stove they were horrified to see human bones.

Working their way aft, they found tiers of wooden bunks all empty except for two. There, huddled side-by-side, were the withered bodies of two dead Japanese.

This discovery ended the search and the boarding party returned to the *Margaret Dollar* immediately to tell of their discoveries to Captain Payne. The captain radioed Seattle Coast Guard and reported what had been discovered. He was directed to tow the derelict to Seattle, so the crew attached a line to the little junk and the steamer set off at AHEAD SLOW so as not to swamp the craft. The 85-foot long *Ryo Yei Maru* was underway for the first time in nearly eleven months.

Customs officers and U. S. Public Health Service inspectors boarded the steamer off Port Townsend. After inspecting the junk, Dr. L. P. Seavy, a U. S. Quarantine officer, the first man aboard declared:

> There is mute evidence of the clean-licked human bones, which clearly points to cannibalism.

On November 1, Customs Officers discovered in the pilot house a thin cedar board upon which Tokizo Miki, the dying skipper of the craft, had scrawled a meager record of the events leading to the tragic end. The Japanese script was interpreted by the Japanese consul in Seattle.

> We, the above named twelve persons, departed from Kisaki, Kanawga [*sic*] Prefecture on December 5, fifteenth year of Tasisho (1926). While at work fishing, a part of the engine was broken. Eight bushels of rice which we had on board has been exhausted. No ships have passed us. All hope is gone and only death can be awaited.

The inspectors discovered nine envelopes in which Captain Miki had carefully placed a lock of each man's hair to be returned home for burial in Japan. Locks of hair of two of the crewmen who had died the same day were in the same envelope.

On November the craft was towed to Pier 41, Seattle and it was there on November 14th, that Customs officers made the dramatic discovery of a diary describing events from the time the vessel had left Japan. It had been kept by Sutejiro Izwa until he died March 17th, after which date it was taken over by Gennosuke Matsumoto, who was the last to die and whose body was found huddled alongside that of the captain. The diary was interpreted by Consul Kawamura:

Dec. 5, 1926   Zero a.m. From Misaki harbor we sailed on off Choji on our eighth sailing

Dec. 9.   Fishing with good result – taking 200 pounds red fish and 4 sharks and 4 other fine fish

Dec. 12.   Ship's crank shaft broke early today and we are helpless. We tried to hoist sails. But on account of strong west winds we could not sail as we desired. The ship drifted on out of control.

Dec. 14.   Snow is beginning to fall without wind. We decided we must use rice sparingly. While we were eating breakfast we sighted northern direction a ship about 20 toms [*sic*]. We signaled them by raising our flag but they were out of sight.

Dec. 16.   At 7 a.m. we sighted a T.K.K. steamer and thought at last the favor of God was upon us. We raised 2 flags and kindled a fire on deck and made great noise. But the steamer proceeded off our track. We sighted a fishing boat at 10 a.m. in a southwesterly direction and we signaled in various ways in vain, as it was out of sight in 30 minutes. West wind began to blow. We are drifting helplessly.

Dec. 18.   For 18 hours this day we sailed west. We rested at 4 p.m. and had a conference. There was no hope of meeting a steamship and we decided to head for Bonin Island [about 500 miles southeast of Yokohama] and try our luck in meeting a steamer then, but this would take three or four months to reach it [at out slow rate of drift].

Dec. 19.   West winds all morning. Waves running high and we drifted on west wind for 30 hours. We are headed for Bonin island and we think how long it takes to wash us there. If we are out of luck our fate is ended.

Dec. 20.   A jewel north wind is blowing and everything O.K. When the westerly winds were blowing day after day the captain began to talk of taking big chance and heading for America. The crew objected to that plan.

Dec. 21.   We are helpless and drifting before the wind going west. We all worshipped *Konpira* [Shinto god for seafaring men] at the shrine [aboard ship]. We drew lots [to determine which way we would go] and so we headed west.

Dec. 23.   Boat still drifting. At 5 p.m. we caught a 160-pound fish. We almost despaired of sailing west [because of no wind] yet in going toward the east it would take 4 months to reach America. It is too late to hope to meet a boat, and it is not manly to wait.

Dec. 26.   Unable to head west, we have at least turned toward the east. We have finally decided to risk all and head for America.

As we have seen, the writers of the log did not make daily entries. How unbearable was it to remain becalmed as a mere speck in the vast ocean? Soon after the decision was made to strike for North America, and they trimmed their sail for that direction, the near calm and slight west wind which was moving the vessel to the east abruptly reversed. The next day's log tells the story:

Dec. 28.   Drifting westward with heavy wind shoving at the stern. If this keeps up 10 days we may be carried to land. This day we caught bonita. We dried the fish to preserve them. The rice is giving out. It is after midnight. As the captain is without definite course, his heart is filled with trouble. We dare not express to each other our innermost thoughts.

We [again] prayed to *Konpira* and promised him that we would never again ask of him [anything] unreasonable. Even our deepest prayers do not draw pity from our angry god! Oh, *Konpira*! Have pity on us or we shall throw away thy charms. No— No— No— No— Oh, let us not think such heresy! *Konpira* is still there. He is for right and justice. The evil that we think is in our minds. Have mercy on us, oh, *Konpira*. We heed your warning and suffer in all humility. Please pity and forgive us!

Dec. 31.   We are drifting again. This is the last day of the year. Greetings and a happy new year to everybody! Pray God to help us.

Jan. 1 [1927].   New Year Day the sixteenth year of Taisho [the era fixed by the reigning Japanese emperor]. We celebrated this day by mixing rice and red beans and enjoying the luxury of *koya jofu* [dried bean cakes]. We confessed to each other many of our innermost thoughts – and then came the night. At 7 p.m. we are again becalmed and drifting.

Jan. 3.   We have had three good days of weather and our spirits have been high as we celebrated New Years Day for three consecutive days. But fear is in our hearts again – whither are we bound? The sea is all about us and we have no compass to guide.

Jan. 4.   Praise be to *Konpira*! He has sent us rain. We gathered it in canvases and shall hoard it as a miser hoards his gold.

Jan. 7.   We are still groping our way about the sea. We have tried to set our course by the sun, but all is in vain. We drift, drift in an endless sea.

For the next ten days there are no entries then suddenly the log keeper declares very tersely:

Jan. 17.   We have repaired our engine

But the Japanese interpreter in Seattle observed the diarist was "obviously suffering hallucinations for no previous reference to repairs had been made," The very next day an entry read plainly and simply: "We are still drifting."

But the despair was suddenly broken some days later:

Jan. 27. A ship! A ship! Happy madness seizes us as we sight a steamer. We build a fire — we wave, we shout, we dance — but oh, *Konpira*! The stranger does not see us and is gone over the horizon . Alas, again we are drifting we know now whither. The seas is mighty. Oh *Konpira*! Are you without mercy?

Feb. 1. We caught 1 fish and ate it for dinner.

Feb 13. Sickness is upon us. Hatuzo Terada has lain in his bunk past 5 days and is wasting away. We have caught more fish to eat. Yukichi Tsume Mitsu has a hurt leg and has taken to his bunk. Who shall be next.

Many days pass with no entries in the log for the men are desperate. How do they spend their time? Finally, on March 5, an entry merely reads: "Today at breakfast we had no food."

The following day, Captain Miki wrote his message on the piece of cedar board.

March 9. Denjiro Hosai this day died of illness. Tsumetaro Naoye now sick. Big bird was caught. [It was later determined that the birds were caught on tuna hooks baited with human flesh.]

March 17. There being no wind, we repaired the sails. Sutejiro Isawa died. [Isawa-san had kept the diary up till this time. Matsumoto continued it until his death.]

March 22. There appeared a seal. We thought we were not far from shore. Tsupiuchi became ill from several days ago.

March 27. Clouds and a southwest wind. As it was an adverse wind we drifted. Terada and Yokota died today. We caught a large bird.

March 29. Rain. North-northwest wind changed to south-southwest winds at 3 p.m. We are drifting average of 4 miles an hour on account of the strong wind. Tokichi Kuwata dies at 9 a.m. and Tokakichi Mitani died during the night. We caught a shark.

From this time on, the diary entries are short and terse as if the very act of writing was a tremendous chore. The common entries were mainly about the incessant drifting – ever drifting lazily with no sounds but their own movements about the ship and the occasional murmur of the sea on the near-calm days; sickness and deaths.

April 6. Tsunjiuchi died.

April 14. Yiukichi Tsunemitsi died.

214

April 19.   Yoshishiro Udehira died.

April 27.   We have drifted 140 days now. Our strength is gone. We are waiting our time to come.

May 5.   From morning to 6 p.m. it was clear. And I [Matsumoto] being ill, I could no longer stand at the wheel but I had to guide the ship. I cannot lose my life.

May 6.   Captain Tokizo Miki became very ill.

May 10.   No clouds. Northwest wind. hard wind and high waves. Ship adrift with rolled up sails. Ship speeding forward south-west. I am suffering the captains complaints. Illness.

Thus the final entry by the dying Matsumoto. The *Ryo Yei Maru* continued in the North Pacific Drift for nearly six more months before the lookout on the *Margaret Dollar* sighted her off the northwest coast of Washington.

—0—

On November 3, 1927, Captain Robert Dollar, President of the Dollar Steamship Company, telegraphed Japanese Consul Kawamura in Seattle expressing sorrow at the tragedy. He disclaimed all salvage rights to the *Ryo Yei Maru* then offered to carry the craft as deck cargo to the owners in Japan on the *SS President Madison* which was soon to sail to the Orient. Captain Dollar recommended that the vessel be sold and the proceeds be distributed to the families of the fishermen.

The families cabled their answer declining the offer saying the evil spirits on the bewitched vessel would cause the people of the village where she was owned to leave.

She, the ship, was cursed by *Konpira* from the moment she was launched in the spring of 1926, they lamented, for she was the first ship of her kind to flaunt tradition, being the first "great ship – five times the size" of vessels that had been used by Japanese in that area throughout centuries.

To offset the wrath of *Konpira,* they said, on her maiden voyage, the crew sailed her 250 miles down the coast to *Konpira's* shrine, where the ancient ritual of dedicating the vessel to the god was scrupulously observed.

It was to no avail.

On November 3, the two withered bodies were cremated in Seattle. On November 7, black-robed Chyoaui Ike, a Buddhist priest, chanted last rites before an improvised, incense burning alter in a Seattle mortuary. On the alter were the weathered cedar board with is scrawled message of last hope, an urn containing the ashes of the two bodies, and nine small envelopes with the locks of hair.

The death ship's career ended December 19 when she was towed to Richmond Beach, on Puget Sound north of Seattle, where it was soaked with oil then it was burned where she had been beached.

There is a morbid irony in the translation of the vessel's name for *Ryo Yei Maru* means "Good and Prosperous." □

—77—

Admiral Benson With Her Nose in the Air
Stranded February 15, 1930 —abandoned

Lost in the fog as she entered the Columbia River, the passenger liner *Admiral Benson* (Captain C. Graham) stranded at 6:45 p.m. near Peacock Spit. The Point Adams and Cape Disappointment Coast Guard Stations dispatched 36-foot motor lifeboats immediately on notification.

The skipper did not send an SOS but rather played down his stranding by only requesting assistance.

Whoops!

The "Always Ready" Coast Guard ordered its cutter *Redwing* to the scene but the cutter failed to respond as her boilers were cold.*

---

* On being "Always Ready": At the beginning of the American Naval action at the historic Battle of Santiago in the Spanish-American War, when without notice the U. S. Navy's heavy fighting ships should have left the blockade and instantly responded to the Spanish ships' sudden efforts to escape the harbor, the only American fighting ship "ready for action" with full steam up was the battleship *Oregon*. As a result, by the time the other ships were ready, the *Oregon* had sunk all the Spaniards and won the engagement nearly single hand-

The 3,049-ton 300-foot long vessel was built for 200 passengers but as this was the era of the Great Depression, there were only 39 plus the 65 in the crew. Although everyone was rescued over a two-day period – the ship did not seem to be at any risk of sinking or capsizing – some of the tourists let their extreme displeasure in having to slide down a wet rope be known.

> ## Slippery Roller-Coaster
>
> **Mrs. A. B. Reynolds, Portland, was the first to be evacuated by breeches buoy. She got dunked, came up gasping after swallowing sea water, lost her hat, had a frenzied trip and on landing declared, "I always wanted to ride one of those things."**

After her experience, the Coast Guard took the rest of the survivors off a few at a time in their 36-foot boats.

Captain Graham had every intention of refloating his ship. On the morning of February 18th, the last of the passengers left followed by non-seaman staff – stewards and musicians. Then the crew turned its attention to refloating the ship. But the wind kicked up, the sea seemed to be revolting because the ship was in its water, and hope for any fast solution to the stranding was vanishing by the minute.

The Coast Guard, in running its breeches buoy had to handle lines that ran 400-yards to the ship which was west of the north jetty. Although by now the skipper was becoming somewhat dazed at the prospect of losing his ship, Captain Graham stayed on board, a lone figure, as everyone else had been evacuated.

It was not until February 24, that the captain signaled the Coast Guard that he was ready to abandon his ship.

What happened?

It appears that in taking a course from the Columbia River lightship, the ship either veered or drifted northward in a thick mist (fog) with the officers taking a bearing on the wreck of the *Laurel* that had been lost about eight months earlier, instead of on a range buoy. The captain was found guilty of negligence and had his license suspended for six months.

edly. For the dramatic moments refer to *Battleship Oregon; Bulldog of the Navy*. See bibliography

Admiral Benson became a spectacle and a warning to ship captains of potential disaster at the Columbia River Bar.

The great warning to mariners about entering the Columbia River has never changed. Ship masters must be constantly vigilant as to the hazards and wait for rough water to calm. One of the first ships over the bar, the *Tonquin* (Captain Jonathan Thorne) on March 22, 1811, lost two of its boats and eight men within a few hours trying to sound the bar in poor conditions. The *Laurel* had been lost on June 16, 1929. Some years later, lost in another fog, a ship actually rammed the beached remains of the *Admiral Benson*.

The *Benson* was never refloated, but salvage crews, using a tram on a fixed line, removed most of the cargo, instruments and other valuables. The vessel settled into the sand by the hull with the bow sticking into the sky on a sharp angle. ☐

Disaster Hits Grays Harbor Fishermen
13 Boats Lost, 17 Fishermen Drown in One Day
April 5, 1933

Grays Harbor Hit By Worst Disaster In Port's History

The first newspaper reports proclaimed that 19 fishermen were feared lost but as more details became available, the Coast Guard reduced the count to 17.

A violent gale suddenly descended trapping trollermen outside the bar. In all, about 200 boats were at risk scattered from Astoria to north of Grays Harbor. As the storm abated, wreckage was strewn along the beaches. The Aberdeen *World* proclaimed it was the "worst tragedy in the history of the fishing industry" on the harbor.

There were over 40 boats still at sea the following day riding out the storm unable to cross the bar due to the continuing high winds. There was fear that some of the boats might run out of gasoline before they could get in.

The Coast Guard saved two men then issued a report of the wreckage ashore and known missing boats by 2 p.m. April 6th:

Axel (Astoria) Swan Johnson, Alex Backlund missing.
Wreckage on south jetty.
Pacific (Hoquiam) Alex Forsal on board. Only the name plate found on beach.
Caroline (Astoria) Oscar Hauru rescued by Coast Guard but his son Emil, missing.
J-232 (Astoria) Nick Hekkila. Bow of boat found on beach.
Ellen (Westport) Wayne Wade, Victor Bjornson, D.L. Beatty. Name plate only found on beach.
Annie (Aberdeen) Jack and Wayne Salno. Boat seen upside down on bar, then found on shore at Grayland.
Alki (Aberdeen) Charles Pietola and Joel Salo.
Norma B and 2 numbered boats (Astoria) Ellias Bellman, Walter Manula, John Kullander
Numbered boat (Astoria) Matt Lehtinen

Small boat (Astoria) Uno Sjoros
M-384 (Bay Center)
J-3179 (Astoria) Alfred Haas of Portland
Large white boat (Seattle) believed to be carrying at least 2 men
Thelma (Bay City) Virgil Pickernell and a second Indian plausibly refuged in
      Willapa Bay but the Coast Guard said it was sure the *Thelma* went
      down.

The Coast Guard's M. J. Bernhardt, in charge of the motor lifeboat that picked up Oscar Hauru, Astoria, and William Lappalaine, Aberdeen, said that the same huge wave that swamped the *Thelma* flooded his engine compartment. He reported that he saw four boats go over. Most boats foundered when caught in giant troughs at the south spit.

Coast Guardsmen asserted there would have been many more lives saved if fishermen had followed the simple expedient of donning lifebelts when entering dangerous water on the bar.

Night Searching at Sea

The big Coast Guard cutters, *Redwing* and *Snohomish,* had been sent to the scene and maintained all night patrols looking for survivors. But a spokesman, who refused to be named, said that night searches are far less likely to find a struggling survivor or a body than daylight searches. He said it had always been Coast Guard policy to turn out for night searches when there was a person known to be missing if weather permitted.

Henry Hendrickson, Astoria, on the *Alf,* said while his boat was being tossed about on the bar, a really big comber pitched another boat onto his deck. The impact threw Hendrickson into the water except one of his feet caught in the rigging allowing him to pull himself back aboard while his partner steadied the vessel.

> Of the 15 to 25 men who were believed to have been thrown into the sea, only two were rescued by the Coast Guard.

Hauru had been saved from the *Caroline,* then from the rescue boat he saw his son Emil go down as the lifeboat sailors made frantic efforts to pick him up. At least 15 times, the Coast Guard worked their boat close to the boy only to have great breakers toss them apart. During one episode, the boy vanished.

Lappalaine was rescued by the same Coast Guard boat. His little "tent boat" was drifting onto the south spit when the Coast Guard, at considerable hazard, managed to pull in close enough to take him aboard. At least 40 more small fish-boats, on seeing the raging breakers on the bar, turned out to sea to wait for better weather. Two Coast Guard motor lifeboats, carrying extra gasoline, patrolled with this off-shore flotilla to be able to service any of the boats that ran out of fuel.

Women and children – hundreds of them – as well as fishermen who had not been out on the sea, set up a 5-mile long beach patrol looking for the missing fishermen.

Hulls of some of the boats, a keel, a pilot house, a deck rail, masts, heaps of tackle, a rudder, hull planks and other parts from the boats, were being washed ashore on the high tides. Some men from outside the area tried to claim salvage on boat parts, especially engines, but were summarily over-ruled by fishermen who banded together and ran them off.

Emil Reikkola, a veteran local fisherman, who had spent 13 years in the off-shore trolling business, described the scene of the rough sea from his 37-foot long troller *Walrus* as "mountainous" during which waves washed over his prow giving him difficulty keeping his own boat under control. He said at times he seemed to be among many boats all trying to make it safely over the bar then, after a giant comber crashed in their midst, he seemed all alone.

Riekkola said the storm came up with amazing speed and fury. He had been out all morning on a smooth sea when the wind whipped up so he decided to quit work and head for safety inside the bar.

Loss of the *Alki*

One of the first boats down, the *Alki* was sighted by a nearby vessel plowing through the water at top sped. She was down at the stern, all her rigging was gone and her crew of two was clinging to the bow. The boat rolled completely over with engine still roaring, then resumed, in its battered condition, toward the bar until water drowned the engine. Her crew, Charles Pietola and Joel Salo, were swept to death by a comber that swamped the boat.

Ellias Bellman, of the 30-foot troller *Norma B,* reported missing at Grays Harbor, brought his vessel into Astoria. He was outside the Grays Harbor bar and was in the clear of the bar breakers, when he reversed course to go after the *Derna* which had just had its cabin smashed and was lifeless with a disabled engine. He said aboard the *Derna* was a single elderly gentleman whom he urged to get into the *Norma B* but the man refused. But suddenly the storm whipped up a comber that swamped his *Norma B* with such a whack it took away the mast and all gear.

His immediate attention was to his own now disabled craft and he did not see what became of the *Derna.* He took an oar and managed to turn his boat into the wind then six huge waves, one right after the other, struck. Bellman hung breathlessly to the anchor windless while wreckage flew around him battering him black and blue. The boat was filling with seawater and was drifting to the south. From about 1 p.m. Wednesday until about 1 p.m. Thursday, Bellman bailed frantically to keep his boat afloat and when possible, to try to restart the engine. No luck with the engine but he bailed enough to clear the galley stove. He got a fire going by shorting battery wires in oil. He said he would have "frozen to death" without the fire.

Early Thursday he determined his powerless craft was drifting toward the breakers at Willapa Bay entrance. With his revolver at hand he said he considered ending his life rather than to be tossed about on the Willapa bar then be thrown into the churning sea to drown. As death seemed to be approaching, his engine started. He headed out to sea.

The cutter *Redwing* ran between him and the shore looking for survivors and wreckage but it was now night time, he had no lights, and was not seen. Finally, a troller, the *Lulu,* came alongside and the two boats plodded through the waves to the *Columbia River Lightship.* After a little tinkering on his engine there, he and the *Lulu* made it over the Columbia bar into Astoria.

While he was at sea after being battered and damaged, he had no food to eat except 6 eggs. He ate them raw. □

Vazlav Vorovsky with mud-hook down, is stranded and broken.

—79—
Soviet *Vazlav Vorovsky* Succombs in Yankee Land
Stranded April 3, 1941 —sank

The Soviet Union held its sea captains in high esteem for it was they who brought life-saving munitions from North America to its ports. The *Vazlav Vorovsky* (Captain Simon Tokareff) was not a very big ship as freighters go, but this 1912 British-built vessel of 4,793-tons did its share. That is, it did until the fateful day of April 3, 1941. The *"Vaz"* as some of the Coast Guard men later called her, was 374-feet long with 52-foot beam. Under the pilotage of George Conway, a licensed bar pilot, the freighter was moving out-bound, a little after midnight, with a full load of freight, making limited headway in the face of a 40-knot southerly gale that sprung up.

The captain and the pilot tried to turn the ship to head back toward Astoria when the helmsman suddenly lost control over the rudder. Almost at once, the ship stranded on Peacock Spit only half-a-mile from Cape Disappointment lighthouse.

The crashing breakers, pushed by the gale, claimed the ship right from the start by pounding on it so hard the hull creaked.

223

Soviet freighter _Vazlav Vorovsky_ went hard aground on Peacock Spit during storm. Coast Guard, in 52-foot lifeboat _Triumph_, rescued crew. Ship broke up, sank.

The Coast Guard responded promptly with three motor lifeboats, including the 52-foot _Triumph_ from Point Adams Coast Guard Station. Chief Motor Machinist's Mate George W. Cooper commanded the _Triumph_ on that rescue. He told the authors about the conditions of the rescue of the 37 members of the ship's crew. *

The sea was coming over us and I was amazed that we did not roll in the breakers. We had a rough enough time just reaching the _Vaz_. We coordinated the other two boats [36-foot motor lifeboats] and between us we were able to take the crew off the ship. We were amazed to observe that two of the crew were women. I was afraid the ship would break up and sink risking our boats. We did not have a Russian interpreter on the _Triumph_ but somehow word was conveyed to us that the captain refused to leave the ship.

Just 24-hours later, Captain Tokareff, seeing his vessel start to break up, agreed to let the Coast Guard take him ashore. The _Vazlav Vorovsky_ broke into three parts. The cargo of heavy machinery and general freight, worth $1,750,000 was a total loss.

In mid-morning after the grounding, Chief Cooper recalled he

---

* This interview was in 1974 when Lt. Cdr. Cooper, (USN-ret) lived in Grants Pass, Ore. Cooper was also the skipper of the _Manana II_ on station off the bar the night of the Japanese Navy's attack on Fort Stevens in June 1942. Cooper was the closest American to the Japanese and considered ramming the enemy. For his experience, see _Silent Siege-III_ in biblio.

**Mary Ann Tichenor Cooper
with cut-glass goblet from
the *Vazlav Vorovsky***

went back to the *Vazlav Vorovsky* ferrying some officials. While there, he retrieved a wine goblet which he gave to his wife.

Local fishermen stopped by the broken ship to pick up whatever they could carry away.

The high tides following the breakup deposited thousands of shipping cases of goods on the beaches. Men from the 249th Coast Artillery, stationed on both sides of the mouth of the Columbia River, retrieved much goods, especially dozens of cases of butter. All of this was excellent "booty." Some of the butter got into the mess halls and other cases were kept by a few of the soldiers who, with their wives, had set up housekeeping. □

—80—
Daring Coast Guard Rescue Saves *Lamut* Crew
Stranded April 1, 1943 —abandoned

Teahwhit Head is a jagged double point 100 feet high just 2.4 miles from La Push, Washington. The head is considered to be a part of what's called the "Quillayute Needles" although Quillayute Needle is an 81-foot tall spire in its own right just over one mile to the west-northwest of Teahwhit Head. For a large ship, a freighter in this case, the *Lamut,* to tightly lodge itself at Teahwhit Head between the rocks, was indeed an Act of God as no pilot could put it there purposely.

Soviet freighter *Lamut* became stuck at Teahwhit Head near LaPush. In center on ledge, left of arrow, is Coast Guard Beach Patrol on emergency rescue mission.

—map from *Silent Siege-III*

NORTHWEST COAST BEACH PATROL

With the ship laying in her side, there was no chance to salvage cargo from the *Lamut* when the ship was forced between rocks during wild storm. Only the ingenuity of the Coast Guard saved the crew.

For shear drama of men against the sea, the rescue of the crew of this Soviet freighter is an outstanding feat in the annals of Coast Guard history. The ship became hung up between the rocks about 11 p.m. on April 1, 1943, according to the Coast Guard's records. The 75-knot wind was whipping the sea and the vessel while heavy rain mercilessly pelted everything under it. In this daze, the Soviet ship ran in between the rocks and tipped onto its starboard side.

> The stranded *Lamut* was discovered by Tyler Hobucket, a Coast Guard Beach Patrolman, while he walked his beat. Using his back-pack radio, he called his headquarters at LaPush and told them of his discovery.

In the initial excitement of the crash, the crew, unaware of the rocks around them, tried to lower a lifeboat. The effort proved to be a disaster for a davit cable broke dropping the bow of the boat into the water critically injuring 19-year old Antonia Shmeliova. Koshova Alexandra, also 19, was killed when a rolling oil drum struck her on the head and knocked her overboard. *

A Coast Guard 36-foot motor lifeboat from the LaPush Beach Patrol Station attempted to reach the *Lamut* early in the morning, but was unsuccessful. Meanwhile, a shore party hacked a trail through the swampy rain forest to the beach. Two miles south of the wrecked ship the Coast Guardsmen broke through and began the hard and dangerous climb over wet, slippery, spray-swept rocks to the top of the cliff against which the ship was pinned.

From a narrow ledge near the summit, the shore party could look down on the slanting deck and huddled survivors of the storm-wracked ship. On the other side of this towering barricade of rock on which they were perched, they could see the sandy beach at the head of little Strawberry Bay only large enough to shelter a few fishboats from high winds. The beach patrolmen did not have special equipment and could not wait for the rescue group that was following overland with equipment and ropes.

How to get a line down to the ship when they did not have any rope with them was their concern. The patrolmen at the scene had to improvise. Each man wore over-the-ankle boots. If they took all of their boot laces and tied them together would this make a light line that would reach the vessel? One of the men unlaced a boot and measured the lace. Multiply that length with the number of laces available. Would this length reach the deck of the ship? A nice idea but not long enough. What could they use?

On the belt of each man was a small metal first aid kit. Within this kit was a long roll of gauze bandage. If all ten of the bandage rolls were tied together the needed length would be available – barely. But gauze stretches. They promptly assembled this emergency "rope," tied a rock to one end, then gingerly drop-

---

* Her body was discovered at the high tide line on the nearby beach after the storm by Coast Guard Beach Patrolman Tyler Hobucket. She was very pregnant and very naked except for a bright red pair of panties.

Surviving women crew members from wrecked Soviet freighter *Lamut* were given clothing by Seattle Salvation Army. A Coast Guardsman rescuer said the lady sailors were "husky, bulky" and had "big feet" so the Salvation Army bought each lady a pair of carefully fit shoes.
—Photo by Glenn Barkhurst

ped the weighted end over the side of the cliff to the deck of the ship below. Then a heavier line was tied to it on the ship and by doing this several times each time with a heavier line, the cable became strong enough to carry one person at a time from the ship to the ledge near the top of the cliff where the rescuers were waiting.

One by one the survivors were pulled to the safety of the ledge. From there, they made the climb to the top then down the other side to the beach. The injured girl had been lashed to a stretcher. Pulling her from the ship to the ledge and on over the top was especially difficult, but the patrolmen finally got her to the beach.

By this time, additional helpers had gathered on the beach. First aid to the injured was given by a surgeon of the U. S. Public Health Service and an Army medical detail.

The Russian crew of 40 men and 9 women, obviously happy to be alive, trudged through the swamp with their rescuers to waiting Coast Guard trucks and ambulances. They were taken to the Marine Hospital (operated by the Public Health Service) in Seattle for observation. The elapsed time between the time of the wreck and the rescue was just 24 hours. The Seattle newspapers made a big play on the subject.

This incident illustrates the dedication and ingenuity of the men who made up the Coast Guard's Beach Patrol. They were tough, courageous, and smart. □

—81—
Saga of the *Diamond Knot* and Canned Salmon
Collision August 13, 1947 —sank

What's one's first thought after being curled and asleep in a bunk in a ship when the sudden wrenching crash and jar knocks one onto the deck at 1:15 in the morning? So it was on August 13, 1947 for the *MS Diamond Knot* (Captain C. N. Goodwin) about six miles west of Port Angeles in a heavy fog.

The *Fenn Victory*, (Captain Joseph Gaidsick), a 10,681-ton freighter, crashed the starboard side of the *Diamond Knot* only half the big freighter's size at 5,525-tons. The bow of the freighter hit the smaller vessel at a right-angle causing a gash that extended 14-feet into her side. The ships radioed SOS. Quickly, the salvage tugs *Matilda Foss* and *Foss No. 21* arrived from Port Angeles.

On board the *Diamond Knot*, cutting torches were used to separate the ships. Free at last, the damaged ship, carrying a super-load of freshly processed canned salmon from Bristol Bay, Alaska, was taking on water in two of its holds. The tugs headed for shallow water near Crescent Beach but at 8:45 a.m., still in deep water, the ship started to settle and ten minutes later, the tugs were forced to cut loose.

The *Diamond Knot* rolled on her starboard side and sank under the Strait of Juan de Fuca in 135 feet of water. In her holds were 7,407,168 cans of salmon worth a small fortune. In addition, there were hundreds of gallons of bulk fish oil in tanks. The major insurance claims were staggering being over $3,395,000. There was also lost a cannery tender, and an automobile that had been on the *Diamond Knot's* deck: $16,000. The sum of bills from crew members who lost of personal items was another $12,000.

The insurance companies, reeling from the losses, decided to go fishing for the fish that was once already caught and now rested in tin cans in the sunken ship. Time was of the essence.

A diver, Walter McCray, anchored his barge *Diver III* above the *Diamond Knot*. When he and his assistant Fred Devine came up from the under-water survey, McCray and others went into consultations with Walter Martignoni, a salvage master of San

Francisco just four days later. It was determined that raising the ship was impractical and just the cargo was to be brought up.

How?

Try a super vacuum cleaner! The first effort was to go after the bulk fish oil. This was done by attaching a suction hose to the lowest part of the tank. Then, install an air hose in the top of the tank, the tank otherwise sealed, the hose run to the surface. As pressurized air was forced into the top of the fish oil tank, the oil was forced into the lower hose then out the end of the hose at the surface into containers. It worked and over $20,000 in fish oil was reclaimed from the *Diamond Knot*. Would this system work on tin cans of fish?

The planning for the next operation had to be closely coordinated. Many divers would have to be located and brought to the job as the work, to be successful, would have to continue day and night and regardless of the weather. This was against the possibility that the canned fish would spoil if haste was not the order of the day. With receiving barges anchored over the wreck, the divers cut away a section of the hull exposing some 2-million one-pound cans of salmon. With the suction hose in place, air compressors forced water through jet openings in the bottom of the ship at 300-pounds pressure. This pressure tore open the sea water soaked cardboard cartons exposing the tin cans. The "vacuum cleaner" sucked up everything in front of the hose, mostly cans of salmon and sea water to a rate of about 800 cans a minute. The cans were spewed into the barges as amazed newsreel cameramen and newspaper photographers shot pictures. A shuttle of barges had to be ready as each barge, when filled, had to be towed away and another moved quickly into place. Each carried about 300,000 cans.

The siphoning out of the *Diamond Knot* finally stopped on October 29, that date being 77 days after the ship went down.

The tally:

> 7,407,168 cans sank with the ship
> 5,744,498 cans sucked from the sunken ship
> 4,179,360 cans salable
>   240,000 cans inaccessible – left in the wreck
> Miscellaneous number of cans scattered and unclaimed
> Gross recovery of product in dollars: $2,100,100.

When the lengthy investigation then the hearing to determine cause of the collision was concluded, it was decided there had been mutual fault. No lives had been lost on either ship but, Captain Gaidsick of the *Fenn Victory*, in a deep depression because of the blot on his record, later hanged himself

Although small attempts to salvage sunken cargo by suction had been experimented with earlier, the method applied on a large scale by vacuuming of the holds of the *Diamond Knot* proved the system was practical for major jobs. ☐

—82—
Andalusia Snagged
Stranded November 4, 1949 —sank

The SOS sent by the radioman on the *Andalusia* (Captain George Lemos), brought the Coast Guard cutter *Fir* and a motor lifeboat to the ship which was snagged on a reef just four miles east from Neah Bay. The ship of 7,770-tons, was loaded with five million feet of Canadian lumber.

The skipper had been awakened on November 4, 1949 at 4:25 and told that there was fire in the engine room. Details of exactly what was happening were confused because of the assorted languages among the foreign crew. They could not understand each other. The Coast Guard took off most of them, including a woman stewardess, then fought the fire. They had it out in an hour-and-a-half.

In the meantime, salvage tugs, where the SOS had been monitored, showed up looking for work. By four days later, the insurance people had finished their inspection then grim-faced, told the captain it was a toss-up if his ship and its lumber could be saved as the hull was cracked and water was coming in. With that, and a gale blowing up from the west, Captain Lemos had the Coast Guard take him and the remainder of his crew ashore.

A review of the charts showed that the *Andalusia* was on a jagged reef surrounded by deep water. The freighter was balanced on this fulcrum of rock therefore the chances seemed to be about even for survival or death. If freed, the vessel could sink or, the ship could stay afloat due to the huge cargo of lumber. The salvage men considered the odds then, combining the tugs, tried to

ANDALUSIA

unhook the freighter from its perilous pointed perch putting pulling power together. It didn't work.

Five days after being stranded, with a stiff gale howling through the rigging, the vessel broke apart prompting a terse message to the owners.

> ALL SALVAGE OPERATIONS UNSUCCESSFUL. VESSEL HAD BROKEN IN TWO. AFTER SECTION SANK. DURING HEAVY WEATHER NOVEMBER 9, BROKE ABAFT FUNNEL IN TWO PIECES. AFTER PART NOW SUNK IN 50 FEET OF WATER; FORWARD PART FAST ON REEF. TUGS ENDEAVORING TO FREE FORWARD PART AND SALVE ON "NO CURE, NO PAY" BASIS, BUT DOUBTFUL WHETHER THEY WILL FLOAT IT FREE.

The fore part of the vessel eventually sank freeing the deck load of dimension lumber. But salvage by local folks was not a take-it-home-and-keep-it matter as shipwrecked cargo often is, for this was foreign (Canadian) lumber subject to duty if landed in the U.S. The Customs agents had a field day with those folks it could locate. □

—83—
Yorkmar in Trouble but She Was Saved
Stranded December 8, 1952 —salvaged

During a typical northwest coast winter storm, the steamer *SS Yorkmar* (Captain Oscar Kullbom), in ballast, was off the Grays Harbor bar. The pilot boat could not cross the roaring bar so the freighter had to stay at sea another two days. Finally, the skipper was allowed to cross the bar to avoid damage by the ocean.

Under way, the *Yorkmar*, nearing the north jetty was caught by a high wind as the tide crested nearly throwing the ship ashore leaving her stranded, broadside, near the beach. When the tide retreated, the vessel was sitting almost on dry sand.

Fred Devine, a noted salvage man, brought in his *Salvage Chief* to refloat the vessel. But he had to sit out three days on his tugboat because of high seas.

After getting the salvage started, and while the Coast Guard maintained constant watch to determine if it had to move in to take off the 37 crew members, the tugboat put in to Aberdeen for more hawser. This was because what it had brought to the scene had been broken in salvage attempts. At one point, an anchor line broke forcing the *Salvage Chief* to drop the line to the stranded ship to keep herself off the beach.

The owners, Calmar Steamship Corporation, brought in San Francisco salvage master Walter Martignoni for ideas. Between he and Devine, and a calm sea that finally arrived, the tugboat again took her place. With anchors and lines again placed, and with the tide in his favor, Devine started his gentle but firm pull and the *Yorkmar* slowly started for deep water. But she got only about 200 feet when the tide ebbed with the ship again stranded.

By now it was December 18th. Ten days had passed since the mishap. When the 12-foot high tide was nearing its crest, the *Salvage Chief,* along with the tug *Sea Lion*, acted as a sea-anchor to brace the *Salvage Chief.* With propellers churning sea water, the two tugboats slowly worked the freighter off the beach and into deep water. The pull was undoubtedly aided by the fact that the 7,200-ton ship was riding high as it did not contain a heavy load of freight.

The *Yorkmar* got steam up as the tow moved out to sea to be certain of not ending up on the beach a second time.

During the investigation that followed, the Coast Guard determined that the captain of the freighter tried to cross the Grays Harbor bar without a pilot's license. But the examining officer for the Coast Guard contended that a...

...realistic approach is meant in enforcing the navigation laws and the captain acted in a way which his best judgment told him was proper.

The charges against Captain Kullbom were dropped. The freighter went to Portland for dry-docking. Following inspection, and a replacement for her bent prop, the captain and the *Yorkmar* sailed again. ☐

Although *Seagate* appears peaceful, she is hard aground, soon broke in two then sank.

—84—
Stranded *Seagate* Seized For Salvage – Sinks
Beached October 31, 1924 –abandoned

Blaming a faulty gyro compass and heavy fog, the *Seagate* was about 100 miles off course on its run to Vancouver B. C. from Japan. The vessel stranded September 9, 1956 on Sonora Reef (47°18'54N - 124°18'31W) southeast of Cape Elizabeth, off the Washington coast. Its crew was off-loaded by the Coast Guard.

Although salvage tugboats worked for a number of days to pull the ship into deep water, their efforts were for naught and they left. The *Seagate*, now abandoned, slipped off her perch by herself then stranded near the beach about 30 miles north of Grays Harbor. A Coast Guard cutter, the *Wachusett*, on patrol out of Seattle, found the derelict ashore south of the Quinault River, about one mile south of Cape Elizabeth. There was a race by large salvagers for the prize but the small tugboat *A. G. Hubble*, from Grays Harbor, beat the larger tugs to the scene and put three men on the deck of the freighter. It did not seem much of a prize however for the vessel broke in two pieces and eventually sank. ☐

U.S. Coast Guard 52-foot self-righting motor lifeboat *Invincible*.

—85—
Barbara Lee and the *Invincible*
Barbara Lee: Stranded January 28, 1960 —salvaged
Invincible: Capsized January 28, 1960 —salvaged

"There was heroism and tragedy on the gale-lashed, scud-shrouded Grays Harbor bar" on January 28, 1960 wrote Clark Cottrell, a reporter for the *Aberdeen Daily World.*

The 56-foot crab boat, *Barbara Lee,* was standing off the heaving bar waiting for calmer conditions when her skipper radioed the Coast Guard at 2:45 p.m. giving his position and a weather report. He asked for bar conditions and informed that he was going to bring his boat over the bar. When situations as this one arise, in adverse weather and poor visibility, the Coast Guard may send an escort boat to patrol the bar whether requested or not. On this date, the crew of the 52-foot motor lifeboat *Invincible* (CG-52300) was alerted, then the boat cast off for the bar.

Normally, the Coast Guard vessel dispatched on bar patrol under such conditions remains inside the bar near buoy No. 8 but in this case, the coxswain of the *Invincible* was unable to accurately observe the bar conditions so proceeded outside for a better look. After affecting a rendezvous and holding a shouting conversation between the boats in the howling wind, both vessels proceeded in crossing the bar, the *Barbara Lee* being slightly in front and about 300-feet to starboard of the *Invincible* during the first part of the transit. The Coast Guard acknowledged that the *Barbara Lee* had not requested assistance.

After the storm, the beach claimed what was left
of the *Barbara Lee*.　—Westport-South Beach Hist. Soc.

The *Barbara Lee* was overwhelmed in the breakers on
the north spit while giving aid to the *Invincible* and its
four-man crew after the *Invincible* capsized then righted
itself but had lost its power. When the *Barbara Lee*
swamped, two of the three men on the boat were washed
overboard and drowned. The third man was rescued.

When the skipper of the crabber, Robert Bolam, saw the
Coast Guard boat in trouble, he immediately put about to render
assistance. Bolam also radioed the Coast Guard base saying that
the *Invincible* had capsized and they were in the breakers and he
was trying to take the 52-foot *Invincible* in tow but the line kept
breaking. That was the last contact with either boat.

The third man on the *Barbara Lee*, Harold Pernula, was also
washed overboard but he was miraculously rescued by the
Invincible in the midst of the turmoil.

The Coast Guard immediately dispatched a 36-foot motor
lifeboat from Westport and the cutter *McLane* from Aberdeen as
well as the cutter *Yacona* from Astoria to render aid.

The storm's winds were howling between 50 and 60 knots.

At 8:17 p.m., the *McLane* located the powerless *Invincible*
and the disabled 36-foot lifeboat, which quit running when it developed a broken oil line. The 52-footer has drifted six miles north

Service for victims of the storm was held at the Fisherman's Memorial at Westport, Washington.
—Westport-South Beach Hist. Soc.

of its last reported position at the bar.

Both the *Yacona* and the *McLane* patrolled the area searching for the missing crab men, Bolam and Ted Sigurdson. Both were commercial fishermen and both had drowned when swept from their boat.

At 7 o'clock the next morning, the hulk of the crab boat was found stranded off the mouth of the Copalis River. The wheelhouse was smashed. There was no one was on board. There was wreckage on the beach which included two life jackets.

Immediately after the cutters had put lines aboard the damaged *Invincible* and the disabled 36-boat, they were unable to cross the Grays Harbor bar due to the continuing storm. Headquarters ordered the cutters to each tow a boat through the crashing sea all the way to Neah Bay, the nearest haven.

The *McLane* remained at Neah Bay to tow the lifeboats back to Grays Harbor after minimum repairs had been made. The *Yocona* was immediately ordered back to sea to patrol off the Washington coast as the three Grays Harbor boats were out of service at Neah Bay.

The *Invincible* while flipped, had its windows smashed, which caused a facial gash to one of her crew. The other men were shaken and soaked but all right. She also lost her running and towing lights and her searchlight. The engine could not be restarted as the craft had taken water down its stack. Damage to

The *Barbara Lee* was rebuilt and sailed again.
—Westport-South Beach Hist. Soc.

the 36-boat was minimal and its crew of three was unharmed. Other than having the broken oil line which put the boat out of business, heavy waves broke the running lights.

The *Barbara Lee,* owned by Roy Furfiord, was salvaged from the beach and taken to a shipyard in Hoquiam for major rebuilding.

On July 28, 1962, Captain E. V. Carlson, USCG, Operations Officer for the 13th Coast Guard District, presented the nation's highest lifesaving award, the Treasury Department's Gold Lifesaving Medal to Mrs. Mary Louise Sigurdson, widow of Ted Sigurdson, and one to Mrs. Onalue Bolam, widow of Robert Bolam. The ceremony, at the Fishermans Memorial on Point Chehalis in Westport, were posthumous tributes for

> ...extreme and heroic daring [while attempting to aid the stricken *Invincible*] after taking a large breaker that immobilized her engine and left her drifting seaward with the tide. In the process of rendering aid, the *Barbara Lee* foundered and Bolam and Siguardson perished.

At the close of the simple ceremony, wreaths were left at the Fisherman's Memorial as the Veterans of Foreign Wars squad fired a salute. □

Coast Guard Rescuers Drown
During Valiant Rescue Try
January 13, 1961 — January 11, 1991

> Seven men died and three Coast Guard rescue vessels were lost, including the valiant 52-foot motor lifeboat *Triumph* (CG52301); a 36-foot motor lifeboat (CG36454); a 40-foot patrol boat; and the commercial fish boat *Mermaid*, at the Columbia River bar on January 13, 1961.

The earliest report read:

One man was dead and six more were missing in gale winds and churning seas at the mouth of the Columbia River that sank three Coast Guard boats and one fishing vessel. —*The Daily Astorian*

As the days wore on and details became available, the story got worse.

Swells of from 10 to 20 feet were breaking on the bar and wind howled at 45 miles per hour. The cutter *Yocona* from Tongue Point Coast Guard Base and two 36-foot self-righting motor lifeboats from Point Adams Coast Guard Station, as well as a helicopter from Coast Guard Astoria Air Station, and beach patrol parties on both sides of the mouth of the Columbia River looked all night for possible survivors. They went unrewarded.

End of an Era

This rescue mission brought to a tragic end the long life of the *Triumph*, the 52-foot self-righting motor lifeboat that had been stationed at the Point Adams Station. The *Triumph* was one of two sisters designed in 1934 for the rough Columbia River bar and the Grays Harbor bar. The boats had come to the northwest coast under their own power from the Atlantic coast in the mid 1930's by way of the Panama Canal. The *Triumph's* mate was the *Invincible* (CG52300) based at Westport, Washington. During the career of the *Triumph*, the lifeboat had gone to the aid of hundreds of stricken vessels large and small.

Lost At Sea

On January 12, 1961, near 4:20 p.m., a 40-foot patrol craft commanded by Darrell J. Murray, and a 36-foot lifeboat (CG-36454) commanded by Seaman Larry Edwards, departed from Cape Disappointment Station immediately to help the *Mermaid,* a 36-foot crab boat which was near buoy No. 1 outside the river. The 40-footer took the fishboat in tow. Two brothers, Bert and Stan Bergman from Ilwaco, Washington were on board.

The fishboat had radioed that it was drifting into the breakers on the Washington side of the river at Peacock Spit because it had lost its rudder. That message was relayed to shore by Roy Gunnari, Chinook, who was at sea in his boat. At 5 o'clock, the 40-foot patrol boat sent a message that it had the *Mermaid* in tow but as the bar conditions had worsened, questioned the wisdom of trying to make a bar transit with the tow. Point Adams responded saying for the 40-foot boat to stay where it was that the *Triumph* was on the way. The 52-footer, commanded by Boatswain's Mate John Culp, headed for the bar from Point Adams Station five minutes later.

Up until this time there was no thought of a pending disaster until 7:29 p.m. when the *Yocona* at Tongue Point east of Astoria and the cutter *Modoc*, based at Coos Bay, 200 miles to the south, were ordered to the scene.

The *Triumph* took the tow from the 40-footer then the two smaller boats headed for the bar to check conditions. The 40-foot patrol craft took heavy water in the stern and rolled over. Its three man crew were washed overboard. The 36-boat (CG36454) from Cape Disappointment Station came on the scene and luckily located the three men from the 40-footer and took them aboard. Very shortly afterward, another comber swamped the *Triumph* turning the 52-foot lifeboat upside-down. Apparently this was near buoy No. 7 off the tip of Peacock Spit. The *Mermaid*, near buoy No. 7, rescued one man, Engineer Joseph Petrin from the *Triumph*, but the others on board disappeared with the boat.

The *Mermaid* despite no rudder, worked itself out toward the sea through the breakers with its engine.

Taking water in the stern, the 36-boat radioed it was immediately heading for the safety of the *Columbia River Lightship*. In the meantime, word was received from the *Mermaid* that the 40-foot boat and the *Triumph* had capsized. Men were reported in the water. The mate on the pilot boat *Peacock*, said he got a radio appeal from the *Mermaid* for help after the *Triumph* was lost, but he could not respond as it was too dangerous to go into the breakers.

About 9:30 p.m., with the *Mermaid* now in tow by Boatswain Paul Miller's 36-boat, a huge wave, estimated to be between 25 and 40 feet high, rolled in and was about to break. His 36 rode over the top but the wave broke on the *Mermaid* which snapped the tow line. The fishboat, with its two crew and a survivor from the *Triumph* on board, simply vanished. Miller stayed in the area looking for it but saw nothing. In the meantime, Captain Kenneth McAlpin, Columbia River Bar Pilot, who was aboard the *Diaz de Solis*, a Spanish freighter outbound, said he saw the big wave capsize the *Mermaid* and that the boat had vanished. It was at this point that the all night search began.

> Nervousness on shore was intensified for those with short-wave radios who tuned in and listened to the terse messages as they flashed between the vessels, helicopter and shore search parties.

During the long stormy night, dozens of flares were dropped but there were no signs of the missing boats or survivors.

At 10 o'clock, word was flashed from a beach patrol advising that Engineman Gordon E. Huggins from the *Triumph* was alive and on the beach. He had been lying on the beach for between one and two hours when a two-man ground party from the Cape Disappointment Station found him. On seeing them, Huggins recalled "they looked like angels." But the ground men reported no sign of the boat.

During the night, the body of Boatswains Mate First Class John Culp was found on the Washington side. He was the commander of the *Triumph*. Huggins and Culp were the only two Coast Guardsmen identified during the night.

The crews from the 40-foot patrol craft and from the 36-boat were on the *Columbia River Lightship* having sought refuge there when it was judged impossible for the damaged 36-boat to transit the bar and make it back to Cape D Station. To assure the safety of the men on the way to the lightship, the bar pilot boat *Peacock* convoyed the Coast Guard boat to the lightship.

The voyage out to the lightship was novel-making material in itself. Forcing its way out of the Columbia River and into the ocean, the 36-boat ploughed through heavy swells taking a severe beating from the sea along the way. It took on water. On arrival, the men tied the boat to the lightship then clamored up a ladder to the deck. In the morning, on looking over the side, it was observed that the 36-boat had parted its line and had sunk.

During these deadly adventures, the cutter *Yocona* was continuing its search. The 110-foot long *Modoc* was to arrive at the Columbia River at the end of its speed run from Coos Bay, in the early afternoon.

Ten life jackets that were lost from both the *Triumph* and the 40-footer washed ashore along with small bits of wreckage.

Engineman Huggins, resting in bed at Ocean Beach Hospital at Ilwaco, Washington, said there were five men, including himself, on the *Triumph*. His boat apparently rolled while maneuvering to pick up the broken tow line from the *Mermaid*.

When she rolled, he was below deck in the engine compartment.

Huggins testified at a Board of Inquiry:

MERMAID

Astoria, Oregon, Saturday, January 14, 1961

Name plank from *Mermaid* washed ashore near North Head.
—Astoria Public Library

I was down below when it happened. The [*Triumph*] rolled completely over. The watertight door on the compartment was dogged shut. When the boat rolled, it stayed upside-down between 10 and 15 minutes. Although I tried to get the door open, it wouldn't budge. When the boat righted, the strain caused the door to fall off so I could get out. No one else was there and breakers were crashing over the boat. It was taking water by the bow.

Huggins recalled he tried to start the engine but it would not "catch." He sheltered himself beside one of the deck structures as the *Triumph* rode the waves for better than 45 minutes when a comber washed him off the derelict. In the next few minutes, he was hit and swept along by the off-shore breakers. As he tried to swim, his feet touched bottom and he discovered he was walking on sand – the beach below the tide line. He struggled out of the water then collapsed on the beach where the ground party found him.

—0—

●A piece of the pilot house from the Coast Guard 40-foot patrol craft washed up on the beach where it was recovered about 1½ miles north of Ocean Park. This is on the North Beach Peninsula in Washington.

●The men who had sought safety on the lightship were transported to Cape Disappointment Station.

●The remains of the *Mermaid* were found on the Long Beach Peninsula. The two-man crew was still missing.

●The *Yocona* and the *Modoc* were tied up at a dock in Astoria awaiting developments.

●Beach patrols on both sides of the river continued in the search for wreckage, survivors or corpses.

●Bar conditions were such that the trans-river ferry service, particularly on the Washington side, caused cancellation of at least one run of the boat,

●The storm had its affect in Astoria's harbor when the *Chokai Maru* and the *Empire State* drifted together after the Japanese freighter dragged its anchor. There was minor damage.

●The people in the families of the casualties included:

> Stan Bergman (*Mermaid*) left his wife and three children
> Bert Bergman (*Mermaid*) left his wife and one child
> Boatswains Mate John Culp (*Triumph* - commander)
>   left his wife and two children
> Boatswains Mate John Hoban (*Triumph*) left his wife
> Seaman Gordon Sussex (*Triumph*) – single
> Engineman Joseph Petrin (*Triumph*) – single
> Seaman Ralph Mace (*Triumph*) – single

●The weather reports indicated another storm was coming.

Another storm was certainly on the way – many more in fact, but especially a storm almost 30 years later to the day.

The newspaper reported:

Two dead, one missing after crippled fishing vessel sinks

Investigators from the National Transportation Board and the U. S. Coast Guard have launched separate probes into a Coast Guard rescue Friday that ended with the deaths of three people.   —*The Daily Astorian*

The Coast Guard's terse announcement said that Petty officer Charles Sexton, who was 37, an instructor at the National Motor Lifeboat School on Cape Disappointment, on the Washington side of the Columbia River, and David Haynes, 28, a fisherman from Astoria, were drowned on Friday January 11, 1991 when the *Sea King,* a commercial fishboat, rolled over and sunk while the Coast Guard's 52-foot motor lifeboat *Triumph* was towing it over the heaving bar. *

---

*The *Triumph* mentioned here is a replacement boat of the same 52-foot size as the earlier *Triumph* that was lost on the Columbia River bar in January 1961.

The Coast Guard further said one other person, John Blunt, 42, of Mantua, Ohio, was missing and was possibly trapped in the sunken boat.

The *Sea King* had left Astoria's East End Mooring Basin two days earlier for bottom fishing.

Lt. Cmdr. Dan Neptun, commander at Motor Lifeboat Station Cape Disappointment, said the capsizing was a surprise because just two minuets earlier both the *Triumph* and the *Sea King* messaged that everything was going well.

A Dolphin helicopter from Air Station Astoria had been called to the rescue, but had to abort trying to lift the crew from the *Sea King* when its rescue basket cable broke.

Haynes, one of the deceased, was being hoisted from the boat at 10:45 a.m., about 2 hours after the distress call, when the *Sea King* suddenly pitched and the overhead steel cable on the fishboat banged into the rescue basket and broke the line. This caused Haynes to fall about 12 feet to the deck.

Helicopter co-pilot Lt.jg Bill Harper believed that the cable might be tangled in the helicopter's blades.

The first indication from the left [pilot] seat was a sudden jolt followed by a vibration that diminished in a couple of seconds. It was typical of a malfunction associated with the rotor head or tail rotor. The first thought in my mind was to get the aircraft back to Astoria.

About one hour later, a substitute helicopter from the satellite station at Newport, on the Oregon coast about 125 miles south, arrived. (Astoria's other two helicopters were grounded. The transmission on one had been damaged in an earlier rescue mission and was not flyable. The other helicopter's engine was disassembled for overhaul.)

Before the broken cable had occurred, Gary Strickland, Astoria, of the *Sea King,* had been lifted to safety and two Coast Guardsmen had been successfully lowered to the craft where they operated five pumps that were keeping the fishboat afloat.

Petty Officer Dennis Hall of the 13th District Coast Guard Headquarters in Seattle, said that unpredictable and worsening weather and high seas dictated that no further efforts for hoisting anyone be attempted. He said waves were reaching 20 feet high and the winds were gale force at 40 knots with higher gusts.

The Coast Guard believed the situation was in hand as the *Sea King* was under tow and the pumps were working. As the tide was ebbing, the rescuers, wanting to diminish risk, elected to wait beyond the bar staying at sea until the weather calmed a little.

> **The Coast Guard takes its role of lifesaver very seriously and mounts backup forces to its rescue systems whenever possible. During this period, the cutter *Iris* put out from its base at Tongue Point to act as escort. In addition, three motor lifeboats along with a hovering helicopter were on the scene ready to accompany the *Triumph* and her tow across the bar.**

The scene was described by Commander Richard Lang of the *Iris*:

Everything looked good. We were at least two-thirds of the way over the bar [when] the *Sea King* was lifted up and rolled to port by a large wave, [but no bigger than any other wave that day], passed under the *Iris* and the *Sea King*. As the swell passed under her she didn't come back up [but] slowly settled until she was lying absolutely on her side. We could see people scrambling to get around the side of the boat so they wouldn't be caught underneath. A couple of them made it up on to the side of the boat. The *Sea King* slowly settled in and sank.

Lt. Neptun said he thought the *Sea King* was about 300 yards east of buoy No. 7 on the bottom in about 60 feet of water probably with Blunt inside.

Rescuers aboard the *Triumph* quickly cut the 800-foot long tow line and attached marker floats. The floats sank in the storm.

New Prototype Boat Serves Well

On the scene was the Coast Guard's new high-performance $2.3 million prototype self-righting motor lifeboat. This 47-foot vessel was trailing the *Sea King* in the flotilla and literally swooped into action. Haynes came to the surface and was pulled on board the 47-boat.

At this point, a rigid-hull inflatable boat from the *Iris* had lost power and was then drifting dangerously close to Peacock Spit. The 47-footer rushed to its side, attached a tow line and pulled the craft, with its five-man crew, into the safety of deep water.

Quickly after it cast off the tow line, the 47-boat raced full speed to Cape Disappointment Station in just 15 minutes – half the usual time needed by the regular 44-foot motor lifeboats. The

Prototype high-speed, high-technology self-righting 47-foot motor lifeboat, *CG47200*, is assigned to Cape Disappointment Motor Life-boat School. —U.S. Coast Guard

47-boat's speed was 31 miles per hour.

On arrival at Ocean View Hospital in nearby Ilwaco, Haynes was pronounced dead. It was 6:19 p.m. The Coast Guard said Haynes was in cardiac arrest when he was pulled from the sea and that his rescuers applied CPR to him as the 47-boat raced to the station.

Nearly one hour after the other five men were picked up, Sexton was spotted. He was picked up with no vital signs observed and was taken by a helicopter to Air Station Astoria. At 6:05 p.m., he was pronounced dead at Columbia Memorial Hospital. Both he and Haynes drowned.

On Search

A flotilla of the cutter *Iris*, six motor lifeboats, the Columbia River Bar Pilot boat and two helicopters searched for the missing man until 7:30 p.m.

The following day, the search continued until mid morning when rough weather and rising seas forced the hunt to stop. The *Iris* had divers aboard to enter the *Sea King* seeking Mr. Blunt if the boat had been found.

Rescued during this episode were:

Jeffery Lippenlt, 24, Machinery technician - Cape Disappointment
Jeffery K. Courson, 28, Boatswains mate - Cape Disappointment
Chris Bennett, 24, Rescue swimmer - Air Station Astoria

Whenever one is knocked down, one must recover quickly and be ready for the next blow which might be worse. The "Always ready" Coast Guard is no exception. □

U.S. Coast Guard 44-foot self-righting motor lifeboat.

Appendix
United States Life-Saving Service
Extracted From General Information, 1906

Life-saving stations, lifeboat stations, and houses of refuge are located upon the Atlantic and Pacific seaboards of the United States, the Gulf of Mexico and the Lake coasts. All stations on the Atlantic coast from the eastern extremity of the State of Main to Cape Fear, North Carolina, are manned annually by crews of experienced surfmen from the 1st of September to the 1st of May following. Upon the Pacific coast they are open and manned the year around.

All live-saving and lifeboat stations and fully equipped with boats, wreck guns, beach apparatus, restoratives, etc.

Houses of refuge are supplied with boats, provisions, and restoratives, but not manned by crews; a keeper, however, resides in each throughout the year, who, after every storm, is required to make extended excursions along the coast, with a view of ascertaining if any shipwreck has occurred and finding and succoring any persons that may have been cast ashore.

Houses of refuge are located exclusively upon the Florida coast, where the requirements of relief are widely different from those of any other portion of the seaboard.

Most of the life-saving and lifeboat stations are provided with the International Code of Signals and vessels can, by opening communication, be reported; or obtain the latitude and longitude of the station, where determined, or information as to the weather probabilities in most cases, or, if crippled or disabled, a steam tug or revenue cutter will be telegraphed for where facilities for telegraphing exist, to the nearest port, if requested.

All services are performed by the life-saving crews without other compensation than their wages from the Government.

Destitute seafarers are provided with food and lodgings at the nearest station by the Government as long as necessarily detained by the circumstances of the shipwreck.

The station crews patrol the beach from 2 to 4 miles each side of their stations four times between sunset and sunrise, and if the weather is foggy the patrol is continued through the day.

Each patrolman carries Coston signals. Upon discovering a vessel standing into danger he ignites one of them, which emits a brilliant red flame of about two minutes' duration to warn her off, or, should the vessel be ashore, to let her crew know that they have been discovered and assistance is at hand.

If the vessel is not discovered by the patrol immediately after striking, rockets or flare-up lights should be burned, or, if the weather is foggy, guns should be fired to attract attention, as the patrolman may be some distance away at the other end of his beat.

Masters are particularly cautioned, if they should be driven ashore anywhere in the neighborhood of the stations, especially on any sandy coasts where there is not much danger of vessels breaking up immediately, to remain on board until assistance arrives, and under no circumstances should they attempt to land through the surf in their own boats until the last hope of assistance from the shore has vanished.

Often when comparatively smooth at sea a dangerous surf is running which is not perceptible 400 yards offshore, and the surf when viewed from a vessel never appears as dangerous as it is. Many lives have been lost by the crews of stranded vessels being thus deceived and attempting to land in the ship's boats.

The difficulties of rescue by operations from the shore are generally increased in cases where the anchors are let go *after entering the breakers*, as is frequently done, and the chances of saving life correspondingly lessened.

Instructions
Rescue with the lifeboat or surfboat

The patrolman, after discovering your vessel ashore and burning a Coston signal, hastens to his station for assistance. If the use of a boat is practicable, either the large lifeboat is launched from it ways in the station and proceeds to the wreck by water, or the lighter surfboat is hauled overland to a point opposite the wreck and launched as circumstances may require.

Upon the boat reaching your vessel, the directions and orders of the keeper (who always commands and steers the boat) should be implicitly obeyed. Any headlong rushing and crowding should be prevented, and the captain of the vessel should remain on board, to preserve order, until every other person has left.

Women, children, helpless persons, and passengers should be passed into the boat first. Goods or baggage will positively not be taken into the boat until all are landed. <u>If any be passed in against the keeper's remonstrance, he is fully authorized to throw the same overboard</u>.

Rescue With the Breeches Buoy or Life Car

Should it be inexpedient to use either the lifeboat or surfboat, recourse will be had to the wreck gun and beach apparatus for the rescue by the breeches buoy or the life car.

A shot with a small line attached will be fired across your vessel.

Get hold of the line as soon a possible and haul on board until you get a tail block with a whip or endless line rove through it. This tail block should be hauled onboard as quickly as possible to prevent the whip drifting off with the set or fouling with wreckage, etc. Therefore, if you have been driven into the rigging, where but one or two men can work to advantage, cut the shot line and run it through some available block such as the throat or peak halyards block, or any block which will afford a clear lead, or even between the ratlines, that as many as possible may assist in the hauling.

Attached to the tail block will be a tally board with the following instructions in English on one side and French on the other:

MAKE THE TAIL OF THE BLOCK FAST TO THE LOWER MAST, WELL UP. IF THE MASTS ARE GONE, THEN TO THE BEST PLACE YOU CAN FIND. CAST OFF SHOT LINE, SEE THAT THE ROPE IN THE BLOCK RUNS FREE AND SHOW SIGNAL TO THE SHORE.

If the instructions are being complied with, the result is shown in Fig. 3.

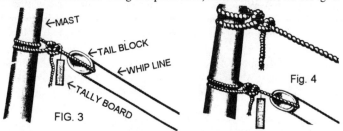

FIG. 3

Fig. 4

As soon as your signal is seen, a 3-inch hawser will be bent on the whip and hauled off to your ship by the life-saving crew. If circumstances will admit, you can assist the life-saving crew by manning that part of the whip to which the hawser is bent and hauling with them.

When the end of hawser is got on board, a tally board will be found attached, bearing the following directions in English on one side and French on the other:

MAKE THIS HAWSER FAST ABOUT 2 FEET ABOVE THE TAIL BLOCK; SEE ALL CLEAR AND THAT THE ROPE IN THE BLOCK RUNS FREE, AND SHOW SIGNAL TO SHORE.

If these instructions are being obeyed, the result will be shown in Fig. 4

Take particular care that there are no turns of the whip line around the hawser. To prevent this, take the end of the hawser UP BETWEEN *the parts of the whip before making it fast.*

When the hawser is made fast, the whip cast off from the hawser, and your signal seen by the life-saving crew, they will then haul the hawser taut and by means of the whip will haul off to your ship a breeches buoy suspended from a traveler block, or a life car from the rings, running on the hawser.

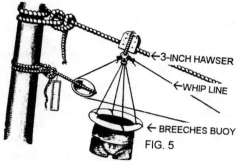

FIG. 5

Fig. 5 illustrates the apparatus rigged, with the breeches buoy hauled off to the ship.

252

If the breeches buoy is sent, let one man immediately get into it, thrusting his legs through the breeches. If the life car, remove the hatch, place as many persons into it as it will hold (four to six) and secure the hatch on the outside by the hatch bar and hook, signal as before, and the buoy or car will be hauled ashore. This will be repeated until all are landed. On the last trip of the life car the hatch must be secured by the inside hatch bar.

In many instances two men can be landed in the breeches buoy at the same time by each putting a leg through a leg of the breeches and holding on to the lifts of the buoy. Children when brought ashore by the buoy, should be in the arms of an older person or securely lashed to the buoy. Women and children should be landed first.

Circumstances may arise, owing to the strength of the current or set, or the danger of the wreck breaking up immediately, when it would be impossible to send off the hawser. In such a case a breeches buoy or life car will be hauled off instead by the whip, or sent off to you by the shot line, and you will be hauled ashore through the surf. □

U. S. LIFE SAVING SERVICE—ANNUAL REPORT-1896

ACTIVITY/DUTY: Beached steamer "Bawnmore"

DATE: August 28, 1895

STATION: Coquille River (Oregon)

British Steamer "Bawnmore"

Stranded 16 miles south of station in dense fog through error of compass. Word was brought to station in the afternoon. Took surf boat and beach apparatus to the scene arriving at midnight, finding the ship's company of thirty persons on the beach where they landed in their lifeboat. Next morning fired a line over the vessel and boarded her to set up beach apparatus, by means of which the property of the crew and passengers, provisions, cooking utensils, sails, etc., were landed and a temporary shelter was set up on the beach. Worked each day in saving and landing cargo until Sept. 5, when the vessel, which had taken fire on Aug. 30 from lime in cargo, was enveloped in flames and consumed. Life-saving crew watched over the goods recovered until Sept 9 when the underwriters took charge of them.

The *Milwaukee* Monument on Samoa Spit

About The Authors

Bert and Margie Webber

Bert and Margie Webber have collaborated on several books about the Northwest several of which deal with the Oregon coast.

Bert Webber is a research photojournalist who earned a degree in journalism from Whitworth College, and a master's degree in Library Science after studies at Portland State University and the University of Portland.

Margie Webber graduated from the University of Washington with the BS in Nursing and worked for many years as a Registered Nurse. Her work on the books pulls from her other talents including photography, editing and active research assistance on many field trips.

The Webbers appreciate music for relaxation. Margie plays piano and organ and is in English Hand Bell ensembles. Bert plays baritone horn in the Southern Oregon Symphonic Band and serves on the Board of Control. For listening, their favorite instrument is the pipe organ.

The Webbers live in Oregon's Rogue River Valley. They have four children and eight grandchildren. □

Bibliography

Separate listings for books and newspapers

BOOKS AND GOVERNMENT DOCUMENTS

Bailey, J. H., *Moro Bay's Yesterdays*. Gates & Bailey. 1982.

Friedman, Norman. *U.S. Submarines Through 1945*. Naval Institute. 1995.

Gibbs, James A. *Oregon's Seacoast Lighthouses*. Webb Research Group. 1992.

_____.*Shipwrecks of the Pacific Coast*. Binford & Mort. 1957.

_____.*Pacific Graveyard*. Binford & Mort. 1950.

_____. *Oregon's Salty Coast*. Webb Research Group. 1994.

_____.["Shipwreck Jim"] *Peril at Sea*. Schiffer. 1986.

Johansen, Dorothy O. and Charles M. Gates. *Empire of the Columbia*. Harper & Row. 1957.

Light List - Pacific Coast United States 1934. US Dept. Commerce - Lighthouse Service. US Gov. Print Office. 1934.

Light List - Pacific Coast and Pacific Islands. Coast Guard. 1983. Dept. of Transportation. US Gov. Print Office. 1982.

Marshall, Don. *California Shipwrecks*. Superior. 1978.

_____. *Oregon Shipwrecks*. Binford & Mort. 1984.

Moore, Capt. Arthur R. *A Careless Word...A Needless Sinking*. American Merchant Marine Museum [Kings Point, NY]. 1983.

Morison, Samuel E. *History of United States Naval Operations in World War II*. Vol. XV. Atlantic. 1962.

Ricketts, Edw. F. and Jack Calvin. *Between Pacific Tides*. Stanford Univ. Press. 1968.

Rush, Philip S. "Japanese Submarines Along the U. S. Pacific Coast During World War II" in *A History of the Californias*. Private print. 1958.

Ships in Gray; The Story of Matson in World War II. Matson Navigation Co. Private Print. 1946.

Tide Tables for the Year 1906. Dept. of Commerce and Labor - Coast and Geodetic Survey. Gov. Print. Off. 1905.

United States Coast Pilot 7 – Pacific Coast: Calif. Ore. Wash. Hawaii. US Dept. of Commerce. NOAA. 1982.

Watts, Anthony J. and Brian G. Gordon. *The Imperial Japanese Navy*. Doubleday. 1971.

Webber, Bert. *Battleship Oregon; Bulldog of the Navy*. Webb Research Group. 1994.

_____. *Retaliation; Japanese Attacks and Allied Counter-measures Along the Northwest Coast*. Ore. State Univ. Press. 1975.

_____. *Silent Siege; Japanese Attacks Against North America in World War II*. YeGalleon. 1984.

_____ *Silent Siege-II; Japanese Attacks On North America in World War II*. Webb Research Group. 1988.

_____ *Silent Siege-III; Japanese Attacks On North America in World War II – Ships Sunk, Air Raids, Bombs Dropped, Civilians Killed*. Webb Research Group. 1992.

_____. *Wrecked Japanese Junks Adrift in the North Pacific Ocean*. YeGalleon. 1984.

Webber, Bert and Margie Webber. *Battery Point Light and the Tidal Wave of 1964, Crescent City, California (Includes St. George Reef Light)*. Webb Research Group. 1991.

_____. *I'd Rather Be Beachcombing*. Webb Research Group. 1993.

_____. *Lakeport, Ghost Town of the South Oregon Coast*. Webb Research Group. 1990.

_____ *Terrible Tilly," Tillamook Rock Lighthouse, The Biography of a Lighthouse*. Webb Research Group. 1992.

Wilson, Nancy. *Dr. John McLoughlin: Master of Fort Vancouver, Father of Oregon*. Webb Research Group. 1994.

NEWSPAPERS AND PERIODICALS

Bahr, Mike M. "*Brother Jonathan* saga continues; ill-fated ship found, court fight next?" in *Triplicate* (Crescent City, Calif.) Feb. 25, 1994.

_____. "Knight wants Crescent City to get artifacts; Del Norte Historical Society may play crucial role in ship's future" in *Triplicate* (Crescent City, Calif.) Feb. 25, 1994.

_____. "State Makes New Effort to Claim Wreck" in *Triplicate* (Crescent City) Aug. 18, 1995.

"CG Board Gets Picture of Sea Tragedy Here" in *Daily Astorian* Jan. 16, 1961.

"Coast Guard Probe Slated Into Disaster" in *Daily Astorian*. Jan. 17, 1961.

Cottrell, Clark. "Fishermen Die While Assisting CG Patrol Craft" in Aberdeen *Daily World*. Jan. 28, 1960.

"Cruiser Milwaukee is Believed Total Loss; Samoa Beach is Scene of Wreck" in *Humboldt Times*. Jan. 14, 1917.

"Fighting to Save Corona's Load of Freight" in *Humboldt Daily Standard*. Mar. 2, 1907.

"Fisher Folks Search Beach For Missing; Tragic Scenes Mark Day" in Aberdeen *Daily World*. Apr. 6, 1933.

"H-3 Wrecked; Crew is Saved; Submarine is Ashore at Samoa" in *Humboldt Times*. Dec. 15, 1916.

"Honor Due 7 Lost" in *Daily Astorian*. Jan. 17, 1961

"Hunt For Wreckage Continues," in *Daily Astorian*. Jan. 16, 1961.

Kennett, Andrea and Alex Friend. "Cause of Sea Tragedy Probed" in *Daily Astorian*. Jan. 14, 1991

"Lone Survivor Relates Events of Ship Loss" in *Daily Astorian*. Jan. 13, 1961.

Merriman, George. "Skipper of S.S.Emidio Visits Crescent City" in *Triplicate* Jul. 3, 1971.

"19 Fishermen Lose Lives, Fear; 13 Boats Founder; 40 Others Still Out" in Aberdeen *Daily World*. Apr. 6, 1933.

Riley, Joan. "Brother Jonathan Search Continues; Pacific Gold Wreck Awaits Discovery" in *Treasure Diver*. Sept. 1989.

Rothberg, Don. "1 Dead, 6 Lost at Sea; 3 CG Boats Sink" in *Daily Astorian*. Jan. 13, 1961.

"The Strange and Beautiful Story of a Jap Sub and a Garbage Scow" in *Chronicle*, (San Francisco). Jan. 27, 1942.

Sullivan, Sean. "Lifesaving Citations Presented Widows" in *Aberdeen Daily World*. July 28, 1962.

Van Syckle, Edwin. "Mystery Hulk May Be Nora Harkins, Belief" in *Daily World* (Aberdeen, Wash.) n.d.

Index

Page numbers for illustrations are shown in **_bold italic_** type
Ship names are in _italic_ type   (fb) = fish boat

257

258